BERTOLT BRECHT'S GREAT PLAYS

BERTOLT BRECHT'S GREAT PLAYS

ALFRED D. WHITE

BARNES & NOBLE
BOOKS
10 East 53d St., New York 10022
(a division of Harper & Row Publishers. Inc.)

First published 1978 by
THE MACMILLAN PRESS LTD
London and Basingstoke

Published in the U.S.A. 1978 by
HARPER & ROW PUBLISHERS, INC.
BARNES & NOBLE IMPORT DIVISION

Printed in Hong Kong

Library of Congress Cataloging in Publication Data

White, Alfred D
   Bertolt Brecht's great plays.
   Bibliography: p.
   1. Brecht, Bertolt, 1898–1956 – Criticism and
interpretation.   I. Title.
PT2603.R397Z8995   832'.9'12   77–22637

ISBN 0–06–497618–1

To my wife

Contents

List of Plates

Grateful thanks are due to Gerda Goedhart for permission to reproduce Plates 7a and 7b. The author and publishers have been unable to trace the copyright holders of the remaining Plates, but we will be pleased to make the necessary arrangements at the first opportunity.

Acknowledgements

The author and publishers wish to thank the following who have kindly given permission for the use of copyright material:

Eyre Methuen Limited, for extracts from 'Brecht on Theatre' by John Willet, and short quotations from the works of Bertolt Brecht: 'The Life of Galileo', translated by Desmond Vesey, translation copyright © 1960 by Desmond Vesey; 'Mother Courage', translated by Eric Bentley, copyright © 1955, 1959, 1961, 1962 by Eric Bentley (original work published under the title of 'Mutter Courage Und Ihre Kinder', copyright © 1949 by Suhrkamp Verlag vormals S. Fischer, Frankfurt am Main); 'The Caucasian Chalk Circle', translated by James and Tania Stern with W. H. Auden, copyright © (Act 5) 1946 and 1960 by J. and T. Stern and W. H. Auden (original work published under the title of 'Der Kaukasische Kreidekreis', copyright © 1954 by Suhrkamp Verlag, Berlin)

Eyre Methuen Limited and Hope Leresche & Sayle, on behalf of John Willet, for an extract from 'The Good Person of Szechwan', translated by John Willet, copyright © 1962 by John Willet (original work published under the title of 'Der Gute Mensche von Sezuan', copyright 1955 by Suhrkamp Verlag, Berlin)

Suhrkamp Verlag, for extracts from 'Arbeitsjournal', copyright © 1973 by Stefan S. Brecht. All rights reserved by Suhrkamp Verlag, Frankfurt am Main.

Every effort has been made to trace all the copyright holders, but if any have been inadvertently overlooked the publishers will be pleased to make the necessary arrangement at the first opportunity.

Preface

This short book is about a closely interconnected group of Brecht's plays in which the elements of his greatness appear in their most concentrated and complex form, and by which his stature can be measured. It is not concerned with his development before these plays were written nor with his verse, narrative, dialogue and theoretical work or with his other plays except in their relevance to the four plays in hand. This involves no denial of the greatness of much of his other work. Despite limations of scope and length, I hope this book will however suggest what made the dramatist Brecht write as he did, how one may approach his texts and what is to be borne in mind when a production of them is envisaged. The plot of each play is summarised – not just to help those who have not yet read or seen the plays, but because absolute clarity of the story-line is a primary consideration for Brecht. Then an attempt is made to characterise each play and explore some of its salient features.

My thanks are due particularly to Mr D. Richards for help and advice, to students of University College, Cardiff, with whom I have discussed many of the ideas in this book, and to my wife for acting as partner in many mealtime thinking-aloud sessions and for reading the typescript and preparing the index.

A.D.W.

July 1977

1 Life of Brecht

Eugen Berthold Brecht was born in Augsburg on 10 February 1898, of middle-class background. His father, a Catholic, rose during the first twenty years of this century from a subordinate secretarial position to the directorship of a paper-mill, and appears – though tolerant of his son's work – to have been a typical ambitious, nationalistic bourgeois of the time. Brecht's mother, a Protestant, who died in 1920 after long suffering from cancer, lived in his memory rather as the passive, tolerant, rural element. She was the bookish one of his parents, the odd one out of the family. He seems to have been an arrogant child (though not an only child), joined in games only when he could be the leader, and was excused exercise at the grammar-school he attended because of a weak heart. He had a good grounding in literature and in (Protestant) religious knowledge. With a group of classmates he spent much time mounting productions in a puppet theatre. In 1914 he published in the schoolboys' journal *Die Ernte* his first drama *Die Bibel* ('The Bible'), already noteworthy for its unimpressed attitude to heroism and to the putting of beliefs above people. In 1914 – unsurprisingly, in view of the atmosphere in Germany at the time – he was affected by patriotic frenzy, but his general attitude was rebellious, as seen in a speech on German Dynasties which gained him the lowest possible mark, and an essay of 1916 with a pacifist theme. He read voraciously – from Shakespeare to Verlaine and trashy novelettes – and gathered around him a group of literary young men, of whom Caspar Neher was to remain closely associated with him all his life: Brecht was intense and faithful in his friendships, though already prone to let personal rancour rule his dealings with people whose views he disliked. They shocked the town with torchlight processions, spent nights out in the meadows, swam, lazed, climbed trees and read their works to each other. Their leader found it wiser to write about swimming and climbing trees than to join in. He took up the forename Bert instead of the Eugen hitherto used, and dressed sloppily as a mark of revolt against bourgeois standards. His mother sighed in vain over his foul language and the erotic entanglements which started, by his own account, when he was 17. After Rose Maria Aman, Paula Banholzer occupied his attention. His attitude to sex was un-bourgeois, lacking in the refinements and neuroses typical of our century,[1] but full of natural zest – and natural egotism. For all his sensitivity towards women, he was obsessed with keeping his independence: he tried to avoid marriage proposals, pregnancies, and distractions from his literary work, whose material was his various passions: the contemplation of transience; friendship; sex; the fascination of the fairground with its swingboats and peep-shows; water, trees and clouds.

As a student in Munich, from October 1917 on, he registered as a student of medicine, attended scientific and literary lectures and frequented the theatre. He just had time to study the dramatist and balladeer Frank Wedekind in person before his sudden death. When the call-up – long delayed because of his weak heart – finally threatened Brecht, he qualified as a medical student for the ambulance service and was able to avoid the front line. In October he duly became a medical orderly in a hospital for the war-wounded in Augsburg. What he saw here marked him for life, though he was assigned to the venereal disease section. He wrote his first famous poem *Legende vom toten Soldaten* ('Legend of the Dead Soldier') – whose catchy presentation of the grotesque excesses of German militarism (the dead soldier is exhumed and declared fit for active service) was later to earn him a high place on the Nazi blacklist. That he sang it to the wounded, and that he was a soldiers' representative in the short-lived Bavarian Republic after the war, however, may well be inventions. The complex revolutionary movements of 1918–19 in Bavaria interested him as instructive adventures, rather than serious politics. He had left-wing sympathies and was friendly with leading revolutionaries in Augsburg; but, as yet, violence in revolutions seemed to him as senseless as the violence of the imperialist war. He was more interested in earning money by writing so as to avoid returning to University; he made contact with Lion Feuchtwanger, the novelist, then dramaturg (literary adviser, editor and adaptor) of a Munich theatre, who was however just as prone to exploit Brecht for his own ends as to help him. Brecht was now prolifically writing poems as a private amusement (some of the more printable verse of this period appeared as *Hauspostille*, 'Manual of Piety', in 1927), stories and film treatments to make money, and also – with rather more difficulty – plays. *Baal* (written 1918, successive versions up to 1955: all Brecht's plays went through a bewildering series of recastings, restylings, rewritings, alterations to suit particular theatres or actors – nothing was ever finished) gives – in reaction to the would-be spirituality of the then fashionable epigones of literary expressionism and in line with Wedekind's principles – a new earthiness to the theme of the asocial vagrant poet and lover, which had long been a rather pale poetic convention. *Trommeln in der Nacht* ('Drums in the Night', written 1919 and continually altered until its première, Brecht's stage début, in 1922) has its setting in the Spartacist risings of the time, but the typically proletarian protagonist turns his back on ideals and violence and goes home to his non-virgin bride. Some one-act plays of 1919, notably *Die Kleinbürgerhochzeit* ('The Petty Bourgeois' Wedding') show the influence of Karl Valentin, a noted Munich comedian whose sympathetic yet sharp approach to human stupidity impressed him greatly and whose friend he became.

Germany in the twenties, the Weimar Republic, never really emerged from the slaughter of World War I which preceded it before entering the violence which portended its close and the horrors of Nazism. Brecht reflects an age which sees life as brutish and basic, people as self-centred and violent, even nature as uncaring rather than maternal. Even the pacifism of the age is aggressive; having seen the hospitals of 1914–18, Brecht was eventually to be willing to espouse a cause which promises universal brotherhood, to embrace violence in the interests of ending violence. Willett (pp. 66–74, 88f.) has shown how typical a child of the twenties Brecht is: in his fascination with gangsterdom, sport, jazz, the Anglo-Saxon and the oriental, the cabaret, and finally Communism, he swims with the tide. Even his moods of despondency are typical of an era when 'no one had enough ego in themselves to do anything', as he claims in a note describing his rootlessness and shiftlessness, his feeling of being expendable and ephemeral, when he moved from one furnished room to another in the early twenties (*Tb.*, 213: *c.* 1930). Conceptions of his life and work which see him as unusually aggressive, or riddled with guilt, or living so unbalancedly that he needed eventually to turn to Communism as a sort of religious retreat, are seeing him out of context. The portrayals in his work of man as lonely, lost in the mass, devoid of personal value, are not unique to him. Nor was he unusual among Weimar intellectuals for his behaviour, particularly in his literary feuds. A hard-hitting style was in favour from the expressionist generation on. It did not endear him to people; his friend Walter Benjamin complains of his aggressiveness about matters of literary taste – but admits to intransigence himself.[2]

From 1919 to 1921 Brecht wrote theatre criticism for a left-wing Augsburg paper but was also much in Munich. His diaries are full of drunken and violent scenes often revolving around sexual jealousy among his Augsburg circle. Paula Banholzer made him the father of a son Frank (born 1919, killed fighting for Hitler 1943). From 1920 he tried to establish himself in Berlin, a fitter scene for his ambitions. A first visit was cut short when he retreated precipitately from the apparent dangers of the right-wing Kapp Putsch. On a second visit he negotiated with publishers and dramaturgs and was fêted as a coming literary figure, but quickly tired of the febrile life of theatrical and literary circles – and the lack of firm contracts. He joined forces with another struggling dramatist, Arnolt Bronnen, to match whose forename he adapted his own to

Bertolt, Nickel-framed glasses gave an ascetic, old-fashioned, pedantic look which Brecht had affected even as a schoolboy; he now added a flat cap – an attempt to give his slight and unmemorable physique some character, and also useful to draw over his eyes so that no one could see if he was concentrating or sleeping.[3] In due course glasses and cap were joined by the leather jacket which gave him an image somewhere between motor-cyclist and Moscow commissar,[4] but was offset by a silk shirt (often dirty). In 1922 he spent time in hospital suffering from undernourishment, and made a bad start to a producing career by quarrelling with the cast in a play by Bronnen.

Im Dickicht der Städte ('In the Jungle of Cities', 1921–2) is one of the works showing the fascination for Brecht of America, the land of action. The squalor and stagnation of German – especially Augsburg – life disgusted him (*Tb.* 11: 18.6.20). Impressions of Berlin add to the characterisation of the city; the plot is a gratuitous fight to the death between two men of Chicago moving beyond the routine constrictions of urban life and communicating somehow in the loneliness of the mass – if only negatively. It has affinities to absurd theatre, but Brecht is actually turning away from asocial individuality, and the play can be interpreted in a social light. In 1922 he was awarded the Kleist Prize and thus established his reputation. *Drums in the Night* was produced in Munich; Brecht assembled a cast and worked with them in bars, in the countryside, informally, and generally interfered in the production. His easy way with actresses made Marianne Zoff, a singer, his mistress since 1920, jealous. She was pregnant – their daughter, born 1923, became the actress Hanne Hiob – and Brecht unwillingly remained in Munich, increased his theatre experience by taking a post as dramaturg with an index-linked salary – no small point in the inflation era – and married Marianne, only to drive her mad by his hatred of babies, generosity with her property and habit of inviting friends to share their tiny flat in the Akademiestrasse. He insisted (his usual pattern) on freedom to consort with other women, whilst not allowing her any latitude. They were divorced in 1927.

In 1924 he produced his *Leben Eduards II*, an adaptation of Marlowe's *Edward II*, in Munich; Brechtian theatre begins with this production, in which in pursuance of an idea of Karl Valentin's soldiers wore white make-up to show their fear in battle. In the same year he finally moved to Berlin, where, together with Carl Zuckmayer, he was dramaturg at the *Deutsches Theater*, a Max Reinhardt theatre run by Erich Engel,[5] the first producer of *In the Jungle of Cities* and later of *The Threepenny Opera*, with whom Brecht carried on many amicable arguments.[6] From 1927 he worked with Erwin Piscator. Despite his attachment to things and people that reminded him of Augsburg, a Berlin circle formed. Elisabeth Hauptmann became his secretary, translating material from English sources. Emil Burri, a young writer and boxer, was his mentor in sport-ing affairs, then the rage in Berlin; Paul Samson-Körner, a more famous boxer, lent his friendship to get him publicity; but the only sport Brecht personally participated in was driving. From 1923 he was in constant contact with Helene Weigel, the Jewish actress who influenced his later work more than perhaps anyone else. This unsentimental figure was re-sponsible for all the organisation which was to allow him to go on work-ing in his own way through a troubled era. Their first child, Stefan, was born in 1924; the second, Barbara, in 1930. They married in 1928 (giving a shock to Carola Neher, another actress Brecht thought much of, and causing Elisabeth Hauptmann to attempt suicide).

Acquaintance with the prose of sporting magazines helped him to develop the unemotional blank verse style which is one of his char-acteristic contributions to German literature; but more public attention was drawn by ostentatious feuds with such established poets as Franz Werfel. On all occasions he attacked the pretentious and much-admired literature of the day and praised detective fiction. Of older writers, only Feuchtwanger and Alfred Döblin impressed him. Thomas Mann was bour-geois, subjective, annoyingly patronising – and too successful. Brecht, with three children to support, struggled financially until a long-term contract with a publisher, Ullstein, guaranteed him 500 Marks a month. Ullstein lost heavily on this. So far, Brecht had developed a nihilistic set of opinions, perhaps more to *épater les bourgeois* and publicise himself than from deep necessity. Early defences of communism (such as *Tb.*, 65: 15.9.20) merely show a pose. But a change was coming about. Between 1926 and 1930 a series of studies convinced him that the Marxian an-alysis of economic and social problems was correct and that a rebel from the middle classes such as himself should join world Communism and work for the dictatorship of the proletariat. In July 1926 he noted that so far he had written plays piecemeal, but if he were to become serious about writing he would have to make a plan, a system, a tradition, a style for himself. At least half-consciously, he sets out to become an all-round author of classical, Goethean mould, rather than a specialist in one or two genres like his major contemporaries.[7] The material he already has: 'As heroic landscape I have the town, as point of view relativity, as situation the influx of mankind into the great cities at the beginning of the third millenium, as content the appetites (too big or too small), as training for the public the gigantic social battles' (*Tb.*, 208: late July 1926). The next year he could write that his early plays had been, with-out his knowing, presentations of material ripe for Marxian interpreta-tion: 'this Marx was the only spectator I had ever come across for my plays' (15, 129: *Der einzige Zuschauer für meine Stücke*). That Marxism answers certain questions is Brecht's main reason for embracing it. What difference it makes is apparent in the two versions of *Mann ist Mann*

('Man is Man', 1924–6; revised 1931): in the earlier one the brainwashing which alters the hero's personality and very identity (perhaps Pirandello influenced the theme) is already interpretable as an artistic statement of how hollow liberal theories of the free individual are, but is comical; in the later one, while still funny, it is unmistakably rejected as part of a capitalist-imperialist exploitation.

In 1928 Brecht conceived and executed the plan of adapting Gay's *Beggar's Opera*, put in much work with Kurt Weill on the music, collaborated in the production, and had *The Threepenny Opera* – his first real box-office success – on the stage by 31 August. It shows a transition towards putting Marxism on the stage: to equate bourgeoisie and underworld is radical enough, but no substitute for close social analysis, and Macheath is more of a rascal than a villain. The production inaugurated Ernst Josef Aufricht's *Theater am Schiffbauerdamm*, which with its intimate ensemble (Helene Weigel, Carola Neher, Lotte Lenya, Peter Lorre, Ernst Busch and others) Brecht for a time thought of as 'his' theatre. The intended successor to the original hit, however, was a mistake, and Brecht withdrew his name half-way through. By now he was more interested in a constructive parody of opera, having more relevance to social themes; this was *Aufstieg und Fall der Stadt Mahagonny* ('Rise and Fall of the City of Mahagonny', 1928–9). Mahagonny is the urban jungle again, now based on business, and the only capital crime there is lack of money.

From about 1929, when Brecht witnessed the bloody dispersal of a May Day march by the Berlin police, whose president was a Social Democrat, he determines to aid the Communist cause in practical ways, though he apparently never became a party member. With the rise of Nazism, he may have looked to Communism's Russian connection as the only counterweight to militaristic German nationalism.[8] He wrote the *Lehrstücke* – didactic pieces: largely simple, paratactically constructed, stylised operatic texts on problems in bringing about social advance – for instance, in *Die Massnahme* ('The Measures Taken', 1930), the Communist who does not want to give up his individuality (well-meaning but too impulsive: he is a forerunner of Shen Teh and Grusha in the later plays) in favour of party teachings on revolutionary method (apparently inhumane, but thought out as the best long-term answers). Some formal aspects are influenced by the Claude-Milhaud opera *Christophe Colomb*, a narrative and didactic work with ritual elements; and Brecht took the plot of at least one of his didactic pieces from a Nô play.[9] Composers Brecht worked with were Paul Hindemith and then the politically more congenial Hanns Eisler. It was the era of *agitprop* theatre, and like the hundreds of socialist troupes in Germany at the time Brecht seeks a new audience in the schools and the trade unions which will be open to his message. But the plays are not party-line propaganda; they concentrate more on problems of belonging to a collective, not on positive aspects. By and large these texts are for amateurs. But the most brilliant product of this period is a play for the professional stage, *Die Heilige Johanna der Schlachthöfe* ('Saint Joan of the Stockyards', 1929–31), whose heroine discovers for herself the truth about the exploitation of the American proletariat and dies proclaiming war on the capitalists. The play is structured according to the phases of the trade cycle as ascertained by Brecht's Marxian studies. Echoes of the Saint Joan story (Shaw's play had been staged in Berlin), blank verse forms, and parodies of the German classics show Brecht's use of the literary tradition. The play remained unperformed in Germany[10] until 1959; and *Die Mutter* ('The Mother', 1931) could only be put on by young committed actors, not in an established theatre. It takes a less pretentious approach to the class war: the heroine learns about Communism and progresses in Leninist awareness, the audience learns from her and with her; frequent apostrophes to the audience and interpolated songs draw attention from the individual figures to the wider implications. Brecht had by now emerged as a Marxist writer, though not as a socialist-realist dramatist plugging Soviet achievements; with the rise of nationalism the professional theatre froze him out, and he went into film with *Kuhle Wampe*, a depiction of the poverty and hopelessness of many Berlin workers of the time. By now his circle had crystallised. Elisabeth Hauptmann was intimately concerned in his discovery of Marxism and of the Japanese Nô play, translated the *Beggar's Opera* for him and wrote much of certain of his works.[11] Margarete Steffin researched for him and watched over his Marxist orthodoxy; she was the only one of his mistresses with whom he had a relaxed and leisurely relationship.

Hitler's rise to power meant immediate exile (followed by withdrawal of German citizenship in 1935) and poverty through loss of royalties. In Vienna, Helene Weigel's relatives and the critic Karl Kraus helped the family. In Lugano, Brecht attempted to assemble a circle of kindred spirits. In Paris, he made some money from the ballet scenario *Die sieben Todsünden* ('The Seven Deadly Sins', 1933), which shows how one gets on in the world by avoiding vice – that is, by being unnatural. Poverty forced him to accept from Karin Michaelis the loan of a house in Thurö, Denmark; but before long, with money provided by their parents, he and Helene Weigel bought a house near Svendborg, the home of the family for the next few years. Margarete Steffin was in attendance, and Barbara had been smuggled out of Germany by an English welfare worker. The Danish theatre showed some interest in the exile's work, though as it turned out he had little success there. An early visitor was Ruth Berlau, a Copenhagen actress and Communist, later Brecht's assistant, mistress, photographer and archivist – important to a writer who in successive hurried moves left many boxes of temporarily abandoned work behind.

He pressed friends – Hanns Eisler, the aesthetician Walter Benjamin, the Marxist thinker Karl Korsch – to join him in Denmark, where he had an extensive working library on Marxism, salvaged from Berlin, to attract them. Whilst advising exiled anti-fascists not known to the régime to go back to Germany and work underground, he also respected those who, like Caspar Neher, simply remained in Germany and kept out of politics, tacitly denying their socialism.

A visit to Russia in 1932 had strengthened his feeling that this was the path to the ending of force and oppression, though violence and injustice were still found on it. He did not want to live in exile in such a geographically and culturally distant country, but in 1935, seeing no prospect of an early return home, went to see whether he could live in Russia. Piscator was doing so and wanted Brecht to work with him on a German-language theatre. But Brecht was unimpressed: the theatre in question became a party-line affair with no appeal, the talents of Piscator and Carola Neher were fallow, his friend Tretiakov was in disgrace and Meyerhold, whom he admired, suspect to the authorities. In the next years, Piscator had to leave Russia, Tretiakov and Carola Neher died in labour-camps. Brecht, listing friends in Russia whom he knows to have been arrested or never hears from, is harsh about circumstances there (*Aj.*, 1, 36: Jan 1939). Had he settled there he would have been in physical danger. Neither the Popular Front period of 1935–7, nor the Hitler-Stalin Pact – each a compromise with anti-Communist parties, and a weakening of the party's purity which Brecht as an intellectual could not be expected to understand – reduced his suspicions of Stalin's politics.

He visited London on business in 1934 and 1936, and got a contract to assist with the script of a Richard Tauber film; but all his suggestions were ignored, and even a £500 fee could not compensate him. In New York he had frustrations of a different order: the Theater Union planned to put on *The Mother* but did not espouse his ideas about presentation. Travelling to New York at their expense, he criticised everything from the quality of the cast to the lack of political (i.e. Communist) awareness in the whole organisation, so that a quarrel was inevitable. Thus in both capitalist and socialist countries Brecht found it impossible to realise his theatrical ideas.

With Eisler's help he revised in 1934 *Die Rundköpfe und die Spitzköpfe* ('Roundheads and Peakheads'), a play started in 1929 containing his materialist interpretation of Hitler's anti-Semitism. There was topicality in the poems he wrote for radio programmes beamed at Germany too; and he agreed to be a co-editor of *Das Wort*, a Moscow German-language literary periodical, though this post gave him no influence. With little to distract him, he wrote a great deal in the late thirties. Two prose works, *Die Geschäfte des Herrn Julius Caesar* ('Mr Julius Caesar's Business Deals') and *Tui-Roman* ('Tui-Novel'), remained weighty fragments.

In 1937, moved by the Spanish Civil War (though he refused to go any nearer to it than Paris, not wanting to be shot at), he wrote a short propaganda piece *Die Gewehre der Frau Carrar* ('Señora Carrar's Rifles'): unable to keep out of the war, the mother unwillingly turns revolutionary. This play's conventional structure is a concession to the circumstances of the 1930s, which condemned the plays by which Brecht set most store (basically those written between 1929 and 1934) to be misunderstood and rejected all over the world. Similar concessions are seen in *Furcht und Elend des Dritten Reiches* ('Fear and Misery of the Third Reich', 1935–8), which uses realistically written scenes for emotional effect in demonstrating the everyday terror under Hitler. *Leben des Galilei* ('Life of Galileo') was also written to be practicable on the existing stage. But at the same time Brecht started the series of *Messingkauf* dialogues on the nature of theatre, which codify and develop ideas and ideals that originated in his practice of the 1920s. He also spent much time studying philosophy and psychology. After the end of the Spanish civil war, and the Munich agreement, he planned to go to America. While awaiting visas he and his family (including Ruth Berlau and Margarete Steffin) were able to move to the island of Lidingö near Stockholm. Two short plays, *Dansen* and *Was kostet das Eisen?* ('How much is iron?'), written in 1939 for workers' theatres in Denmark and Sweden, use caricature and exaggeration in transposing recent international events to the personal level. *Der gute Mensch von Sezuan* ('The Good Person of Szechwan') was begun in Denmark, but put back in favour of *Mutter Courage und ihre Kinder* ('Mother Courage and her Children'). This was followed by *Das Verhör des Lukullus* ('The Trial of Lucullus', 1939), an opera text on militarism.

The series of great plays, unlike the ones preceding them, present little overt Communist thought or topical propaganda. Brecht knew that topical messages date quickly; after 1930 he wrote propaganda plays only if immediate production seemed likely, and from 1938 is often willing to write in such a way that even audiences hostile to Communism can accept the plays – though under the surface his convictions are always present. The secret of these plays' quality is Brecht's ability, just at the point when Hitler seems triumphant, even concluding an alliance with the Soviet Union, to disregard the world situation (at least with the creative side of his mind) and write plays equally far removed from topicality and from portentous seriousness. He takes up a perspective of the future, seeing today if not *sub specie aeternitatis*, at any rate from the superior viewpoint of tomorrow: the attitude evoked in the famous poem *To those born later* (9,722; *B. Poems*, 318). Thus he can be ironic about life in a harsh era. He sets the plays in distant times or places (personal experience of anything seems actually to have inhibited him from using it in a play); and whilst stamped by the experience of exile, none of these plays is (as some of his best poems are) *about* exile. Brecht tried to get the plays performed in Switzerland and America, but until after 1945 it was only the Zurich *Schauspielhaus* that actually presented them.

On the German occupation of Denmark and Norway Brecht left Sweden for Finland, where the writer Hella Wuolijoki accommodated the family on an estate near Kausala (though Ruth Berlau was excluded and had to pitch a tent nearby). Mexican visas arrived, but as there was none for Margarete Steffin, and Brecht had no intention of giving up any of the women in his life, he stayed put. He wrote *Herr Puntila und sein Knecht Matti* ('Mr Puntila and his Servant Matti', 1940), a comedy with farcical elements set in the Finnish countryside and based on the class relationships between the indispensable and independent-minded chauffeur Matti, the irresolute landowner Puntila who is generous when drunk and humourless when sober, and Puntila's daughter Eva who is attracted to Matti but must make a more suitable match. When Hella Wuolijoki had to sell her estate Brecht lived in a small flat in Helsinki and worked on *Der aufhaltsame Aufstieg des Arturo Ui* ('The Resistible Rise of Arturo Ui', 1941), which transfers Hitler into a Chicago gangster setting – and iambic metre.

By the time visas finally arrived, the safest way to the U.S.A. seemed to be via Moscow and Vladivostock: so the defender of Communism travelled the length of the Communist world to embark for capitalist shores. The fares were paid by the actor Fritz Kortner.[12] Margarete Steffin had to be left behind in Moscow, to die a few days later of tuberculosis. On 21 July 1941 the Brecht family arrived in America, where friends awaited them and a house was ready in Santa Monica, Hollywood. Brecht hated America's gold-digging atmosphere, lack of taste and tradition, commercialised film industry, lack of decent bread, and way of judging people according to their moneymaking potential. He avoided the petty intrigues of the exiled German community too, except that he kept up his hatred of Thomas Mann, allying himself with Heinrich Mann and Alfred Döblin, who had both been helped by Thomas Mann and both felt put in the shade by him. Brecht participated in film scripts, losing any illusions he had about the film industry in the process; from *Hangmen also die*, a Fritz Lang film quite unsatisfactory by Brecht's standards, he made enough to live on whilst writing an adaptation of Webster's *The Duchess of Malfi* (1943–6), in which the actress Elisabeth Bergner was interested, *Die Gesichte der Simone Machard* ('The Visions of Simone Machard', 1941–3) – a drama after a novel by Feuchtwanger – and *Schweyk im zweiten Weltkrieg* ('Schweyk in the Second World War', 1943), a re-use of Hašek's celebrated character in new situations. Though Kurt Weill was interested in a Broadway staging, the play proved politically unsuitable. Then came the one great work of the American period, *Der kaukasische Kreidekreis* (*The Caucasian Chalk Circle*). Work on stage plays took

Brecht out of the Hollywood orbit and into the world of Broadway. Ruth Berlau had moved to New York and he visited her there in 1943, when he met the composer Paul Dessau, who later wrote music for some of his plays. Ruth Berlau later bore Brecht a son, who however died after a few days; always a stormy person, she was more than usually difficult and alcoholised after this.

His son Stefan became an American citizen; but after the end of the war Brecht was looking constantly at the German situation, hoping in vain that after Hitler's defeat the workers would at last create a German revolution. He was active in a broad-left organisation, the 'Council for a Democratic Germany'. His main work was discussing a new version of *Galileo* with Charles Laughton, who then played the lead in it in Beverly Hills and New York (1947). Brecht wanted to return to Europe, but not to either part of a Germany demoralised by Hitler, devastated by war, demolished by reparations and divided by the allies – unless he got good offers and the use of a theatre. Plans to try a start in Switzerland were accelerated in autumn 1947 by a summons before the House Committee on Un-American Activities to answer charges of Communist leanings; he took refuge in vagueness, loss of memory, perverse interpretations of his writings produced in evidence, and the fact that he had never been a party member. A day later he was out of Senator McCarthy's reach on a plane to Europe. In Zurich he met Caspar Neher again, and at Chur had the opportunity of producing a play as practice for a return to Berlin; he adapted Sophocles' *Antigone* for the purpose (1947). Helene Weigel played the lead; Ruth Berlau made a photographic record of the performance usable as a model or pattern for further productions.

He did not go to Berlin until invited, arriving in the Eastern sector on 22 October 1948 to produce *Mother Courage* in the *Deutsches Theater*. He did not underestimate the difficulties; acquaintance in Zurich with actors who had spent the Nazi period in Germany had shown him they had learnt nothing from the catastrophe and had developed a style of acting which carefully avoided all contact with realities. There was also mistrust between the writer and the authorities, but preliminary agreement was reached for the establishment of a standing company – the Berliner Ensemble – under Helene Weigel's management. Back in Zurich, Brecht applied for an Austrian passport, in order to be able to travel freely in both parts of Germany, and also thinking of working at the reformed Salzburg Festival as well as in Berlin. He gained Austrian citizenship in 1950, but the outcry there when it became known made him finally give up the impracticable Salzburg idea. So he settled in Berlin and tried to get other prominent artists to do likewise and form a group of kindred spirits. The Berliner Ensemble was opened on 12 November 1949 with *Puntila* – his new play on the Paris Commune of 1871, *Die Tage der Commune* ('The Days of the Commune', 1948–9) was thought politically too advanced.[13] The theatre was not yet the territory of a Marxist proletariat, but a cultural tradition which the government supported without *élan* and whose audience was basically middle-class. The Ensemble opened up sources of support among the masses – taking theatre to the workers by touring productions to factories and encouraging works trips to the theatre, usually combined with discussions between the working population and the theatre staff. Productions included some of Brecht's adaptations of the classics – Lenz, Hauptmann, Molière; new East German plays; and Brecht's own writings. The second generation of Brecht's team was trained and developed – notably the directors Benno Besson (later at the *Deutsches Theater*, Berlin), Manfred Wekwerth (chief director after Brecht's death) and Peter Palitzsch (later in West Germany). Brecht also adapted plays by Shakespeare, Anna Seghers and Farquhar to improve the repertoire.

Having returned to Germany aware that many of the attitudes which led to the rise of Hitler survived, and having returned to East rather than West Germany in the hope that this was the progressive, if not perfect, German state, Brecht gave much time to propaganda for peace and Communism, in speeches, open letters, poems and discussions. But he also had continually to defend his art and ideas against a fossilised party orthodoxy; and even when the result of such arguments did not displease him (he and Dessau altered the condemnation of war in *The Trial of Lucullus* to except wars of self-defence, in deference to political pressures), they added to his unease, shown in an increasing need to be right in every argument, if necessary by shouting the opponent down. He might attack the party bureaucracy – but did not allow his assistants the same freedom.[14] When he and Eisler planned reworkings of Goethe's *Faust* showing the bourgeois side of the great German hero, Walter Ulbricht personally condemned their ventures. In the early fifties the party demanded more production from workers and artists, but not on lines Brecht could agree with. The independently thought-out productions of the Berliner Ensemble existed, for some years in a vacuum; many people Brecht would have liked to work with went West. When the government's stress on more production (and less reward) led to the rising of 17 June 1953, Brecht's view that there were indeed grounds for discontent was neutralised by his fear of American provocation and intervention. A letter of his to Walter Ulbricht, attempting a balanced view, was published in a truncated form which made it seem an uncritical acclamation of the party. Though bitter, Brecht used the following period of compromise to encourage the reform of the cultural organisations in East Germany; with the formation of a Ministry of Culture headed by his friend Johannes R. Becher, he gained better official support. His last play, *Turandot* (1953), has little to do with previous versions of the theme, but is bound up with the *Tui-Novel*, satirising the intellectuals in capitalist and other states who prostitute their brains for money and influence. He still had female company. Helene Weigel continued to fascinate him as well as being the indispensable organiser. Ruth Berlau was increasingly dependent on him, liable to alcoholic depression and capable of spectacular attacks of jealousy. Käthe Reichel was a young actress to whom he gave special attention on and off stage. Käthe Rülicke was in favour, and finally there was Isot Kilian. The last two years of his life were outwardly successful: established in a model theatre, he was honoured in various ways in East Germany and Russia and had great success in Paris with *The Caucasian Chalk Circle*. But the reception of his work in East Germany did not satisfy him.[15] Even the official record admits that in the early fifties the work of the country's most famous dramatist 'could not become accepted without conflicts' (*nicht . . . durchzusetzen war*).[16] Influential critics had condemned him as decadent when they found no spontaneous rising of the masses in *Mother Courage*; and attacked him for being too traditional, or not traditional enough, or not comprehensible enough to the masses (as if they knew best what could be put across). He was patronised as a non-party-member who couldn't quite keep up with the party aesthetic line.[17] A high point of official uninterest was reached when the party organ *Neues Deutschland* disregarded the première of *The Caucasian Chalk Circle*. Brecht also begrudged the time wasted in public activities and retired as often as possible to work in his country house at Buckow. He died of a heart attack on 14 August 1956 after suffering the after-effects of virus flu for some months.

Though within his own circle Brecht made no secret of his feelings, he was reluctant to bare his private life to the public at large. He stylised himself and lived behind façades: the angry young man, the commissar, the sage. Autobiographical elements in his literary work are few: even his poems do not allow one to build up an image of Brecht the lover. The way he regulated his love-life by contracts excluding inopportune claims for his undivided attention gives the impression of coolness; yet passion sent him across the American continent to face Ruth Berlau's ungrounded suspicions and jealous scenes. His work shows the same unpredictable blend of coolness and passion; and the loves of his mature life were all women associated with his work. Similarly, a surface flippancy covered feelings: when alone, but only then, he might sit uncomfortably and leave his cat the best place on the sofa.[18] He embraced the intellectual paradox of supporting the use of force for peaceful and useful ends; he thought of himself as a creature of opposites, quoting with obvious involvement a statement about Delacroix: 'In him a warm heart beat in a cold man' (*Tb.*, 186: 10.2.22). Moods of melancholy could take him to a state of depressive near-schizophrenia worthy of a Hofmannsthal (*Aj.*, 2,681: 31.8.44); but in general he was always active, and never spent an idle quarter of an hour.[19] A diffidence born of a feeling that he ought to be able to cope with people and things (*mich zurechtfinden*) better than he in fact could (*Tb.*, 215: 1931) did not prevent him wishing to triumph over mankind by being 'allowed to do what is right, without scruples, harshly' (*Tb.*, 209: 1927). Such Nietzscheanism is seen in his private life in his not suffering fools gladly (he could be repellent to people he suspected of stupidity or uncongeniality), and in outbursts of temper when he felt let down by poor work from his collaborators. His life was too short, fragmented and passionate to allow him to gain serenity: yet, as we shall see, it was an important ideal for him.

2 Brecht's Ways of Thought

The young Brecht hated Bolshevism as being too orderly and regimented (*Tb.*, 61: 12.9.20). His intellectual attitudes were undisciplined: he doubted his ability to keep to a single philosophical system (*Tb.*, 32: 24.8.20). The less rigid and more meditative quality of oriental thought had more appeal to him; he discovered an affinity with Lao Tzu as soon as introduced to his work (*Tb.*, 66: 21.9.20). Oriental aspects can be seen in such poems as *Of swimming in lakes and rivers* (8,209; *B. Poems*, 29), where the individual progressively abandons himself to the influence of water and becomes an aquatic object with no will of his own to contradict nature. A nihilism or cynicism typical of the twenties is also visible. His early works show a keen sense of the morbidity of nature alongside the wish for communion with it;[1] the nauseating and the attractive are not separated. Similarly, a sharp awareness of man's proclivities to exploit and terrorise man does not exclude a romantic wish to see mankind brought closer to perfection. Marxism is a means to that end.

He describes (*Tb.*, 221: 1935) how, where the German upheavals of 1918–19, Eisenstein's films and Piscator's theatre had not made him turn to Marx, he was forced to recognise the nature of capitalism when he wanted to use the wheat-exchange of Chicago as the background for a play. Finally he got the impression: 'From every viewpoint except that of a handful of speculators this grain-market was one big morass. The planned drama was not written, instead I began to read Marx . . .' (20,46: *Der Lernende ist wichtiger als die Lehre*). This reading never means sinking himself in the attitudes of the Communist party: he still has his own development, his attitudes and idiosyncracies; and he continually checks Marx against contemporary reality, as suggested in the poem *Thought in the works of the classics* (9, 568; *B. Poems*, 269). His thought always directs itself to the solution of his personal problems as man and author. Truth is for him, in a truly Marxian sense, concrete. 'By years of practice he had made himself incapable of understanding bloodless abstractions at all'.[2] Marxism and Communism satisfy Brecht's curiosity as to what makes people and societies work, and his humanitarian impulse. There is no evidence for supposing he embraced Communism as a mother surrogate or as an authoritarian organisation which would absolve him from having to exercise rational self-control and make decisions of his own – psychoanalytical explanations used by presumptuous critics to propagate the view that Communist beliefs are something to be explained away rather than taken seriously.[3] Had he so deeply wanted to lose himself in a mass he could not, as he did, have coolly regarded himself as a bourgeois who happened to have espoused the proletarian cause (*Aj.*, 1, 143: 5.8.40). Marxism's attraction for him is that of reason, not of belief. 'The moment Brecht realised there was another way to improve conditions in the world than the discredited religious and ethical nonsense, he embarked on this humanitarian path and followed it with exemplary steadfastness. This was not the choice of a religion, but the finding of reason.'[4]

For our purposes Marx's thought is that of the early and middle periods. Brecht was certainly familiar with the political economy of *Capital*, but, for the plays we are to consider, this is not called on. Brecht tends to provide a critique of parts of the superstructure of bourgeois ideology – family, science, charity, religion – more than he looks at the economic substructure. His models of capitalist society are, from the viewpoint of Marxian economics, very simple. Even *Saint Joan of the Stockyards*, dependent on Marx for its whole structure, only uses the circulation sphere; *The Good Person of Szechwan* involves only the primitve capitalism of the manufacture stage. Marx's characteristic thought as relevant to us may be summarised (following his sketch in the Preface to *A Contribution to the Critique of Political Economy*) as involving the tenets (1) 'that legal relations as well as forms of state are to be grasped neither from themselves nor from the so-called general development of the human mind, but rather have their roots in the material conditions of life'; (2) that the economic structure of society is based on relations of production which men enter into with each other – relations corresponding to the stage of development of production and not dependent on men's free will; (3) that the economic structure of society is 'the real foundation, on which rises a legal and political superstructure and to which correspond definite forms of social consciousness'; (4) that material life conditions social, political and intellectual life – 'it is not the consciousness of men that determines their being, but, on the contrary, their social being that determines their consciousness'; (5) that material productive forces, as they develop, demand changes in the relations of production and property between men; (6) that these changes come about in a social revolution, whereby the new material conditions, having developed within the existing society, change the economic foundation and consequently the whole superstructure; (7) that 'the bourgeois relations of production are the last antagonistic form of the social process of production; at the same time the productive forces developing in the womb of bourgeois society create the material conditions for the solution of that antagonism.'

This world-view is a materialist use of historical dialectics as developed by Hegel, for whom history is a flux of contradictions seen as analogous to philosophical concepts (theses). Theses are to Hegel not independent, but automatically engender their opposites (antitheses). From thesis and antithesis proceeds a synthesis, which combines them without really superseding them. In history, the universal synthesis is the self-realisation of the harmonious world-spirit. Marx interprets the flux of contradictions as a succession of kinds of society which alienate man – that is, force people to sell their labour and renounce the values it creates, thus alienating them and inhibiting their free self-development as individuals. The synthesis he replaces by the concept of man's freeing himself from alienation by revolutionary practice which removes contradictions.

To Marx revolutionary practice is a subjective category (*Theses on Feuerbach*, I). To Lenin, however, only matter exists, and our perceptions only reproduce it; so nature and history are objectively dialectical. Brecht scorns this view as too simple. He developed his Marxism in discussion groups dominated by the theoretician Karl Korsch, and, sharing his opposition to Stalinist orthodoxy,[5] sees Marxism more as science than as philosophy and more as method than as dogma: a tool for interpreting the movement of history and criticising bourgeois society, not a unified world-image or complete system, still less a statement of Utopian historical ideas to be realised (20, 152: *Dialektik*; 16, 531: *Was den Philosophen auf dem Theater interessiert*; *M. Dial*, 36; cf; Engels, Letter to C. Schmidt, 5.8.1890). 'Scientific socialism is not at all concerned with the painting of a future state of society.'[6] It is a theory of conflict. Class struggle is central to Marx's and Lenin's view of society as it so far exists. Brecht too shows a world in which man is a wolf to man, a marauder, selfish and grasping.[7] This can be changed, eventually, by the means taught by Marx – the revolutionary change of economic relationships; but there is nothing simple about this, and one must continually re-examine the present state of society, which is changing all the time in its dynamic flux of contradictions. Marx charges one to see all things dynamically, according to the principle of change.[8] Brecht follows Marx closely, is a connoisseur of the progressively shifting interactions of the various components of society, and points out how the same phenomena can be unitary in one context and contradictory in another. 'in nations the proletariat sees things fighting against one another; as a unit it sees them as against itself, the proletariat. only recognition of their unitariness and disunitariness allows it a reasonable political line' (*Aj.*, 1, 86; 31.1.40). Or, concretely concerning Germany in 1918–19:

the SPD, i tried to explain, had precisely that amount of power that the allies and german imperialists allowed it and procured for it. – 'and why did they not grasp more power?' he said. – 'there was a certain fear of revolution', i said. . . . it is continually impossible to make circumstances in germany clear to people who have not heard of at any rate two theorems of dialectics, the one about opposites acting as a unit and the one about the leap from quantity to quality' (*Aj.*, 2, 720).

Dialectics here is a means of analysis allowing the common interests of apparently opposed parties to be recognised, and also an explanation of the discontinuity of history. For Marx, we have seen, the new conditions ripen within the old. A given order of society can contain the consequences of its development up to a given extent, beyond which they must assert themselves in a revolutionary movement changing the society – but before that extent is reached no revolutionary movement could succeed. Only the quantitative accumulation produces the qualitative leap.

Marx had ideas, based on the situation at various times of his own life, on the probable course of the social revolution. He altered these views as history developed. For Brecht to stick to Marx's final views, the best part of a century later, would have been undialectical. He believed that capitalism would be ended by crises and unemployment – rejecting Marx's pauperism theory.[9] If Brecht had around 1930 a phase of starry-eyed acceptance of the inevitability and closeness of the victory of the proletariat and the withering away of the state, the experience of Hitler and Stalin did away with it and made Brecht develop a longer time-scale incorporating the possibility of short-term reverses; his private concept of 'gedewei' (*Geduldserweiterung*, extension of patience) was much needed from 1933 to 1953. In any case, describing the Communist state is something to which Engels is more prone than Marx (the withering away of the state is best described by Engels, in Chapter III of *Socialism: Utopian and Scientific*). Brecht too holds back with unambiguous results, preferring hopeful travel to arrival,[10] doubt to certainty. 'one chinese picture roll THE DOUBTER' has first place in an inventory of his possessions (*Aj.*, 1, 73; 8.12.39). He concentrates on change and unlikeness, not stability and harmony; he contradicts himself freely; he knows his name will be forgotten when changes in the world have made his work oudated (9, 562: *Warum soll mein Name genannt werden?*); he does not believe perfect relationships between people are possible in any conceivable society, for he can see no possible end to dialectical development and contradiction.[11]

This is the approach of a playwright, whose chosen genre is based on contradiction and struggle. Beyond the age of thirty or so most playwrights need an intellectual structure to allow them to write the plays they still have in them, and Brecht found the structure of the Marxist dialectic most congenial. The Marxism of his plays is in the underlying attitudes, the dialectical structure, rather than in superficial content or in any following of the Communist aesthetic line. The basic structure, furthermore, involves certain directions of movement in his dramatic work. Some, perhaps most, writers are unable to deal with social questions until they have sorted out matters of individual belief, and for them the personal is primary, the social something to move towards. Brecht is of the opposite type: he cannot deal with individual matters until the social aspect is secured. The didactic and other plays of his early thirties concentrate on the social and his adaptation to a particular way of viewing it. The plays we are more concerned with here build on this foundation and move back towards defining the place of the individual within its structure.

Brecht, unlike his friend Korsch – who had been excluded from the Communist party in 1926 – was not content to confine his Marxism to theory; the Soviet Union is after all 'the first workers' state in history',[12] theoretical criticism automatically means an impulse to practical improvement. In the practical field Brecht was impressed by Lenin's combination of theory and pragmatism.[13] Marx is indeed close to pragmatism in the philosophical sense, believing 'In practice man must prove the truth, that is, the reality and power, the this-sidedness of his thinking' (*Theses on Feuerbach*, II). Only concrete applications can allow one to judge of a philosophical theory. Brecht was fond of the English proverb, 'The proof of the pudding is in the eating.' The dialectic is fed not by abstruse philosophical considerations, but by real cases (*Aj.*, 1, 85ff.). Theory and practice are inseparable. So if Brecht was suspicious of Korsch's lack of enthusiasm for practically changing society, he was equally opposed to the unintellectuality of the Stalinist party line. Korsch led him in opposition to Bolshevisation – the extension of the Moscow line to Communist parties outside Russia.[14] Brecht demands a Marxism of equal intellectual rigour and practical effectiveness.[15]

He joins issue with Stalin about the nature of the superstructure: culture has for him, as for Engels (letter to J. Bloch, 21.9.1890), its own history independent within certain limits of the substructure, and can anticipate the substructure's future or try experiments about it (20, 76–8: *Thesen zur Theorie des Überbaus*). So the demands of socialist realism as formulated by A. A. Zhdanov in the thirties – the veristic or mimetic reproduction of a real milieu recognisable to the recipient, the moral demands for equality and justice attached as a message, the inevitable rosy revolutionary future – are alien to him. His work has to lay bare dialectical processes at work under the surface, and to encourage thought (not just moral feeling) about social change as a historical phenomenon.

Only thus can it have a function and influence reality. And for this it needs to use discursive and allegorical treatments. The apparently philistinic views of Georg Lukács on realism, holding up Balzac as a timeless ideal, seemed to Brecht and a few others (such as Ernst Bloch) to condemn official Communist art to sterility.[16] He was forced to explain that he was against socialist realism because he was for socialism and for realism.[17] He even defends expressionism: Toller's unrealistic plays opened many people's eyes to social realities. The effect, not the means, counts. Anger at inhumane conditions can be awakened in many ways, by presentations in objective and in imaginative form; art participating in the struggle of the working class needs formal principles derived from that struggle, not from bourgeois models (19, 293–5: *Praktisches zur Expressionismusdebatte*; 19, 327: *Volkstümlichkeit und Realismus*; *B. on Theatre*, 110; 19, 380: *Über sozialistischen Realismus*). Class awareness is a necessity for critical revolutionary practice – and in the Popular Front period Brecht felt Lukács did not possess it (*Aj.*, 1, 13: July 1938) and was too inclined to compromise with the bourgeois.

Orthodox Marxism has difficulty in accommodating anything indeterminate or apparently subjective: not only non-mimetic art, but quantum theory in physics and mutation theory in biology. Brecht on the other hand took readily to quantum physics. His acceptance of its philosophical implications as a refutation of determinism – seen in various notes from his American period – has, in dealing with society, the implication that while we can make forecasts on the basis of statistical probability no individual fate is quite determined. So past historical events were not inevitable. Chance played a part in struggles which were often close-run. Future movements, of individuals and masses, are also not completely foreseeable. The relationship of mass and individual is a fruitful source of tensions for Brecht: the individual's decisions are important, and real, and the sum of individual decisions makes history. Rigid Utopian ideas of whither the dialectic of history is tending are dismissed. Scope is allowed for the imagination: the individual can produce something new and alter the world.

The keen eye for contradictions is a prerequisite of humour as well as of dialectics (14, 1460: *Flüchtlingsgespräche* XI). Brecht is reported to have opined that the Russian and the Italian soldiers were the best in World War II: 'they know what they're fighting for.'[18] The dialogue form is important too: dialectics originated as the art of finding truth through conversation. Philosophical dialogues from Plato through Galileo to Diderot fascinated Brecht, who uses the form himself at the time of the great plays in *Flüchtlingsgespräche* ('Refugees' Conversations') and the *Messingkauf*: the arguments between different figures may end in a consensus, but not in a forced harmonisation which would make any of the participants give up his individuality. The fascination of the oriental for Brecht is another source of a certain detachment. Brecht worked on adapting Mo Di (Mê Ti), in whose writings the concepts of Yin and Yang, the universal duality, and their harmonious interwork-ing, first appear.[19] The balance of opposites may be seen in his life and work in this among other ways: whilst his activism as a Communist is perfectly serious and wholehearted, it is balanced by serenity *vis-à-vis* the events of life (Hermann Hesse's ideal too, in *Steppenwolf*). This serenity appears in his life – though never for long; for instance, in the ability to write *Puntila* whilst tensely awaiting the outcome of the Battle of Britain; and in his work – in many exile poems as implicit negation of the single-minded hatred shown by many other opponents of Hitler. In *The Mask of Evil* (10, 850; *B. Poems*, 383) he regards with sympathy the swelling veins which show 'what a strain it is to be evil'. Serenity also helps to explain the difference between Brecht's great plays and the work of many engaged writers, unable to look dispas-sionately at their beliefs and always tense in their attempts to con-convince. For him, 'the simplest [*leichteste*] way of living is in art' (16,700; *Kleines Organon* §77: *B. on Theatre*, 205). Another point where Brecht uses oriental ideals is for what the Marxist classics do not dis-cuss: personal relationships on a smaller scale than the grand move-ment of history. 'That doctrine deals above all with the behaviour of great masses of people . . . But in our demonstrations we'd be more concerned with the behaviour of individuals to one another' (16, 530: *Messingkauf, Was den Philosophen auf dem Theater interessiert*; *M. Dial.*, 35). For this field Brecht – disinclined to borrow Christian concepts of neighbourly love – develops the Chinese idea of deep politeness. Lao Tzu wrote the *Tao Te Ching* only because he was too kind to refuse a poor stranger's request for a précis of his beliefs (*Legend of the origin of the book* . . .; 9, 660; *B. Poems*, 314). The beliefs are seen as socially progressive too: there is a synthesis of Marxism and Eastern gentleness.

The major failure of Brecht's dialectics is a tendency to see ideologies and modes of social organisation other than Communism as mere varia-tions on a theme. Capitalism, parliamentary democracy and fascism are seen as intimately connected (*Aj.*, 2, 823: 16.3.48). Hitler becomes simply the finest flower of capitalism (*Aj.*, 1, 262: 14.4.41), Nazism the continu-ation of bourgeois domination only by more nakedly violent means. This view does not allow Brecht to cope with the problem of anti-Semitism in the Third Reich.

Just as Brecht's theoretical Marxism is the result of independent thought, so his view of the practice of Soviet Communism is unblinkered. He firmly believed that international Communism was the only viable way to social justice and equality, and the Soviet Union the guarantor of its viability – having made life much better for millions, even if it had not produced all conceivable social improvements (*Aj.*, 1, 82: 26.1.40).

He points out that the western concepts of individual freedom and of democracy are tainted by association with capitalism and competition, and other criteria of a society are thinkable. In a state where the masses possess the means of production and no one is allowed to use his talents to exploit others, perhaps new kinds of personality develop (19, 437: *Kraft und Schwäche der Utopie*). It is the tremendous social advances in Soviet Russia that justify Brecht's serene optimism about the future despite Stalinist terror. Esslin (pp. 275f.) claims that Brecht continually proves despite himself that human nature is violent and bad. He forgets that for millions in Russia, and for Brecht, the liberation after 1917 from feudal restraints, exploitation and insecurity was a constant proof of the opposite. The failings of Communism, the show trials and purges under Stalin particularly, disquieted Brecht. In private notes he compares the party bureaucracy with that of fascism (*Aj.*, 1, 307: 27.10.41) and is very hard on the excuses given for Stalin's invasion of Poland in collusion with Hitler (*Aj.*, 1, 65: 18.9.39). But publicly, looking at Soviet Communism in the global context, he always found it possible to support it rather than any capitalist system, to express solidarity with it and support Stalin's right to defend its achievements as he saw fit (20, 111–5: *Über die Moskauer Prozesse*).[20] Similarly he reacted to the Berlin rising of 1953 by supporting the disaffected workers but doing nothing that might make the Socialist state less secure.

The mistakes of Communist governments are for Brecht no reason for returning to capitalism. Rather they are an impetus to work harder for more Communism, for the freeing of each person from alienation and the enabling of everyone to spend his working life producing materially or intellectually in the way best suited to his personality.[21] Brecht's emphasis on production, or productivity, starts very early (20, 49: *Musterung der Motive junger Intellektueller*). Productivity is, for Brecht as for Marx, important for the future of Communism and the self-realisation of the individual. Marx looks forward to a phase 'after the enslaving subordination of the individual to the division of labour, and therewith also the antithesis between mental and physical labour has vanished; after labour has become not only a means of life but life's prime want; after the productive forces have also increased with the all-round development of the individual . . .' (*Critique of the Gotha Programme*). Brecht, rejecting the intensification of division of labour under Stalin, defines Communism as 'a great production' rather than 'a great order', its struggle as being 'of the freeing of the productivity of all men from all chains', the products being 'lamps, hats, musical compositions, chess moves, irrigation, complexion . . .' (*Aj.*, 1, 247: 7.3.41). Here he is following his theatrical collaborator Erich Engel, who in 1928 had said that all intellectually productive workers had 'to make sure that when once the poor enter into possession of the means of production they do not just enter a new grey monotony (*Trostlosigkeit*) as state labourers with no meaning to their existence'. This (together with some thoughts on the role of intellect and imagination in the Marxist system) is proof of a striking affinity between Brecht and Engel.[22]

Moral progress is dependent on social progress, individual liberation on mass liberation. Once society allows people to help each other rather than compete, they can relax and become serene. In a discussion of Communism in *Refugees' Conversations* Ziffel says: 'It is quite sufficient if you say a community should be so organised that what is useful to the individual is useful to all' (14, 1465). A higher egoism is reached through acceptance of the community.

3 Theory and Practice of Brechtian Theatre

Brecht's early theory of theatre is consciously one-sided, in rebellion against German theatre around 1920, 'in which bombastic productions of the classics alternate with empty photographic replicas of real life',[1] and against the last two German literary and theatrical movements – naturalism and expressionism. His mature theory is only the link between general tenets of his Marxism and alterations in his theatrical practice; not a complete theory of theatre.[2] The *Short Organum* is his only systematic statement on theatre; also important are the *Messingkauf* dialogues (16, 499–657; *M. Dial.*) and the notes on individual plays and performances (17, 943–1296).

At the beginning of Brechtian theatre is enjoyment (*Spass*), never quite ousted by the more sedate 'entertainment' (*Unterhaltung*). His early cynicism leads to healthy suspicions of the pretensions of grand tragedy; from the 'inertia of matter' and the 'inadequacy of all things, including ourselves' Brecht prefers to wring enjoyment, as do the comedians Karl Valentin (15, 39; *Karl Valentin*) and Charlie Chaplin. At the end of his life again he demands a spectator capable of 'enjoying himself in a sophisticated manner' (*sich differenzierten Spass zu bereiten*).[3] His notes on *Mother Courage* close with an apology for any over-seriousness and an avowal of intent to amuse (*Mat. C.*, 80); his productions of his own works show this intention at work. But enjoyment also means, from an early stage, that the spectator exercises his intellect on what as a stage action seems strange and incomprehensible. 'The "chaotic" which stimulated our naïver intelligence to bring order into it was our true element' (15, 81: *Über das Theater, das wir meinen*). A similar appeal to the spectator's reason is found in the theories of the expressionist playwright Georg Kaiser, whom Brecht saw as a precursor.[4] From the stimulation of the intelligence, Brecht is able to move to the presentation of political contents. Ideological drama is nothing new. Brecht remarked that medieval mystery plays and the Jesuit theatre of Austria showed didactic tendencies, making them too his forerunners. He wants to deepen the audience's understanding of certain events seen in the past, and this depends on his taking up a perspective outside these events which determines his choice of material.[5] For him this perspective is a social one; so his enjoyable intellectual art is to appeal to material and social interests. In a stratified society great art will serve and appeal to the interests of only one social layer (*Schicht*) (15, 91f.: *Über die Eignung zum Zuschauer*).

The approach of socially committed naturalism, as in some plays of Gerhart Hauptmann, whose emphasis on reproduction of a confined reality allows full sympathy for the oppressed to arise but scarcely has room for analysis of the wider social factors, is no longer sufficient for Brecht, once he sees with Marx (*Theses on Feuerbach*, III) that economic and social processes must not be presented as unalterable and fated, externals that no individual can escape, but rather as produced by people and capable of being modified by people. Naturalism describes the misery of today, not of hope of tomorrow; it is 'ersatz realism' (*Aj.*, 2, 780: 30.3.47). It cannot show the wider scene, though more suitable for immediate propaganda than is the theatre Brecht has in mind. A school of left-wing theatre which has more appeal for Brecht, though still not satisfying him, is the 'epic theatre' of Erwin Piscator in the twenties, which uses bold technical experiments such as the marrying of film and stage action, lavish technology, a strong left-wing message put over directly in the text and the whole style of presentation, and the over-riding of conventional dramatic action among individuals by the showing of large-scale political developments. Brecht supported Piscator when he was attacked for political bias, and he first uses the term 'epic theatre' at this point and in Piscator's sense (15, 104: *Über die Volksbühne*). It is the example of Piscator's attempt to run a left-wing theatre that leads Brecht to analyse the commercial theatre as a means of production, in the hands of capitalists and thus resistant to any new directions involving social change. 'The cry for a new theatre is the cry for a new social order' (15, 172: *Über eine neue Dramatik*). His first major independent statement on epic theatre (1927) already has a socially committed line (influenced by the sociologist Fritz Sternberg), demanding a new style to rejuvenate the whole repertoire (not just something for new plays), which will be part of the ideological superstructure for the effective real social shifts (*Umschichtungen*) of the present; will embrace acting, stage technology, theatre music and use of film, as well as dramaturgy; and 'appeals less to the feelings than to the spectator's reason. Instead of sharing an experience [*miterleben*] the spectator must come to grips [*sich auseinandersetzen*] with things. At the same time it would be quite wrong to try and deny emotion to this kind of theatre' (15, 172: *Betrachtung über die Schwierigkeiten des epischen Theaters*; *B. on Theatre*, 23, but I have altered the translation). Where Piscator was concerned to confront individual fate and general political development, to reproduce reality on the stage, to give the spectator an emotional experience, and to make propaganda, Brecht soon saw the limitations of this development of naturalism, and wanted to make his protagonists representative of social development, to represent (not reproduce) reality in distanced ways, and to allow an intellectual experience leading to a critical attitude. Rather than simply activising and fomenting revolution, he wants to take a long-term view, to adopt the perspective of the rising proletariat – what has been called his plebeian standpoint;[6] to invite the workers to think, learn, recognise their existing social position and formulate ideas for its revision. *The Mother*, a play centred on the Russian revolt of 1905, epitomises this. Brecht wants to encourage the revolutionary activity which, according to Marx (*Theses on Feuerbach*, I) is practical-critical activity. Turning a tragic attitude on its head, the spectator says 'the suffering of this man shatters me, because there is after all a way out he could take' (15, 265: *Vergnügungstheater oder Lehrtheater*; my translation, fuller than *B. on Theatre*, 71). Criticism extends, then, to the behaviour of the dramatic figures as well as to the author's way of dealing with reality. Brecht has always wanted this, starting with the debunking of the current repertoire. In the intervals of a tragedy, he suggests, clowns should appear, bet on the outcome, refer to the hit of the week, and instruct the stage-hands: 'He's on his way out now, you know. Turn the lighting down!' (*Tb.*, 45f.: 1.9.20; 15, 51). This is to draw the public's attention towards the substance: 'Hang it all, the *things* should get criticised, the plot, the words, the gestures, not the execution' (ibid.). Any similarity to Dadaism is merely passing: after holding current culture up to ridicule, Brecht soon feels the need to present an alternative. Criticism remains a constant. Shaw is praised for his cold-blooded attitude to important phenomena, 'because it is the only one that permits complete concentration and real alertness' (15, 97f.: *Ovation für Shaw*; *B. on Theatre*, 10). The material is primary, the aesthetics secondary. Theatre is above all a democratic institution trying to give the audience enhanced possibilities of visualising and performing changes in the world. 'The philosophers have only *interpreted* the world, in various ways; the point, however, is to change it' (Marx, *Theses on Feuerbach*, XI). 'The theatre became an affair for philosophers, but only for such philosophers as wished not just to explain the world but also to change it' (15, 266: *Vergnügungstheater oder Lehrtheater*; *B. on Theatre*, 72).

A critical attitude does not necessarily mean that the theatre attacks the state in which it finds itself. Eastern theorists have claimed the German Democratic Republic needs no critical theatre; Western ones that since Brecht held fast to the concept of criticism even in East Germany, he cannot have been a loyal communist. Both have failed to grasp the point. Criticism allows ways of improving the good, as well as of eradicating the bad, to be seen and practised (16, 671; *Kleines Organon* §22).

It means mainly putting reason to work. All ideologies presumably believe in working against war; Brecht's specific view is that no one can learn to overcome the irrational charms of aggressiveness from a play which merely shocks him and does not also put reason to work against unreason. Wekwerth (p. 280) rightly tells us that theatre of cruelty can get a shock effect from showing physical horror, but that it is more meaningful to go back to the origins of the horror and present to the audience's understanding the mechanisms of social alienation.

For the philosopher who wants to forecast and to influence human behaviour, theatre is a source of examples, 'models' (16, 509f.: *Messingkauf*, introductory dialogue; *M. Dial.*, 13f.). For Brecht, people who think, and who are presented with a new vision of capitalist society showing its outdatedness, must take sides in the social struggle, and further thought will impel them towards Communism – unless their class bonds, their interest in the continuation of exploitation, are too strong. Brecht never claimed he could convert the class enemy![7] Rather, he accepted that his plays would split the audience into camps by class interests. He does not want to celebrate (like the expressionists) some sort of universal brotherhood, easily used as a cover for continuation of the *status quo*, exploitation and so on.

His is a practical theatre, a means to an end; its beauty must spring from function, from its role in the business of living.[8] Nothing could be more alien to it than an aesthetic experience as an end in itself. But, from the mid-thirties on at any rate, Brecht tries not to reduce theatre to a series of dry-as-dust demonstrations. To see possible improvements for the world, to hope for their realisation, to plan them, to realise something of what makes the world what it is and of one's own role (real and potential) in important processes – these are enjoyments, and theatre is called on to make them possible and to surround them with more specifically aesthetic pleasures. Learning, Brecht points out, can be a pleasure, provided it is not merely buying knowledge in order to resell it later (15, 266: *Vergnügungstheater oder Lehrtheater*; *B. on Theatre*, 72); so 'Theatre remains theatre even when it is instructive theatre, and in so far as it is good theatre it will amuse' (15, 267: same essay; *B. on Theatre*, 73).

As Brecht – still following the *Theses on Feuerbach* – sees revolutionary practice materialistically, he reacts sharply to the charge of wanting simply to update Schiller's idealistic notion of theatre as a moral institution. 'We were not in fact speaking in the name of morality but in that of the victims. These truly are two distinct matters, for the victims are often told that they ought to be contented with their lot, for moral reasons' (15, 271: same essay; *B. on Theatre*, 75). He finds other than moral grounds to be against hunger, cold and oppression; other ways than preaching to remove these evils. The lesson of his plays is never a moral, but a statement about society made in the hope of encouraging change. Such statements of Brecht's stress the importance of economic factors in human behaviour to a degree unmatched even by German naturalism.

All plays and films have lessons – if only lessons about how to hold a fork. They project to the audience a view of life, human nature, and cause and effect. These views may be clichés, even dangerous. The spectator is brought to share certain feelings of the persons appearing on the stage and thereby to approve them as universally human feelings, only natural, to be taken for granted. They need not always in fact *be* correct, universally human, natural feelings' (15, 430: *Lohnt es sich, vom Amateur-theater zu reden?*; B. *on Theatre*, 150, but without the last sentence quoted here). Brecht works against this partly by encouraging the feelings he finds preferable – those which help transform the nature of human interrelations (16, 678: *Kleines Organon* §35; *B. on Theatre*, 190); but largely by his opposition to the spectator being made to share feelings of the stage figures.

> I hope to have avoided in 'Baal' and 'Jungle' a great error of other art: its attempt to carry the spectator with it [*mitzureissen*]. I instinctively leave distances [*Abstände*] here and see to it that my effects (of poetic and philosophical nature) remain limited to the stage. The spectator's 'splendid isolation' [in English in the original] is not violated, it is not sua res, quae agitur, he is not lulled by being invited to empathise [*mitzuempfinden*], to incarnate himself in the hero . . . There is a higher kind of interest: that in the parable [*Gleichnis*], the Other, the Confused [*Unübersehbaren*], Strange' (*Tb.*, 187: 10.2.22; 15, 62).

From the outset Brecht turns against the spectator's self-identification (empathy, *Einfühlung*) with the great personage in favour of the spectator's interest in the course of events, against a quasi-mystical, quasi-hypnotic mass emotional experience in the theatre in favour of cool awareness that the effects produced are stage effects. This is the basis of his theory of distancing (*Verfremdung*), which has been translated by 'alienation' and 'estrangement' – both words with undue negative connotations – and literally means 'making strange'. Our term 'distancing' is analogous to the well-tried, clear and suitably neutral French term *distanciation*.

Conventional stage illusion is created by two techniques: the imitation of reality on the stage, and a quasi-hypnosis which induces the spectator to suspend his knowledge of the unreality and improbability of what he sees. Illusion is often destroyed by techniques which draw attention to the unreality of the stage by altering the perspective: presenting two levels of stage 'reality' (the play within a play or deception within the action), planting actors in the auditorium and thus loosening the division between stage and audience, and so on. Brecht's destruction of illusion by distancing is radically different because it refers the stage action to the *public's* reality. The world of the stage no longer claims autonomy, and is 'merely' an act put on for the public, but continues to claim truthfulness and relevance. The actor shows himself as actor, but as a real person – say Charles Laughton; not as a stagey actor hamming a part. In Brecht's world there is not the conventional agreement to suspend disbelief, for there is no consensus about any metaphysical reality which it would be right and proper for the actor to hypnotise the audience into sharing with him. The actor is only an individual who demonstrates on stage the special cases of other, fictional individuals. There are no morals to be handed down with the voice of authority, only suggestions as to how to see things.[9]

Distancing of one kind and another was discovered, or rediscovered, by others at about the same time. Brecht was aware, for instance, of Pirandello's *Six Characters in Search of an Author*, produced in Berlin in 1924.[10] The term *Verfremdung* itself appears in his theory relatively late, apparently a fruit of his visit to Moscow in 1935 and the influence of the Russian formalists. The precise importance of the Russian connection is still much discussed;[11] but Piscator and Brecht were working on lines analogous to Russian developments long before the Russian term (*ostranenie*: showing the familiar as if seen for the first time) appears in Brecht. About 1930, Brecht had combined his anti-illusionistic techniques, worked out to keep the audience alert and critical, with a socially orientated dialectical interpretation of the procedure of distancing. The Russian example had been important: Sergei Tretiakov for the use of documents about the social revolution in such a way as to inform the audience as well as inflaming it; Meyerhold for the fostering of non-naturalistic styles of acting to the point of grotesquerie and for accuracy of work-processes presented – both seen in Brecht's Berlin production of the revised *Man is Man*; Mayakovsky for the emphasis on the theatrical work of art as a product (the concretised work of certain people, and a step in the general social process of production) and on the dialectics of history; all of them for political and social commitment. It was lucky for theatre history that Piscator and Brecht were able – after 1945 – to keep alive elements of a Soviet tradition which in Russia was stifled by Stalin and the hegemony of Stanislavsky's theories and practice.

With *Verfremdung* comes the *Verfremdungseffekt* or *V-effekt* – 'v-effect' seems an innocuous translation. This is any technique which allows stage action to be turned into food for thought by being made to seem strange and even forced: 'one which allows us to recognize its subject, but at the same time makes it seem unfamiliar' (16, 680: *Kleines Organon* §42; *B. on Theatre*, 192). Where the critical spectator is given leisure to be intellectually aware that he is not watching a reproduction of empirical reality, some v-effect or other must be present. The socio-philosophical aim is to sow doubt in the spectator's mind. Conventional patterns of looking at things, always present in the twentieth-century audience,[12] are broken down in favour of naïve, unprejudiced modes of vision, things we take for granted presented in a new light. Particularly at the end of his life Brecht develops the category of artistic naïvety,[13] a return to a healthier, deeper level in our responses to life. What has always been thus and is familiar to us need not always be thus, rather it is odd that it has for so long been accepted unquestioningly.

Marx likes to examine the economico-social system of his time as something inorganic: though aware that, in fact, it grew, he is interested only in using and changing it, not in its past. In Brecht, seeing things in the present without trying to show organically how their contradictions came about leads to the montage principle: elements of present reality are juxtaposed so that their contrasts are apparent, but no explanation is offered. In effect, our experience is broken down into components which we see laid bare, stripped of our habitual harmonisations. It is left to us to reconstruct the relationship of the work of art to empirical reality, at the same time discovering the criticism we can apply to our previous view of that reality. Clearly this dissociation attaches Brecht to general trends of modern art. He at once recognised in Picasso's *Guernica* the affinity to his own procedures (*Aj.*, 1, 117: 24.6.40). Similarly Engel had described dialectical materialism as a quasi-artistic concept, because its analysing power breaks up empirical reality and allows it to be properly assessed.[14]

Paradoxically connected with this breaking-down of reality is the principle of historicisation. Again pointed disregard of the past is the clue. Our tendency if we look at the past is to interpret it in terms of the present. Giving the present such importance lends it, or rather our usually blinkered view of it, a spurious naturalness. To counter this Brecht suggests historicisation, looking at 'a particular social system from another social system's point of view' (16, 653: 2. *Nachtrag* to *Messingkauf*; *M. Dial.*, 103), to show just how much of the present social system is accidental and thus alterable. The present contains contradictions which doom it to change. What seems obvious from today's viewpoint is not necessarily eternally true. This concentration on dynamic contradictions, potential change, means looking at things from a dialectical angle. 'When a material is subjected to the examination of dialectical thought, it distances itself.'[15] A simple instance of this principle at work is the argument in proverbs or quotations – found in *Mother Courage*, *Galileo* and *The Caucasian Chalk Circle*. Long-accepted wisdoms turn out to contradict one another and must be reconsidered and evaluated afresh.

Since to Brecht it is self-evident that the critical attitude is basic to social change and should therefore be fostered in the spectator, and since in his view only a theatre of distancing encourages criticism, he is generally convinced that his theatre is the only true social theatre and that empathy is politically undesirable. By pulling the spectator into a mass experience, the conventional theatre – including most Communist theatre – works like a Hitler rally, and so empathetic theatre is damned even if its aims are politically correct: one goes the right way on one's own two feet or not at all (16, 563–7: *Messingkauf, Über die Theatralik des Faschismus*). What can be felt in the theatre is not enough: the audience needs critical knowledge.

Emotion is allowed to exist in Brecht's theatre, though subordinated to reason. The plays are not 'ice-cold intellectual exercises'.[16] The statements that epic theatre narrates (rather than embodying) an action, works with arguments (instead of hypnotic suggestion), investigates man (rather than taking him for granted) and so on do not exclude emotional responses at all; and they only show 'changes of emphasis' compared with conventional dramaturgy (17, 1009f.: *Anmerkungen zur Oper 'Aufstieg und Fall der Stadt Mahagonny'*; *B. on Theatre*, 37). 'Every thought that is necessary has its emotional counterpart, every emotion its rational counterpart' (*Aj.*, 1, 31: 12.9.38). Brecht had a phase of trying to limit (not to abolish) emotion, but repudiates it later in favour of the full, earthy presentation of life (*Aj.*, 1, 180: 25.9.40). There remains a difference from most modern writers, who, with Freud, think they can explain nothing apart from the sexual urge; Brecht, with Marx, thinks he can explain nothing without socio-economic forces. Love and sex are aspects of human life alongside others, interesting mainly in their social effects, not as wellsprings of sensational psychological complexes. What Brecht does oppose is emotions forced on the members of the audience by self-identification with a hero – emotions which may be contrary to their real interests as they would see them if they were invited to think. Brecht cites the film *Gunga Din* as having made him feel an emotional bond with the British – imperialist! – soldiers and scorn the Indian 'natives', despite his intellectual rejection of such attitudes (15, 430f.: *Lohnt es sich, vom Amateurtheater zu reden?*; *B. on Theatre*, 151). The emotions he wants are rational emotions – basically, ones with a definable role in today's class struggles. The individual figure on stage is less important than the class or mass. The audience's attention is to be given to the class, which cannot be accurately represented on stage, by the accurate presentation of the individual, who however is not a mere representative of the class. The audience must not identify with the atypical individual, but be enabled to consider what stands behind him (15, 242–5; *Über rationellen und emotionellen Standpunkt* and *Thesen über die Aufgabe der Einfühlung*). The spectator's and the character's emotions may then diverge: we may be able, for instance, to see more of Mother Courage's predicament than she does herself, to be saddened even where she is happy. Such critical emotions are vital to epic theatre. But these effects cannot be guaranteed by the text alone: a check is required in the form of acting techniques. Empathy leads to acute 'emotional infection',[17] which interferes with the critical attitude, breaking down barriers between protagonist and audience (and between actor and role; Brecht is very suspicious of Stanislavsky and method acting). It thus encourages what he sees as the weakness of naturalism and post-naturalist theatre by imposing on the spectator the same limited view of life that the protagonist – passive in the grip of social circumstances and the existing order – has. In his last years, when opposition to existing theatre practice is less important, Brecht shows magnanimity toward empathetic approaches; he sets up a dialectic of *Einfühlung – Ausfühlung*, feeling-in and feeling-out.[18] The actor has attributed to him a fruitful tension of demonstration and empathy (16, 703: *Nachträge zum Kleinen Organon*).

Much of Brecht is reminiscent of comedy. Tragedy imposes itself on the spectator, makes him acquiesce in its laws, invites him to feel with a figure subjected to an inevitable catastrophe, works with such powers as death, fate, and divine intervention: comedy does not involve inevitable catastrophes or irreversible supernal interventions, and does not suck the spectator into its slipstream, but allows him to remain superior to the action and engage in laughter and criticism, sympathy and *Schadenfreude*, and pleasurable learning. But there must also be, in a good literary comedy, something the spectator will feel seriously affected by. Either he sees a world familiar to him (identification) but subjected to criticism which he is to take to heart (distance); or an unfamiliar world (distance) in which familiar relevant moral problems occur (identification). A typical comic element is the situation in which one or more figures trick or deceive others and the audience shares the secret. The general stage illusion is perforated by a second illusion not shared by the spectator (and dissoluble at any time without permanent ill-effects). Also typical are disguises, changes of role, masks, use of stage tricks for their own sake, caricature, grotesquerie, parody, excess of all sorts, overflowing vitality, large gestures. Apostrophe to the public breaks through stage illusion as needed and makes the spectator a partner in the action. Dialect or uncultured language allows the audience to feel superior and aids distancing. But a certain pathos and seriousness furthering empathy are also useful: the more the spectator is dialectically torn between serious involvement and laughter, the better the comedy.

In this view of comedy much coincides with Brecht. Even in his gloomiest plays he retains laughter and criticism, the feeling that nature

and the fate of the protagonist are not deterministically fated and unalterable, the dialectical alternation of distancing and empathy. Galileo's
manœuvres with the telescope are obvious comic trickery; deception and disguise are the root of *The Good Person*, used with Pir-
andellian gusto, turned into a spectacle in their own right. Azdak in
The Caucasian Chalk Circle is a figure of overflowing comic vitality.
Brecht's exploration of such obsessive characters as Galileo, Shen Teh
and Azdak is reminiscent of Molière. He caricatures: amuses us by comic,
exaggerative, distancing, critical representations.[19] Brechtian comedy
is rooted in his intention to make drama a tool in the productive criticism
of the existing order, and *Theaterarbeit* deals (pp. 42–5) with 'the social
Comical' as the comic aspects of class-divided mankind: basically, the
comedy of the bourgeois as perceived by the rising proletariat. For Marx,
the comic treatment of the ideology of a declining era is the last stage
of its treatment, when it has already been mortally wounded by serious
opposition.[20] Brecht uses this in connection with *Puntila*: the age of the
landowner being past in East Germany, the audience can sit back and
laugh at him. One can hold the bourgeois world up for sympathy (the
tragic approach), or attack it satirically, or show it as objectively out-
dated and comical – Brecht mentions these three approaches quite clearly
very early on (15, 55f.: *Zur Ästhetik des Dramas*) and singles out the comic
approach as the neglected one, the one needing to be worked on. There
is no need to preach against the bourgeois world, mobilise moral opposition to it, or present its conflict with that which is replacing it. It is
simply laughed off the stage; the public need only keep its distance
and be brought to a cool recognition of the basic ridiculousness of what
is presented. This relaxed intention is very different from the intention
of satire, which battles with a still dangerous opponent. In practice the
division between serene comedy and satire is not always clear; and under
the pressure of Hitler Brecht also sometimes has to fall back on a different kind of humour, associated with Schweyk: laughter as a private self-
assertion against an overwhelming and hostile reality which one dare not
oppose directly. But as a general aim Brecht has the comedy which buries
the past and holds a wake over it. An example of an aspect of bourgeois
existence consistently so treated by Brecht is the wedding. From the
early one-acter *The Petty Bourgeois' Wedding* to *The Caucasian Chalk
Circle*, the fine words bandied about at weddings are shown as comically
unrelated to reality, which is a contract for exploitation, sex, food, money.
Brecht thought sexuality in late bourgeois society comical because of
the gap between ideology and reality and the fact that a different society
could cure this (2, 489: *Anmerkungen zur 'Dreigroschenoper'*). Grusha's
wedding is farcical, but Brecht does not forget to emphasise the social
reality: 'Woman hoes the fields and parts her legs. That's what our
calendar says' (2059; 56; 4). In *The Good Person* a comic entanglement

comes about in that Shui Ta cannot be where Shen Teh is – but the fact that both are needed has the serious implication that Shui Ta, who holds the purse-strings, is at least as important to Sun as his bride is. The demonstration of the power of money balances the comic elements, but Shui Ta is not satirically attacked.

Brecht has little sympathy with tragic views of life. 'Tragedy is based on bourgeois virtues, draws its force from them and declines with them' (*Tb.*, 131: 28.5.21). Yet where he looks closely at particular epochs he sometimes takes up the tragic attitude, notably in *The Measures Taken* where the well-meaning protagonist jeopardises a progressive venture by personal weakness; in the analogous situation of Galileo; and in Mother Courage's inability to escape from the vicious circle of war and business. Yet she is not caught up in processes beyond her grasp: she brings about her own downfall by her decisions and what she is caught up in could be altered, if not by her, then by society as a whole. So sympathy for her is not enough, we must remain critical. The balance of sympathy and criticism in Brecht is rarely grasped by critics. Soviet critics were dismayed by Brecht's unsentimental 'revolutionary analysis': they wanted 'revolutionary optimism'[21] even if it meant a glaring inconsistency and the grafting on of a popular rising or suchlike at the end. Westerners, on the other hand, often refuse to see the concept of social alterability, and so see only the tragedy of a situation which they see as representative of the human condition. But to Brecht the tragic features, the sympathy with the declining bourgeois, are secondary; the comic ones, the perspective of the rising proletariat, primary. What is horrible in the play is not necessarily tragic from such a superior viewpoint; when seen from a future perspective, it is cut down to size. The play may not come to a happy end, but one can posit a happy end beyond the end of the play.

Since Brecht's theory originated in the revolt against the existing stage, he labelled it anti-Aristotelian. He polemicised against the canonised ideas of drama loosely associated with Aristotle, rather than against Aristotle himself. He sought replacements for the cathartic emotions of fear and pity: he suggests desire for knowledge and readiness to help (*Aj.*, 1, 198: 15.11.40). But he was closer to Aristotle than he thought; Ronald Gray (p. 83) quotes from Humphry House an interpretation of Aristotle which Brecht could have subscribed to in all main points. To define him as anti-Aristotelian means lumping him together with Claudel, Beckett and other strange bedfellows. Similar confusion surrounds the terms of the later theory, 'theatre for a scientific age' and 'dialectical theatre'. Both mean theatre basing itself on the philosophical and sociological insights of Marx, attempting analysis of reality and thus constructively entertaining people who are used in their daily life to taking up critical and progressive attitudes (16, 671: *Kleines Organon* §21f.;

B. on Theatre, 185). 'Dialectical', used by Brecht with a smile,[22] has the advantage over the paradoxical 'epic theatre' of offering no targets to hostile critics. Another term, 'inductive', emphasises opposition to the deductive logical and dramaturgical procedures associated with Aristotle. To cut through all this Käthe Rülicke-Weiler suggests the term 'Brecht-theatre', and one can but agree. Brecht himself, who rarely wrote a theoretical essay for its own sake but criticisms, polemics, descriptions of stage techniques and the thinking behind them, disliked the impression of dogmatism given involuntarily by his writings. His conversation gave a 'more tentative and lively, and less grandiose' impression than his writing.[23] He thought his theories should be examined only in connection with his stage work. The critics should look first at his theatre, one, he hopes, 'imbued with imagination, humour and meaning', and then use his theories to help analyse its effects. The theories were meant only as hints at the proper performance of his plays (16, 816: *Katzgraben-Notate, Episches Theater; B. on Theatre*, 248).

Brecht took an interest in sub-literary theatrical genres; the fairground puppet-shows of Germany (*Kasperltheater* – comparable to Punch and Judy) were favourites of his, as were early silent films (*Aj.*, 1, 50: 4.5.39). But his plays (like Wedekind's) are no less literary for this; rather (like Shaw when he rejected pretentious dramatic forms for the techniques of the popular theatre) he is giving literature a shot in the arm by widening its range. Another useful technique is adaptation of the corpus of world dramatic literature. As a young rebel Brecht demanded the rejection of all the established classics, but the saving of their plots for their intrinsic value (15, 106: *Materialwert*). Adaptation also involves parody – as with Shaw, whose attitude to the classics and popular plays of the English stage has much in common with Brecht's. Both want to make the audience think and judge for itself.[24] In this process, the audience's recognition of literary structures and phrases it knows in one context, re-used in another, aids the work of historicisation.

Brecht develops a literary style which depends neither on the artificial *Bühnendeutsch* of the classical German stage, a language of purity and lifelessness nowhere found in common speech, nor on the naturalistic imitation of a particular dialect such as Hauptmann's Silesian. The abstraction of the former is avoided by returning to an earlier attempt at universally comprehensible German, the language of Luther's Bible; the particularising effect of the latter is rejected, South German features being used only to give added earthiness, not local colour. Pithy proverbs and apophthegms, Anglicisms, puns, all serve to make truth more concrete.[25] The rhetorical parallelisms of the Bible, the rough-grained verses of the popular stage, the strident rhythms of Kipling, are juxtaposed – but not mingled. The language is by turns stilted, parodistic, poetic, vulgar, to draw attention to the incongruences of the content.[26] The language of a play need not follow a single convention, realistic or otherwise. Brecht avoids too harmonious language, just as he avoids premature resolutions of dialectical conflicts. Often he works from gesture to language, asking first how a person would move in a given situation, then how he would speak. The result is expressive and, so as to represent the true patterns of gestic speech, ungrammatical. 'Ego, poeta Germanus, supra grammaticos sto.'[27] But his universal aspirations also embrace elevated language. If one writes for the sovereign people, one may claim the language of sovereigns as fit to describe the struggles of the masses and fit to be presented to them on the stage (9, 740f.: *Die Literatur wird durchforscht werden*; B. *Poems*, 344f.).

Brecht's early ideas of the place of the protagonist in drama are not only positively influenced by the plot-orientated sub-literary genres, but also negatively influenced by pretentious types of literature such as the grandiose tragedies of Hebbel, patterned on quasi-Hegelian concepts of the workings of the world-spirit. 'That chaps of a certain particular structure get hit on the back of the neck with a shovel is not what the play ought to show. It ought to show how they behave under it, what they say about it and what face they make' (*Tb.*, 31: 21.8.20). The early diaries are full of plans for such stories. A positive literary model is in the early novels of Alfred Döblin; Brecht praises *Wadzek's Struggle with the Steam Turbine* (*Tb.*, 48: 4.9.20). Later, detective novels, which Brecht read insatiably, are a useful parallel: the action is primary, the motives are obscure and must be deduced from the evidence.

Whether the protagonist is the primary element or not, Brecht is always fascinated by the riches of individual character, admires individuals' stature and energy, and puts on stage rounded human beings with quirks and development.[28] According to Brecht, reported by Bernard Guillemin in 1926 — following ideas of the mutability of personality which come from Ernst Mach and entered literature with Hofmannsthal in the 1890s — 'nobody can be identically the same at two unidentical moments. Changes in his exterior continually lead us to an inner reshuffling' (most accessible in B. *on Theatre*, 15). In drama as in life, characters will contradict themselves. Not all need be explained: a Richard III, for instance, must retain the fascination of the monstrous (15, 194: *Situation und Verhalten*).

Early protagonists tend to be outsiders; but growing social commitment leads Brecht towards the insider-protagonist, a member of a social group who develops in an exemplary fashion (Brecht's version of the 'typicality' demanded by Communist literary theory) because of his particular openness to stimuli. Increasingly Brecht writes of proletarians or people who find something in common with the workers, and are thus important to society and its development. Thus Johanna Dark (*Saint

Joan of the Stockyards) abandons her allegiance to religion and capital after being impelled to search for the root causes of social misery. Generally the protagonist is an ordinary person – and even for Galileo, many problems boil down to how to pay the milkman; but not a copy-book proletarian, for rich rounded characters with complexity and self-contradiction are often those who stand between the classes and thus astride the great social conflict described by Marx. 'How is the "ownness" of the individual guaranteed? By his belonging to more than one collective' (20, 62: *Individuum und Masse*). Impelled by a fixed aim incompatible with their social state, they want to live off war without being cruel (Mother Courage), to give away money without earning it by exploiting others (Shen Teh), to explore the universe without defying the authorities (Galileo). The type is prefigured in the sketched story of one Malvi, 'a good man, who had one passion: one expensive mistress: the idea of going straight. She brings him to beggary' (*Tb.*, 52: 5.9.20). They are led into dilemmas which are the psychological manifestation of social conflicts, put up against the manifold contradictions of an imperfect society; they find it impossible to fulfil all their responsibilities, they adapt or perish, they become model cases of the social behaviour of the well-meaning person. 'the individual remains an individual, but becomes a social phenomenon, his passions for instance become social matters and his fate too' (*Aj.*, 1, 139: 2.8.40). The split individual is a model of a split society: bourgeois and proletariat, the old and the new fight within him (9, 793: *Looking for the New and Old*; *B. Poems*, 42f.). Brecht discovered the technique of the unresolved internal contradiction in Shaw (15, 99: *Ovation für Shaw*; *B. on Theatre*, 11). The two sides of the individual distance each other: Shen Teh shows up Shui Ta's unscrupulousness, he her ineffectuality. Most characters act hypocritically in order to save their ruling passion intact against social pressures: Schweyk, Galileo, Azdak.[29] They are acted on by society, in its economic, social and political aspects; and they act on society and make it what it is. As they collect a quantity of motivations on their way through life, they steer towards a qualitative change where external influences force them into a decision – most obviously, Kattrin finally sacrificing herself to her passion for children at the siege of Halle. Such decisions are real dialectical turning-points, and Brecht demands that on stage the alternative course of action be made visible as a possibility. The concept of a fate against which individuals kick in vain is as foreign to his drama as to his thought. By the leap from quantitative to qualitative a new phase of the historical flux is produced (*Aj.*, 1, 393: 23.3.42). The figure and the plot are parts of the progress of history. The circular type of drama found equally in naturalism and absurdism, in which no actions and no decisions make any real difference, is rare in Brecht.

Brecht is classical, not romantic. He sees writing as a craft, not a calling. He instances the hard work and accuracy of Flaubert, Zola, Baudelaire, against the German lack of a technical-artistic ethos (*Tb.*, 122: 20.5.21). The artist must make form work for him, not allow every isolated emotion its full development, renounce reproduction of outer reality in favour of leisurely 'revelation of humanity with all its nuances and shifts of plane' (*Tb.*, 139: 17.6.21). He cannot empathise with every character he wants to depict; rather he exploits the sum of modern knowledge (*Aj.*, 1, 236: 28.1.41). To show an ambitious man he needs knowledge of public political and economic affairs and a grasp of psychology (Brecht was interested in psychoanalysis and in behaviourism, though subscribing completely to neither). But it must all be converted into poetry (*Dichtung*) in his final text (15, 268–70; *Vergnügungstheater oder Lehrtheater*). Any amount of message is no substitute for the peculiar aesthetic quality. Reading an essay on himself, Brecht complains 'ideology. ideology, ideology. never an aesthetic concept; the whole thing is like a description of a food without anything about its taste. we ought to start by arranging exhibitions and courses on the training of taste, that is, on enjoyment of life' (*Aj.*, 2, 929: 10.6.50). This does not mean the writer is autonomous. The food he offers must nourish as well as tasting good. The writer – and the actor – is given the responsibility to criticise society and take a hand in its improvement. In a productive society the social ethos and the artist's ethos go hand in hand; in a socially regressive society art may do well to develop its ethos (*moral*) independently of society (*Aj.*, 1, 358: 16.1.42).

An ideal of cool gracefulness, or elegance, is derived from sport. In the arena, in Brecht's interpretation, trained sportsmen do what they seem to enjoy, please the public, and generate enjoyment by their skills. The theatre too could have audiences of 15,000 and recover contact with the spirit of the age if it would lower the emotional temperature and become elegant, light, dry, concrete (15, 82–6: *Mehr guten Sport* and *Über den "Untergang des Theaters"*; *B. on Theatre*, 6–8). The audience must be able to sit back, relax, smoke, appraise characters and their reactions. Elegance is also characteristic of oriental theatre. Its plays are often loose in construction, exposition handled by apostrophe to the audience, scenery stylised, musicians on stage in view of the audience, sets changed with no curtain; no attempt is made at the illusion of a real world, gestures and action are conventional, and the spectator comes to judge the performance as a performance.[30] That Brecht knew all this is obvious from his later theory, and though acquaintance with Chinese acting came too late and remained too slight to have formed his views on elegant distancing in the theatre, he uses it as a corpus of evidence that non-illusionistic theatre can thrive.

Brecht's plot may consist of a number of episodic, demonstrative actions – as many as happen to be needed – with no overt connection.

The five-act play is practically unknown to him. This is 'epic theatre' applied to the actual structure of the text. The term *episch* in German has to do with narrative form — less with sheer scale, as often in English.[31] Brecht constructs model situations to show social relationships, rather than more or less naturalistic depictions of probable and lifelike procedures. Theatre is not life. It must however learn from life and have an analogous relationship of plan and chance, probable and improbable (15, 117: *Vorrede zu 'Macbeth'*). Brecht found a loose way of constructing drama in Georg Büchner; the neater the tragedy, the more Brecht sees it as a mere anecdote which simply confirms the spectator's view of life. The stage must tackle such characteristic conflicts of our era as the fluctuations of grain prices (15, 174: *Über eine neue Dramatik*). For this an open, or atectonic, dramatic structure is needed.[32] Brecht repeats the development undergone some years before by Eisenstein, whose major films develope montage to deal with plots whose ramifications defy treatment within a conventional dramatic structure. In each case the need to treat new, complex and extensive materials led to new techniques. Brecht began in every genre in old forms, transcending them only when they hindered him (*Aj.*, 1, 18: 3.8.38). Function, not form, is primary; art is practical, not a refuge from real life. The world of the play is not an autonomous one which comes to an end with the resolution of its tension in a catastrophe into whose preparation all the characters are drawn. Brecht's stage figures are independent of the drama — in *Mother Courage*, even quite important figures swim in and out of the action quite arbitrarily. This contributes to the lifelike jerkiness of the action. 'The Augsburger cuts his plays up into a series of little independent playlets, so that the action progresses by jumps' (16, 605: *Messingkauf — Das Theater des Stückeschreibers*; *M. Dial.*, 75). Within these pieces, the deeds of the protagonist show the attitudes to which his social dependences incline him.

Brecht wants to give the drama the possibilities of the narrative: presentation of the action as past and continuously completely present in the narrator's mind, and freedom for the audience to go at its own pace and refer mentally to previous sections of the narration, coolly making comparisons. Brecht does not (except in *The Caucasian Chalk Circle*) use the stage narrator, traceable from the Greek chorus through Shakespeare's histories to Thornton Wilder, but he does have ways of pressing on the audience's attention a perspective chosen by the author. Narration by figures within the play is common, but the function is filled in most of his plays by scene titles, which, like the chapter titles of the old-fashioned novel, give away much of the action of the scene. They are to be projected on to a curtain or other suitable surface before each scene. As well as communicating from author to audience, marking each scene off from its predecessor, and removing tension about the outcome of the scene, they may – in historical plays – give dates and background material, showing the relationship of history and stage action.

All narrative procedures bridge the gap between stage and audience. Brecht's stage is never, from the outset, a closed world. For the first production of *Drums in the Night* the theatre was hung with placards with such warnings as 'Don't gawp so romantically!' to wake the audience from its hypnotic trance. With *Man is Man*, Brecht broke with the convention of natural exposition and let the protagonist present himself, his status and his plans directly in an address to the audience. Figures temporarily abandon their roles and step into the audience's world. From the popular melodrama Brecht developed the use of asides to audience, for information and comment. Similarly songs from the *Threepenny Opera* on are narrative elements, definite interruptions of the dramatic action rather than parts of it, and they can communicate directly from author to public. Then Brecht loves to have characters telling stories. In *Mr Puntila and his Man Matti*, not only are things narrated which could have been incorporated in the dialogue, but much of the play consists of stories unrelated to the action but filling out the theme. The most pointed narration is the deposition of a witness in court; Brecht loves court-scenes with their more or less dispassionate search for the truth about some social action. Psychology is relevant here only in its social aspects; the actual episode is seen at one remove; and the playwright can show how one arm of the state, the judicature, regards the problems arising in the society it controls. The process of discovering the truth is the material of Brecht's basic exemplar of theatre, the classic 'Street Scene' in the *Messingkauf* (16, 546–58; *B. on Theatre*, 121–8; cf. *On everyday Theatre*, 9, 766–70; *B. Poems*, 176–9). An action of actual relevance is presented in such a way as to make it easier for the spectator to give an opinion on the subject (leading to criticism). Theatre is a section of reality engaged in a play, a game representing some other section of reality. This game makes social-historical complexes, the class and individual forces at work in a historical epoch, visible. It does not claim completeness, it does not provide an exposé of Marxism for those too lazy to read Marx for themselves, and it has little to do with socialist realism, which demands mimetic reproduction of an action having a progressive typicality interpreted in limited ideological terms. Rather Brecht aims at some analogy with reality, and at the collection of attitudes which suggest to the audience possible implications outside the theatre. Here he is followed by Friedrich Dürrenmatt, who however makes cynicism, not productivity, the content of his implied lessons. Against the usual yardstick of realism, 'a work of art is more realistic as reality is easier to recognise in it', Brecht sets up the assertion 'that a work of art is more realistic the more recognisably reality is mastered in it' (*Aj.*, 1, 142: 4.8.40). It is an ambitious aim and means that the plays and productions are more difficult to digest than conventionally realistic products, particularly as the episodically constructed play has a wealth of implications and contradictions. 'the unitary whole consists of independent parts, each of which can be immediately confronted with the corresponding part-processes in reality – indeed must be' (*Aj.*, 1, 140: 3.8.40). Mastering reality is one of the two tasks of theatre: the other, enjoyment, is inseparable from it. 'The theatre must in fact remain something entirely superfluous, though this indeed means that it is the superfluous for which we live. Nothing needs less justification than pleasure' (16, 664: *Kleines Organon* §3; *B. on Theatre*, 181). 'the world is grasped as capable of being changed. a moral imperative "change it!" need not take effect. the theatre simply gains for its audience somebody who produces the world' (*Aj.*, 1, 194: 1.11.40). Causality is important in this theatre as understanding of causes is necessary for mastering the world – in contrast to Aristotelian theatre in which a state of affairs whose causes may remain unexplained produces an emotional reaction (*Aj.*, 1, 136f.; 2.8.40). Deeper structures are to be shown, not necessarily surface reality.

A useful term in the analysis of Brecht's plays, but one with which he himself had difficulty (sometimes defining it more narrowly than I shall), is *Gestus* (untranslatable: attitude as shown in the signs we use in communicating with others). At its widest this means the basic attitude which informs any particular transaction between people.[33] The transaction can be a whole work of art presented to a public, a conversation, a single speech considered as an independent component of a conversation. Gestus concentrates on interactions between people, for Brecht disliked psychological observations which could not be expressed in social interplay and put to work in the recognition and changing of social circumstances. It includes the unspoken 'languages' of demeanour by which we recognise others' behaviour, but language itself also. Its theory is basically Hegelian. What is said in a dialogue cannot be interpreted out of context, but only when placed within the complex interaction of theses and antitheses which is conversation. Theatre aims to communicate from stage to audience a demonstration of social facts, so the basic gestus of theatre is demonstration (see 15, 341: *Kurze Beschreibung einer neuen Technik der Schauspielkunst*; *B. on Theatre*, 136). Within this, different passages of a play represent the gestus of particular social facts and relationships: the gestus of deferring to someone who may give you money, of attempting to convince by logical argument, etc. In analysing the text one may always ask what the gestus of a play, a scene, an episode, a speech is. This helps to fix the inner structure of the play, for the succession and interplay of different kinds of gestus is basic to the dramatist's art. Brecht's scene titles often hint at the gestus of a particular scene. He also suggests setting up 'a scheme of quantums of effect, which one would look for in the scenes, poetic, dramaturgic, showing the history of manners, social-political, psychological (furthering knowledge of human nature), etc. one could make statements about these quantums which could have come from aesthetic, social-historical, psychological textbooks': for instance, isolating the social history shown in scene 2 of *Mother Courage* in a generalisation which could find its place in a textbook: 'the dealers plundered their own armies as well as the inhabitants of the enemy country' (*Aj.*, 1, 206f.; 9.12.40).

Brecht never speaks of establishing aesthetic rules for the stage, only of techniques, functional means to an extraneous end (19, 411: *Notizen zur Arbeit – Über ästhetische Gesetze*). The number of techniques available for furthering the ends he has in view is unlimited; Brecht gives the examples he happens to have at hand, not intending to hold anyone else in the straitjacket of his limitations. Brecht-theatre is an extensible concept. Others following his ethos and attitude in their way, using their imagination, will impose their own flavour on their productions. 'My rules are to be applied only by those who retain independent judgment, a spirit of contradiction and a social imagination, and who are in touch with the progressive sectors of the public and are thus themselves progressive, rounded, thinking people. I cannot muzzle the ox that grindeth out the corn' (16, 600: *Messingkauf – Das Theater des Stückeschreibers*). Brecht hopes to find a tradition which, adapting to unforeseeable conditions of the future, will give scope to the productivity of generations – not a rigid style which, fossilising, will lose touch with reality. Werner Hecht points out: 'Brecht's way of working, that is his technique at the desk and in the theatre . . . delivers to us that which preserves his theatre from fossilisation: the ability to find readings of plays for the contemporary audience; doubt of extant solutions; contact with the audience as a principle; a range of models as impulses for creative work . . . Brecht's method delivers no recipes. There is no "style" in the Berliner Ensemble.'[34] There is only a general attitude: to present things in the light of reason and sensuality (the English way) rather than of pedantry and passion (the German way)(*Mat. G.*, 76). Conversely one should look critically at the techniques Brecht invented, which can only remain valid as long as they continue, despite changing social contexts, to produce the effects he had in mind. They are not fetishes with absolute rights to immortality. Manfred Wekwerth points out, for instance, that Brecht introduced the light, half-height curtain used during scene changes at a time when audiences universally expected a heavy proscenium curtain to descend; but that expectation no longer being present, the Brechtian curtain no longer has its shock effect and has instead become a fetish, the outward sign of a pseudo-Brecht style which does not necessarily correspond to any inward thought.[35] So all that follows about Brecht's stage techniques is to be taken as a report with ideas in it, not as an instruction manual.

The cardinal point of Brecht's theories of distancing on the stage is the work of the actor. Given his head, the actor could – German stars of the twenties excelled at this – by his own aura create empathy and illusion which would undo all efforts at distancing. Brecht early objects to actors spending so much effort learning to feel like Richard III and not being able to carry a glass of water across the stage. They have inadequate elegance, self-observation and technical skills; and they have not the kind of knowledge of human nature one needs for playing poker (15, 111: *Weniger Gips*). They should come down off their pedestal.

The first stage of Brechtian acting proper – preserved for us to some extent in the film of *The Threepenny Opera* – is the supercooled style. The actor takes a distance from the figure, acts dispassionately; he refuses to give way to the emotions implicit in a speech, rather he quotes what he has to say. This stage starts with the historic moment when Helene Weigel, as the maid reporting Jocasta's death in *Oedipus Rex*, delivered her lines with a sense of their importance rather than of their horror (15, 190f.: *Dialog über Schauspielkunst*; *B. on Theatre*, 28). Brecht generalises later: 'If he [the actor] would just restrict himself to bringing out the sense of the words without more feeling than happens to arise as he is talking, then the spectator would once more be enabled to feel something and enjoy food that has not been predigested for him' (15, 412f.: *Erfahrungen*). Distance is gained in various ways. Brecht liked to cast young actors for the roles of old people, which automatically encourages the actor in observation and discourages empathy. A favourite rehearsal technique (practically the only one which his actors recognised as specifically Brechtian) is turning speeches into reported speech. 'She said she was ashamed to offer her son such poor soup . . .' immediately establishes a distance between role and actress. Or speeches are read against the grain: what seems unique and highly charged is taken as routine and requiring no emphasis – in the 1932 film *Kuhle Wampe* the censor objected less to an unemployed man's killing himself, than to his doing it as casually as if peeling a cucumber; conversely, routine ways of talking may be emphasised, so that the audience has to see them in a fresh light and recognise their implications for the critical analysis of the whole society of which they are manifestations.

In fact the actor comments. To do this, he must have a social perspective on his role. Brecht is willing to help here. For instance, his *Zwischenszenen* ('Interpolated Scenes', 1939), extra episodes for classical plays, show such things as how much Romeo is the spoilt child of his class and has no feeling for subordinates – which will affect interpretation of the part. The actor cannot have in himself the materials for

creating by empathetic processes the characters of both Romeo and
Lear (15, 391f.: *Schauspielkunst*); so he must observe, appreciate, analyse
and finally copy reality, rather than exploiting his own psychology. The
analysis means such things as historicising: finding what parts of characters' behaviour are timeless, which belong to the particular epoch only
(*Looking for the new and old*, 9, 793; *B. Poems*, 424). The character is
built up from the outside, not from inner emotion but from attitudes
and gestures. The resulting copy of an observed reality is applied to the
business of speaking a dramatic text which is fiction – to be quoted from,
not believed in (15, 342–4 and 351–2: *Kurze Beschreibung . . .*;
B. on Theatre, 136–8 and 142). The actor continually compares what
the author has written with his own experience of reality, and in the
light of this comparison stresses some features of the text which
the author perhaps did not intend to be stressed; he is reluctant to let the
action take the course intended by the author, he shows that he is
being dragged along, he adds elements alien to the author's conception
of the part (15, 402: *Aufbau der Figur*). A simple example of comparison with a reality obviously outside the play would be the way the
actors in *Mother Courage* stress the 'Adolf' in the name of the King of
Sweden, the invader of Poland. Suggested rehearsal procedures are to
memorise where, at first reading, one found the text odd; to invent and
speak reasons for the oddities of the figure's behaviour ('I was in a bad
mood because I hadn't eaten, and said: . . .'); to exchange roles, copying the other actor or diverging from his interpretation; to improvise in
the style of the author (15, 409–11; *Anweisungen an die Schauspieler*).

That the actor does not depend on his own psychological resources to
build up an interpretation does not mean he cannot put across his own
feelings. In developing his own social perspective he develops emotions
about the figure (not coinciding with the figure's emotions) and finds
ways of superimposing them on his interpretation. Helene Weigel in the
part of Señora Carrar broke into tears during performance, perhaps on
a day when the Spanish Civil War was going badly. It may have been
bad acting; but the actress is entitled to her feelings, as long as they are
those of a thinking, socially committed person (16, 601: *Messingkauf
– Das Theater des Stückeschreibers*; *M. Dial.*, 70f.). Inspiration is
allowed, within the framework of reason; so are tears over Señora Carrar
(not tears arising from identification with her). Sympathy is allowed,
empathy is suspect.[36] The actor remains aware of what he is doing, what
he is transmitting to the audience. Only if the actor is aware can the
audience have its awareness heightened. The actor defends and criticises
the character he plays; but he may defend warmly. In this event the
cool awareness is pushed into the background. At some points of Brecht's
plays tension mounts to a point inimical to cool analysis: in *Mother
Courage* scene 3, for instance. Weigel had all the art of an actress

skilled in creating illusion, and put it to work here – but it had to be abandoned in scene 4, which it could ruin.

As Rülicke-Weiler (pp. 165f.) points out, a representational (as opposed to self-identificatory) style of acting has often been fostered by authors and theatres with a critical attitude to social reality, from Diderot to agitprop. The representational school is more likely to be able to come to grips with the social aspect, the identificatory with the psychological aspect of a role. Since Brecht is content neither with two-dimensional figures which merely represent a class, nor with asocially seen heroic individuals, he requires from the actor a synthesis of the approaches. (It must be remembered that the Hegelian synthesis does not supersede its components, but puts them in their place within the scheme of things.) In Moscow in 1935 Brecht saw a demonstration by the Chinese actor Mai Lan-fang, which led to the crystallisation of his thought on the duality of the actor as actor and figure, and its technical possibilities. The duality is observable in the villain of our nineteenth-century melo-drama, whose 'stage leer' shows the actor's distance from the role; but such forerunners are not actually examples of distancing:[37] the con-scious, primary, social and intellectual aims of Brecht are missing in them. In Mai Lan-fang Brecht noted the use of conventional gestures to show a series of aspects: tea is made; made in the traditional way; in the traditional way by a girl; by an impatient girl; by an actor using gestures apposite to an impatient girl (15, 427: *Über das Theater der Chinesen* §4). There is nothing inscrutably oriental about this: Brecht could have seen the same in classical ballet, had he wanted to. In any case he must substitute for the symbolic and hieratic meanings of the elements of Chinese theatre an analogy to empirical reality.

A further stage of Brechtian acting, dependent on clear recognition of the duality of actor and figure, is reached with Charles Laughton as Galileo in 1947. Its elements are Laughton's eminence and his power of relaxation. The public which admires the actor comes to see him show-ing 'what he imagines Galileo to have been'; 'the demonstrator Laughton does not disappear in the Galileo whom he is showing' (16, 683f.: *Kleines Organon* §49; *B. on Theatre*, 194, but I have altered the trans-lation). He could produce an admirable effect by turning into Galileo, but he does not; he remains two entities in one body, Laughton and Galileo, and so his acting combines two types of gestus: the constant gestus of showing on Laughton's part, whatever gestus the text calls for on Galileo's part. And Laughton relaxes: Brecht imagines him smoking a cigar and 'laying it down now and again in order to show us some further characteristic attitude of the figure in the play' (ibid.). The mysti-cal trance is radically removed from the theatre experience.[38] As with the social function of theatre, so with the acting technique involved: it can all be derived from a single simple everyday example provided by

Brecht in the street scene. The actor, though possessing much more sophisticated skills, is in the position of the bystander demonstrating, after an accident, how it happened. He does not intend to be taken for either the victim or the driver, but to make clear how the victim moved and to convey the flavour of the driver's self-exculpations. The story is primary, the characterisation derived from it. The accident is over, the bystander is not in danger, he can relax and be himself. But his evidence may be important, for instance if there is a prosecution later.

One must admit that Brechtian acting often seems fuller of mystique than of meat. His own descriptions of actors at work consist chiefly of analyses of techniques for building up interpretations, preparing and rehearsing. Weigel and Laughton are the main cases in which he claims the further specific quality of conscious demonstration. Thomas K. Brown concluded after enquiries in the Berliner Ensemble in 1972 that no specifically Brechtian distancing procedure was at work there. Ekkehard Schall was unable to explain how to demonstrate in doing an action that he had made a decision not to do the opposite, or in making a statement that it was false though the character said it in good faith (both demands made by Brecht). His explanation of showing that he was only demonstrating a figure was vitiated by the fact that when on stage he turned temporarily from Coriolanus into Schall, it merely looked as though he had forgotten his lines. Nor were members of the audience being affected in the ways the theory demands.[39] Even in Brecht's lifetime his actors were unclear as to whether they used a peculiar mode of work (*Theaterarbeit*, 412). Angelika Hurwicz seems to think not.[40] It is not easy to see how an actor can learn procedures to enable him to represent two different things to the audience simultaneously. The decision not to perform an action can only be shown by the traditional means of starting to do it and then stopping. And the effect of demonstrating, rather than being, a figure can be gained only if the actor can for reasons implicit in his own personality – think of the relaxed geniality of Laughton, so much more at home on the stage than in life! – and out of the fulness of his enjoyment of acting give the impression of an actor enjoying himself in giving a zestful interpretation of a role. This is a matter of ethos and experience, not properly speaking technical; and Laughton, for one, had this capability before he met Brecht.

It is then perhaps time to debunk the concept of Brechtian acting, to sweep away the abstruse and unrealisable technical demands and leave ourselves with two things: the body of training and rehearsal techniques by which Brecht encourages distancing as between actor and role, and the actor's ethos which makes the spirit of criticism and the spirit of enjoyment parts of his personality on and off stage. Brecht's requirement that empathy between audience and role should be avoided is then to be fulfilled in two ways: by the intervention of distancing elements in text, design and music; and by the constant ground-tone of watching the actor enjoy giving a good performance.

Brecht tends towards a less authoritarian idea of theatrical production than is usual, so that actors, designer and so on are free to impose their own attitudes. He sets up against Wagner's *Gesamtkunstwerk* the idea of a composite work of art which can tolerate differences of approach on the part of its various makers. In the attempt to make the music of *Mahagonny*, like the words, appeal more to the reason than to the emotions he demands music to interpret (not heighten) the text, go beyond (not restate) it, and express an opinion (not illustrate) (17, 1011: *Anmerkungen zur Oper* ". . . *Mahagonny*"; *B. on Theatre*, 38). A little later he praises jazz techniques for their combination of individual freedom to improvise with general discipline (17, 1032: *Anmerkungen zur "Massnahme"*). In 1941 he encouraged Simon Parmet to use his orchestra for independent statements in writing music for *Mother Courage* (*Aj.*, 1, 240: 2.2.41).

Illusionism in décor is done away with. 'It is more important today that the décor should tell the spectator he is in a theatre, rather than, say, in Aulis. The theatre as theatre must take on that fascinating reality that the boxing arena has. The best thing is to show the machinery, the winches and the flies' (15, 79: *Dekoration*). When Meyerhold's company visited Berlin in 1930 Brecht found ideas for continuing his work: both believed in visible lighting. The designer in Brecht-theatre has, like the composer, independence and responsibility. Elegance is a precondition of all his work. Caspar Neher (following techniques of Piscator's) early used the bipartite stage, a three-dimensional room small in the foreground and a wide backdrop showing the social scene; and also static projections of a symbolic nature. Brecht explains that a text set among a small number of people calls for staging which will fill it out by showing the wider functional aspects. To clarify the implications of a simple dialogue in a factory yard, the décor uses financial and other data about the concern in question, showing how it treats its workers and who gets the profits (15, 456f.: *Zeichen und Symbole*).

The stage began to tell a story. The narrator was no longer missing, along with the fourth wall. Not only did the background adopt an attitude to the events on the stage – by big screens recalling other simultaneous events elsewhere, by projecting documents which confirmed or contradicted what the characters said, by concrete and intelligible figures to accompany abstract conversations, by figures and sentences to support mimed transactions whose sense was unclear – but the actors too refrained from going over wholly into their role . . . (15, 164: *Vergnügugstheater oder Lehrtheater*; *B. on Theatre*, 71).

The designer, like other members of the team, works at social facts and presents the mass of data in a form in which the audience can master it and find the exercise useful. He is not afraid of the written word as a design element: it shows he has been thinking (15, 464: *Literarisierung der Bühnen*). Design also means creating areas which reflect social circumstances (a capitalist's house is too large for his actions, a proletarian's too small) and previous users as well as present inhabitants (15, 449f.: *Fixierung des Raums bei induktiver Methode*). Where in conventional dramaturgy spaces express their occupants, here they show their occupants' adaptation to existing circumstances. Whilst Brecht sometimes works with a bare stage, as in *Mother Courage* where a constant white ground suggests the spatial and temporal limitlessness and barrenness of war, his dramatic language needs use of all the theatre's resources. He did not require every word on stage to be audible – provided the set and groupings told the story. The Berliner Ensemble used lavish sets and costumes when indicated: Brecht is said to have insisted on real copper and no papier-mâché for the décor for *Galileo*: 'If I set riches in front of the proletariat, it must be genuine riches.'[41] The totality of the set forms a harmony of its own, different for each production, on which Brecht was very insistent, noticing if something was an inch out of place; props, down to the tin spoon which Weigel as Mother Courage wore through a loop in her padded jacket, combine aesthetic harmony, functional solidity and symbolic value.

The Chinese theatre does without illusion, and Brecht found it worth learning from the way it uses masks, costume and setting to complement the work of the actor; but his practice was already fixed, probably with a certain influence from the Japanese Nô plays, by 1930. Masks do away with the illusion of reality and draw attention to the social fact that a person in the imperialist era is indeed a *persona*, a façade put up to hide or even smother the character rather than express it. Masks are often specified for the ruling classes and their helpers, whose personality is held to be distorted and forced into a rigid mould by their exertions to gain and retain power; less for the workers and men in the street. Shen Teh has a mask when in her vain pursuit of the higher good she becomes Shui Ta. Brecht, fascinated by nuances of costume from the time of *The Threepenny Opera* on, worked out the function of costume fully in the Berliner Ensemble with the help of the costume designer Kurt Palm. Costume is first a social indicator: expensive or cheap, new or old, worn evenly or unevenly, according to the wearer's work and finances; but then it is a personal statement: members of a mass are marked as individuals by variations of clothing, ambition is portrayed by giving a figure clothing above his social station, and so on.

All the theatrical arts are placed on a single level, and their relationship consists of their mutually distancing each other's efforts (16, 699:

Kleines Organon §74; *B. on Theatre*, 204). In practice writing, direction, acting and design are the core. Music is important and independent, but still often given menial functions, notably to indicate that the plane of dramatic action is being left for that of meditation or of unreality (in *The Good Person* especially). Dance gets a mention in the *Short Organum*, but is not prominent in practice: Brecht had to give up the idea of featuring a dance at the end of *The Caucasian Chalk Circle*, one of his few theatrical capitulations.

'it is impossible to finalise a play without the stage . . . only the stage decides between the possible variants' (*Aj.*, 1, 122: 30.6.40). So the play reaches its final form during the very complex process of Brechtian rehearsal. The director takes a modest part here – Brecht calls him *Probenleiter*, rehearsal manager. Brecht did not theorise in rehearsal. Whereas Gordon Craig, whose movement from theatre of reproduction to theatre of representation parallels Brecht's thought, wanted to go on to a theatre of creation pursuing transcendent aesthetic aims under the direction of a super-régisseur whom he calls the monarch, Brecht refuses any offer of a crown and wants a democratic and socialist theatre. He tries as director to see that the basic social aspects come across, he helps his co-workers to understand the dialectics of their roles but does not impose on them with his interpretations (16, 759f.: *Die Spielleitung Brechts*). That Brecht never spoke the lines to suggest an interpretation is however untrue: he did so in rehearsing *Galileo* and recommended the procedure to Benno Besson, whilst forbidding Manfred Wekwerth to use it.[42] He did not theorise, nor psychologise, preferring to work from the outside, from attitudes shown in interpersonal relationships, and pragmatically. He directed from the auditorium.

A lengthy note in *Theaterarbeit* (256–8; and see the notes on *Theaterarbeit* in *B. on Theatre*) distinguishes fifteen stages in the preparation of a production. (1) Analysis of the play – looking for social lessons and impulses, turning-points of the plot, structure of events; writing a short summary; thinking how to get the story line and its social significance clear. (2) Preliminary discussion of a set or sets, production of sketches showing groupings of actors and their postures at various points. (3) Preliminary casting – not type-casting, for the sake of the actor and of realism. (4) Reading through with little expression or characterisation, to familiarise the cast with the plot. (5) Trying out positions, movements, accentuations, gestures, including those invented by the actors; moving towards characterisation. (6) Set rehearsal: marrying intended sets with movements and groupings, so that sets can be completed early and props found. Later rehearsals are with final sets and props. (7) Detail rehearsal of each gestic section, building of characterisation, rehearsal of the transitions from section to section. (8) Run through, pulling elements together and getting relative emphasis and continuity right. (9) Discussion of costume and make-up – only possible when characterisation is fixed; but high heels, beards, etc., can be tried out earlier. (10) Check rehearsals to see if demands under (1) are being met; groupings photographed for examination. (11) Tempo rehearsals: a series of dress rehearsals to fix tempo and running time. (12) Main dress rehearsal. (13) A quick run-through without prompter, with gestures only hinted at. (14) Previews: checking the reaction of audiences, preferably homogeneous ones (students, a factory group) to allow discussion. Correction rehearsals. (15) Public première – the director is not present, actors are given their head.

Rehearsal also included the production of a sort of super prompt-copy showing signs for music and sound-effects, cues and pauses, the end of sections within the scene, and the words emphasised in every single sentence of the dialogue.[43] This leads into the characteristic Berliner Ensemble institution of the *Modellbuch*, 'Model Book' of a production, worked out under Brecht's guidance by Ruth Berlau. It consists of between 450 and 600 photos of the production, keyed to the text. Photos were taken from a single position, in the circle and rather to the side (unless the beauty of a particular piece of business was better shown from elsewhere), and selected to show the main changes of groupings onstage and the most characteristic gestures. They should ideally tell the story even without the help of dialogue. Production assistants took notes during rehearsals of interesting discussions, salient points insisted on by the director, timings for each scene, and so on; these notes, collated, form a commentary in the model book. Photos of costumes and masks against neutral backgrounds, and of sets and props, are appended. Certain model books were eventually printed, others existed in maquette form to be borrowed by other theatres planning to perform plays in the Berliner Ensemble repertoire. Sometimes Brecht made the following of the model a condition for allowing a performance. Properly used, the model book explains the points Brecht would wish to be stressed in production and helps its user to see the problems of the work concerned as Brecht saw them. No director is expected to negate his own theatre's traditions and his own tendencies; but working with the model makes him confront them with Brecht's intentions, an aspect very important when so much of Brecht's thought cannot be read from the plain text. And the model book imposes standards: if the user cannot think of a better solution, he can at least copy what a good theatre did![44] Brecht defends the art of copying, done intelligently; but Werner Hecht has amusingly exemplified the results of too mechanical copying, as when a designer with a very large stage to work on copied the proportions of the Berliner Ensemble set for *The Good Person*, so that what should be a very crowded little shop became a spacious area and the scenic effect was lost.[45]

Most lessons about Brecht theatre in action are of course derived from the example of the Berliner Ensemble during the short period when Brecht was its chief director, dating for practical purposes from the 1949 *Mother Courage*. This was his first opportunity to try out in a series of productions with a static base the concepts he had been writing about all through his exile years, which sum up to his mature view of theatre. The Berliner Ensemble did not have to be miserly with material resources or rehearsal time. Its team consisted of the finest theatrical talents in the most important fields, and they thought out every production, from the basic conception of a drama whose emotional effect is based on its success in analysing the deep mainsprings of society, through important technical characteristics such as the dismissal of atmospheric lighting effects, to the superficial trademarks such as the half-curtain. This thinking-out was done in theatrical, not theoretical, terms. In conversation Brecht attached more importance than in his writings to the imponderabilia of actors' personalities, the sudden inspiration which produces a new and enjoyable theatrical effect, and so on. The result was exciting; East Berlin became the 'obligatory pilgrimage'[46] of all *avant-garde* theatrical artists.

Yet there is another aspect. In the reception of *Mother Courage* Brecht saw dangers for the understanding of his theatre. Despite all attempts to make the protagonist a hyena of the battlefield, people insisted on feeling for and with her as a victim of war. They were politically not ready for the message. The work that followed in the Berliner Ensemble was directed more towards the political education and activisation of the audience than towards the realisation of a true Brecht-theatre. He went on record as saying that the present state of the theatre did not allow the full exploitation in practice of his theories (*Theaterarbeit*, 412). Whereas he had said his epic theatre was unsuitable for short-term propaganda, the repertoire was biased towards political topicality, including Strittmatter's *Katzgraben* as a comment on agrarian reform and Becher's *Winterschlacht* apropos of West German rearmament.[47] And there has long been a strain of criticism which felt the productions of Brecht's own works did not do justice to them. The overriding need, however, was not to satisfy critics insistent on Brechtian purity, but to keep in touch with the audience – many of whose attitudes had survived from before 1945, even from before 1919 (16, 906f.: *Einige Irrtümer über die Spielweise des Berliner Ensembles*). 'The political vision of our public is only slowly getting into focus' (16, 832: *Katzgraben-Notate, Neuer Inhalt, neue Form*).

The realisation of disjunctive theatre was also hampered by the tendency to treat Brecht as a Grand Old Man. He approved of the practice of recording his rehearsals on tape, as an example to posterity of what can be done in a theatre with that Utopian luxury, unlimited rehearsal time;[48] but the result is to enhance, rather than limit, the status of the director. Yet his leadership did guarantee movement in the direction of Brecht-theatre, and his productions and model books remain authoritative until a company arises which, starting from his artistic ethos, can develop independently in his spirit. This company is not necessarily the Berliner Ensemble, which for some time after 1956 seemed concerned to follow more than to develop the master's practice. Helene Weigel was criticised for rigidity and autocracy. After Manfred Wekwerth's departure in 1969 and her death in 1971 there were changes.[49] Her successor, Ruth Berghaus, though an accomplished Brechtian, has been charged with eclecticism, neglect of the Brecht tradition and putting on plays with no didactic purpose. However, Manfred Wekwerth has now returned as director. Another noteworthy Brechtian nucleus was built up in the 1960s by Fritz Bennewitz at the *Deutsches National theater*, Weimar.[50] Brecht's influence in East Germany has grown since his death, despite the persistence of basic doubts about the acceptability of critical theatre under a socialist régime. Much the same goes for the Soviet Union.[51] In West Germany Max Frisch's phrase, that he has attained the 'hard-hitting ineffectiveness of a classic', is still apt (though Brecht would have been critical of the capitalist world's definitions of effectiveness and of classicality). In 1971–2 he outdistanced Shakespeare in number of performances.[52] As for Brecht-theatre, a potential carrier of the tradition is the West Berlin *Schaubühne*, an ensemble of independent artists directed with awareness of Brecht by Peter Stein, and having plenty of time and material resources.[53]

In the United States Brecht is still largely for the radical fringe, having given rise to such way-out phenomena as the *Bertold [sic] Brecht Memorial Guerilla Theater* of Austin, Texas.[54] Truly Brechtian productions are rare in America as elsewhere. A few Brechtian directors have arisen in Europe: Jean Vilar and Roger Planchon in France, Giorgio Strehler in Italy.[55] In Great Britain his influence, mediated by Kenneth Tynan and seen particularly in the work of Peter Hall, has been blamed for much that is boring in the modern classical stage. If that is so, it is a misunderstood and distorted influence. More fun was kept in the Brechtian style by Joan Littlewood's Stratford productions, and the master would have approved of *Oh, What a Lovely War!* But we must still echo Michael Kustow's remark that the 'fruitful ambiguities' of Brecht's later plays have not yet been confronted on the British stage.[56] We seem to skirt round the four great plays this book is about; they are often performed amateurishly, almost never well by any standards Brecht would recognise. The latest production (*The Good Woman of Setzuan*, Royal Court Theatre, London, 1977) runs true to form by cutting important scenes.

1   *Life of Galileo*, scene 2: the Doge tries to attract Galileo's attention (Berliner Ensemble 1957)

2   *Life of Galileo*, scene 12: Laughton with projection of instruments of torture (New York 1947)

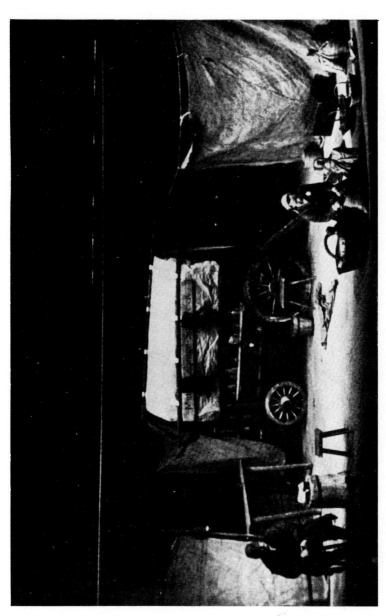

3 *Mother Courage*, scene 6: Courage counts stock and curses war (Berliner Ensemble 1951)

4   *Mother Courage*, scene 11: death of Kattrin (Wuppertal)

5   *The Good Person of Szechwan*, street set (Frankfurt 1952)

6b *The Good Person of Szechwan*, scene 8: Shui Ta supervises the
tobacco factory (Zurich 1943)

6a *The Good Person of Szechwan*, scene 7:
Shen Teh addresses the public (Berliner
Ensemble 1957)

7a *The Caucasian Chalk Circle*, act 2: Grusha rescues Michael (Berliner Ensemble 1954)

7b *The Caucasian Chalk Circle*, act 3: the bridge (Berliner Ensemble 1954)

8　*The Caucasian Chalk Circle*, act 6: Grusha argues with the Governor's Wife (Berliner Ensemble 1954)

4 *The Life of Galileo*

This play contains 'the most complete presentation of Brecht's intellectual world'.[1] The *first version* was written in Denmark in November 1938 and revised early in 1939. It reached the stage in Zurich on 9 September 1943. A *second version* in English was worked out in collaboration with Charles Laughton in California from December 1944 to December 1945, and first performed in Beverly Hills on 31 July 1947. This version, turned back into German by Elisabeth Hauptmann and Benno Besson, and further altered by Brecht (*third version*), was put on in Cologne on 16 April 1955 and by the Berliner Ensemble in a production prepared by Brecht and continued after his death by Erich Engel, on 15 January 1957. Galileo was played by Ernst Busch, sets designed by Caspar Neher. We are concerned mainly with the third version.

(1) THE PLOT

Brecht designated the play 'biography' (*Aj.*, 1, 274: 24.4.41). The term 'Life' in the title attaches it to two earlier plays: the early Marlowe adaptation *Life of Edward II*, and *The Mother*, subtitled 'Life of the Revolutionary Pelagea Vlassova from Tver'. After history made by medieval kings and by the modern proletariat, we have history made by a Renaissance man.

The scenes of *Galileo* are largely prefaced by dates: in some cases a spread of years whose activities are to be exemplified in the scene, in others a single turning-point in Galileo's fortunes.

Scene 1 [1609]: 'Galileo Galilei, teacher of Mathematics at Padua, determines to prove the new Copernican system.' Galileo after his morning wash explains (in a conventional exposition) to his housekeeper's son, Andrea Sarti, a ten-year-old budding physicist, the principles of the new view of the universe: all is in motion; doubt is replacing belief; in astronomy, the earth is thought to revolve around the sun. Signora Sarti, however, has her doubts as to the new age Galileo announces: in order to pay the milkman Galileo will need to take a private pupil, Ludovico Marsili, a young noble interested in horses, who comes to introduce himself and tells Galileo of the latest toy he has seen in Amsterdam: a tube through which one sees distant objects magnified. Galileo sketches such a thing for himself and sends Andrea to the lens-grinder's with half a scudo borrowed from his next visitor, Priuli, the Curator of the University, who has come to turn down Galileo's request for an increase in salary: the Republic of Venice feels it has done enough for a scientist if it gives him a job and keeps the Inquisition off his back; what Galileo teaches brings no money into the state; he should invent something useful, if he wants to be rewarded. Galileo thinks of the telescope, arranges the lenses Andrea (pawning his coat to do so) has bought, and lets Andrea test the effect. Two unwelcome visits have changed the course of Galileo's life.

Scene 2 [24 August 1609]: 'Galileo presents the Republic of Venice with a new Discovery.' In the quest for his salary increase Galileo passes the telescope off as his own invention at a ceremony in which he presents it to the Doge and Senators. The Curator draws attention to its use in war; Galileo's fifteen-year-old daughter Virginia performs the presentation; the lens-grinder sets up the instrument, and while it is being examined Galileo tells his friend Sagredo what he has seen in the skies with it. Virginia brings Ludovico who ironically compliments Galileo; the Doge, a shy man, manages to get Galileo's attention and grant his pay rise.

Scene 3 [10 January 1610; historical events of 7–13 January]: 'By means of the Telescope Galileo discovers Phenomena in the Sky which prove the Copernican System. Warned by his Friend against the possible Consequences of his Researches, Galileo Professes his Belief in Man's Reason.' Sagredo observes the moon through the telescope and Galileo interprets what he sees: the moon is, like the earth, lit by the sun. Giordano Bruno, burnt for heresy ten years before, was right. The Curator storms in angry about the deception with the telescope which he has by now discovered, refuses to be mollified by the promise of better star-charts made with its aid to help navigation, and storms out. Galileo defends himself to Sagredo: he needs money for Virginia's dowry, for books and for food, and his telescope is much better than the Dutch one. Returning to it, he notices that one of the satellites of Jupiter he has observed is missing. He and Sagredo observe – there is an interruption with the stage in darkness to suggest the passing of time – and calculate: Jupiter has no crystal circle and there are no supports in space! Sagredo is afraid: there is no room for God in space now either, and trouble is bound to come – especially as Galileo espouses Bruno's heresy that God is within man. Galileo is more optimistic: he defends his belief in people's reasonableness and thinks that now he has proofs he can avoid Bruno's fate. To prove that reasonableness is common he calls in Signora Sarti, who duly confirms that in her experience the small revolves around the great. Virginia comes on her way to early mass; Galileo treats her interest in the stars very shortly, but does tell her he wants to get a job at Florence: there he can have time for research, and money for the fleshpots. To this end he has – he tells Sagredo – written a servile letter to the Grand Duke of Florence. The thought of the monkish intellectual stagnation there is a challenge to him. But Sagredo remains unconvinced.

Scene 4 [summary of activities of 1610–15]: 'Galileo has exchanged the Republic of Venice for the Florentine Court. His Discoveries with the Telescope Meet with Disbelief among the Savants there'. Signora Sarti is dissatisfied with Florence and Galileo's status there. The young Grand Duke Cosmo (Cosimo in the English translation), curious to see the telescope, arrives early for a demonstration of it arranged by Galileo and has a fight with Andrea, who wants to force the Copernican system on him too dogmatically, until Galileo and the gentlemen of the university arrive. Galileo speaks on the Ptolemaic and Copernican systems and invites the scholars to examine through the telescope the satellites of Jupiter, which he has christened Medicean Stars in honour of Cosimo; but they prefer a theoretical discussion in Latin on the basis of Aristotle's authority, and hint that they do not trust a man whose association with the telescope started with a fraud. Andrea finds them simply stupid. Federzoni the lens-grinder reminds them that Aristotle had no telescope, but Galileo becomes more and more obsequious, even as he grows more and more insistent that they should not close their eyes to changes which are all around them and have already been embraced by artisans and sailors. However, they depart unmoved, promising to submit the matter to the Vatican.

Scene 5 [unhistorical]: 'Undaunted even by the Plague Galileo Continues his Researches.' (*a*) The plague breaks out as Galileo is in the middle of a set of observations with which he hopes to silence his opponents. A coach is sent by the Grand Duke to take him and his household to safety, but Galileo wants to stay at his telescope; while Signora Sarti is arguing with him the carriage goes without them. (*b*) Signora Sarti has disappeared and is reported to be sick with the plague. The street is cordoned off by soldiers. Galileo is afraid of starving but an old woman promises – and later brings – milk, Andrea turns up, having jumped off the coach distraught at his mother's dangerous illness, but still able to listen to the news that Venus describes a circle round the sun.

Scene 6 [unhistorical: in fact Clavius reported in 1611, but the Jesuits dropped Copernicus in 1614]: '1616. The Collegium Romanum, the Vatican's Institute of Research, Confirms Galileo's Discoveries.' Galileo waits among a great crowd of clerics for the verdict of the Jesuits' expert, Clavius, on his theories. The mood is hostile to him: if the earth is part of the heavens, and the heavens consist of worlds, how is theology possible? Galileo must be a slave of his mathematical errors, the earth must be the midpoint of the universe. But Clavius comes and pronounces in Galileo's favour, The Grand Inquisitor arrives to look at the telescope.

Scene 7 [5 March 1616; historical events of 26 February to 5 March]. 'But the Inquisition Puts the Copernican Teachings on the Index.' Cardinal Bellarmin is holding a carnival ball; Galileo comes with Virginia and her fiancé Ludovico. He encourages two clerical secretaries to play chess with the modern 'long moves. Cardinals Bellarmin and Barberini come with lamb and dove masks. Galileo competes with the latter in quoting the Bible, a prelude to a more serious astronomical discussion in which the Cardinals point out the dangers of accusing God of being bad at astronomy. The authority of God is needed to reconcile people to the roughness of the world, and they intend to assert it against Galileo, whom they formally warn to give up the Copernican heresy, notwithstanding the Collegium Romanum's recognition; he may use it as a hypothesis, a poor consolation. The inquisitor afterwards reads the secretaries' transcript of the conversation, and makes sure he knows who Virginia's confessor is.

Scene 8: 'A Conversation.' A little monk with astronomical leanings comes to second, from his own experience, the Cardinals' views: only belief that the eye of God is watching them keeps the poor reconciled to their poverty and gives their life a meaning. Galileo is moved to contradict: they suffer poverty in a fruitful land because they have to pay for the Pope's wars and for presents intended to silence Galileo, and because they are denied modern technology. Galileo might remain silent if heavily enough bribed, but basically he knows that he must go on trying to discover and spread the truth, even if it leads to a catastrophe. The monk joins him.

Scene 9 [historical events affecting the Papacy, but the experiments were undertaken earlier, 1611–13]: 'After Eight Years of Silence, the Enthronement of a New Pope, Himself a Mathematician, Encourages Galileo to Resume his Researches into the Forbidden Subject of Sun-spots.' Galileo holds an experimental lecture for Federzoni, the little monk and Andrea while Virginia and Signora Sarti sew at Virginia's trousseau. Galileo has written nothing for years. He is sarcastic to Mucius, a former pupil of his who has condemned Copernican theories when he should have known better. Virginia and Signora Sarti are more interested in the astrological portents for her marriage. The appearance of a new tract on sunspots interests Galileo's pupils, but he forces himself to remain silent in fear of the Church: sunspots involve Copernican theory. They experiment on floating bodies and Galileo shows that a needle can be made to float on water.

Ludovico comes. Galileo welcomes the interruption and has wine fetched. Ludovico has news from Rome: the Pope is dying and Barberini, a mathematician, will probably be the next Pope. Galileo shows life immediately and wants to start investigating sunspots again, deaf to the warnings of Ludovico and Signora Sarti that Barberini is not yet Pope and, even when he is, will have to think of keeping the nobility on his side. Signora Sarti says she knows Galileo has been secretly working on sunspots for two months, and warns him that Ludovico will drop Virginia if her father persists in heresy. Galileo, however, is unstoppable and annoys Ludovico – whom he likes less with every mouthful of wine (*Mat. G.*, 63f.) – by hinting that he could sow revolt among the peasants. Ludovico goes without taking leave of Virginia, who is putting on her wedding gown to show him. Galileo proceeds to his observations of the sun, as Virginia returns, realises Ludovico is lost, and faints.

Scene 10 [unhistorical]: 'During the following Decade Galileo's Teaching Spreads among the People. Pamphleteers and Ballad-singers Everywhere Take up the New Ideas. In 1632, during Carnival time, many Cities in Italy choose Astronomy as the Theme for the Guilds' Processions.' A couple of poor travelling artistes sing the latest song from Florence, which shows the social consequences of abandoning the geocentric view of the heavens: people want to escape the domination of employers, priests and husbands, as the heavenly bodies have that of the earth; the Bible is discredited. The carnival procession includes tableaux such as Galileo holding a Bible whose pages are crossed through.

Scene 11 [1633; historically 11 October 1632]: 'The Inquisition Summons the World-famous Scholar to Rome.' Galileo, shadowed by an agent of the Inquisition, waits to present his new book to the Grand Duke of Florence; the Rector of the University scarcely notices him, but an ironfounder, Vanni, is very friendly (scientific, technical, and mercantile progress is important to him) and advises Galileo to avoid the consequences of his increasing reputation as a heretic by fleeing to Venice in Vanni's coach. Galileo however trusts to Cosimo to protect him; he himself has after all had nothing to do with the popular interpretations of his work. When an official is rude, Galileo wonders whether to go after all; but it would mean saying goodbye to three months' pay he is owed. The Grand Duke comes, embarrassed, and refuses to accept Galileo's book; an official asks Galileo to step into the Inquisition's coach which awaits him.

Scene 12: 'The Pope.' Pope Urban VIII (Barberini) receives the Inquisitor. He is inclined to defend the new theories, but the Inquisitor stresses the consequences of the growth of doubt in terms of social unrest at a time when the papacy can ill afford it, being involved in religious wars – on the Protestant side, at that. Galileo will make the heavens subject to reason rather than God, whilst his machines will destroy the existing master-servant relationships. If the maritime cities insist on the heretical star-charts, they will have to have them – but the theories on which the charts are based must be rejected. The Pope is now persuaded that something must be done; the Inquisitor strengthens his resolve by pointing out that Galileo cheated in his book by giving the last word in the dialogues to the spokesman of religion as agreed – but making the spokesman of religion a fool. Urban agrees to let Galileo be threatened with torture, which will be enough to make him deny Copernicus.

Scene 13: 'On the 22nd of June, 1633, before the Inquisition, Galileo Galilei Recants his Teaching about the Movement of the Earth.' Galileo's pupils and Virginia wait for the outcome of Galileo's trial. Andrea fears he will be killed, for he will never recant, and his 'Discorsi' will remain unwritten. Federzoni is not so sure. Virginia prays. The set time for his recantation comes and goes and the pupils are glad; but the bell tolls after all, Virginia is glad, and outside the recantation is read. Andrea is bitter when Galileo comes, but Galileo, though altered by suffering, remains calm and rejects the idea that he should have showed heroism.

An extract from the 'Discorsi' is read to show that great machines are more fragile than small ones.

Scene 14 [1633–42]: 'Galileo Galilei lives in a Country House near Florence, a Prisoner of the Inquisition until his Death. The "Discorsi".' Galileo, old and half-blind, is experimenting with a ball in a groove. A monk is on duty to see that he writes nothing. Two geese are sent from someone passing through; Galileo shows appetite, although he has already dined. Virginia insists that he dictate to her part of his weekly letter to the Archbishop, in which he shows orthodox theological knowledge and supplies arguments in favour of the social *status quo*. Andrea, on his way out of Italy to continue his researches in Holland, comes to see Galileo, and reports how since the recantation many scientists have lost heart. Galileo hides his disappointment. He manages to get Virginia out of the way in the kitchen, then – all the time anxious because of the monk who may be listening outside – tells Andrea he has finished the 'Discorsi', delivered the manuscript to the Church, and at great risk made a copy which is hidden inside his globe: if Andrea takes it, he must not betray where he got it from. Andrea takes it and interprets Galileo's behaviour: he recanted in order to be able to work on, retreated from a hopeless position. Galileo, excited, forgetting the danger from the monk, and not stopped by Virginia's return,[2] contradicts him: only fear of pain made him recant. He has delivered the scientific work, but now he feels that is not enough; science has used the new-found instrument of critical doubt to understand the skies, but failed to put it to work to ease the life of people in general; indeed, new machines and discoveries will merely contribute to their oppression, since scientists will have no independence of the oppressing classes; and Galileo lost his chance, when he was relatively strong (this contradicts what was said at the time), to reverse this; he is no longer a scientist or fit to shake Andrea's hand. Andrea disagrees, but Virginia inhibits further argument and he has to leave.

Scene 15 [unhistorical]: '1637. Galileo's Book, the 'Discorsi', crosses the Italian Border.' Andrea waits to go through the customs examination at the frontier and talks to children, one of whom is despised by the others but shows more critical intelligence. The customs men have not time to read all Andrea's books, and do not notice the manuscript which he carries in his hand and reads all the time. Andrea buys and leaves behind milk for a woman who is suspected of witchcraft and thus generally refused milk; encourages the bright boy; and crosses the frontier.

(II) GALILEO, SCIENCE AND THE BOURGEOIS ERA

The play is unusual in its concentration on the content of science. Astronomy and hydrostatics are made present on the stage. But so are the scientist's mentality and the way in which science runs his life for him. The physical demonstrations on stage are part of the plot, and have practical implications: floating a needle is part of a study of hydrostatics important for building bigger ships.[3] In that Galileo is a scientist, we learn from him, not (empathetically) with him. The naïve, critical, unprejudiced vision Brecht noted in the scientists of his own day, which strips away from things the familiarity of *idées reçues* and makes them new in the mind, is exemplified in him. He puts the authority of Aristotle to the test and refutes it by making metal float (1304; 85; 9). The moral victory, at least, goes to the new science against the old obscurantism. Galileo is modern in his attitude to evidence too, declaring he will explore every alternative theory before reluctantly accepting the bold revolutionary one (1311; 91; 9). Doubt is the way to discovery. Novelties may be ephemeral unless existing convictions really have failed to provide satisfactory explanations of things. Brecht means the same attitude to apply to social phenomena; he was as wary of those who always propagate revolution as of unshakable conservatives (20, 6f.: *Über den Gewohnheitspatriotismus*).

Galileo opens with a great speech on the new age he thinks has dawned (1232f.; 20ff.; 1). The telescope symbolises the strivings of this age and of Galileo within it: to provide empirical evidence for the cosmology of Copernicus, according to whom the earth and planets revolve around the sun, whereas in the ancient, officially accepted Ptolemaic system all heavenly bodies are centred on the earth. Giordano Bruno had been burnt at the stake in 1600 after upholding such views; Galileo thinks he would have escaped had he been able to offer physical proof (1255; 41; 3). Such proof depends on the evidence of the senses; Galileo is down-to-earth enough to learn from the workers who, relying on their senses, bring about technological progress (1230; 55; 4). That the workers in fact are interested in astronomy and its implications – that men are open to reason – seems apparent to Brecht in *The Mother*, where Pelagea Vlassova backs up one of her revolutionary arguments by saying no one believes in God any more since the skies are measurable (2, 883). What does not occur to Galileo is that the audience to which he praises the workers' spirit of innovation is one which has everything to lose from an alteration of the *status quo*. He believes that even such people must accept the evidence of their senses and trust truth not to lead them astray. He is wrong. The unwillingness of the Church and its tame philosophers to look through a telescope and believe what they see is powerful enough to conquer him. This subject had interested Brecht since 1920. 'Copernicus' discovery . . . is first shot down, then declared to be correct and perfectly insignificant . . . That is a cheek that cannot but suceeed' (*Tb.*, 43: 31.8.20). It is mainly the cheek with which the Church overrides logic that makes Galileo speechless when told of the decree in scene 7. Brecht suggested parallels with Darwin and Freud, both of whom with their new ideas and methods seemed scandalous to their contemporary establishments, irrespective of their objective rightness or otherwise. To Galileo reason is irresistible. 'The temptation offered by such a proof is too great . . . Thinking is one of the greatest pleasures of the human race' (1256; 42; 3). Signora Sarti supplies the social equivalent when she shows that the small revolve around the great (1257f.; 43; 3). People reason for a purpose: the child puts on his cap when told it may rain (1256; 42; 3). Such utilitarian ideas, typical of Brecht, belong less to the historical Galileo than to a philosophical tradition going from Holbach and Helvétius through Feuerbach, for whom the good is what serves the general egoism, to Lenin.[4]

On a purely scientific level, however, the physical concepts we associate with Copernicus (and with Newton) need modification in the twentieth century; Einstein and Heisenberg dominate our ideas. Brecht possessed A. S. Eddington's book *The Nature of the Physical World*, in German translation,[5] and was able historically to overlook the whole era of 'classical' physics. What is more, he sees it as coterminous with the era of capitalism. In connection with his late play *Turandot*, which deals particulary with the intellectual prostituting his talents for short-term personal advantages, he writes: 'Particularly after I had written *The Life of Galileo*, in which I had described the dawning of reason, I was interested in depicting its twilight, the evening of precisely that kind of reason which towards the end of the sixteenth century had opened the capitalist age' (5, 3*). In a sweeping transposition of history, Brecht considers the beginning of the science of the bourgeois age in the light of the ending of that age – and condemns in it the whole era. This hostile intention, appearing in the second version, is much clearer in the third, where the social questions affecting the status of science are given lengthier and more precise statement in Galileo's self-analysis.

To clarify this we must return to the first version. In the 1930s Brecht is able to see Galileo as a positive model of behaviour for the intellectuals and scientists in Nazi Germany.[6] The play has been described as a dramatic version of the essay *Fünf Schwierigkeiten beim Schreiben der Wahrheit* ('Five Difficulties in Writing the Truth'): Galileo practises the courage, wisdom and cunning to recognise and spread the truth in a hostile world. In the argument about whether to investigate sunspots or not, he tells the story of Keunos, a Cretan philosopher who served an agent of tyranny for seven years without saying yes to the man's question 'Will you serve me?'; after the man's death he said 'No'. Brecht had published this story independently in 1930, and its basic lesson is: wait until the time for resistance is ripe.[7] During his house-arrest depicted in his last scene, Galileo gives the results of his surreptitious writing to a tiler who repeatedly visits him on the pretext of repairing the chimney and smuggles his manuscripts out; but now he has increasing difficulties and has brought back a manuscript which Galileo hides inside a globe. In the 1938 version, Virginia reads Galileo aphorisms by Montaigne which he comments on, showing his questioning and rebellious spirit unbroken; in 1939 this is replaced by a more matter-of-fact element, the révision of a passage of the 'Discorsi' (the passage read in the final version after scene 13). To Andrea, Galileo says that the scientist has a duty to fight for the freedom of science against force, and this means fighting against lies and for the good of mankind. He has failed in this duty. But he still researches, his notes are in the globe though his writings are delivered to the Inquisition, and if anyone came around looking for useful things in the debris of his career (his authority has been shattered by his recantation), they will treat it as the work of a discredited researcher. Andrea takes the manuscript; he believes that Galileo's fall has left most of his work intact. Galileo reflects on the need for the exercise of reason to develop more and turn the new age from one of darkness into one of light.

Details show that, although Brecht disclaimed the intention of proving anything in it (*Aj.*, 2, 747: 30.7.45), the historical play is closely connected with the present. For instance, Galileo's house-arrest is shown as more closely supervised than in reality. His letters are opened. The historical parallel construction is this: in a time of basic social progress (with the rise of Communism), a progressive thinker finding himself under an authoritarian régime (Germany) withdraws under the threat of torture; but recanting his views means that he survives, though shamefully, to work on in co-operation with the tiler (working-class resistance to Hitler) and use his talents to weaken the régime in the long run. Brecht has put aside the revolutionary heroism of *Saint Joan of the Stockyards* and *The Mother* in order to show survival under pressure. Thought and truth are for Brecht necessarily socially good: with Goebbels in mind he had written 'Propaganda for thinking, in whatever area it is made, is useful to the cause of the oppressed' (18, 235: *Fünf Schwierigkeiten . . .*). That Galileo's survival allows him to go on with his scientific work, which aids the proletariat, is more important than the setback of his recantation – which however makes him a closer model for a German scientist who by 1938 will have made many surrenders to Hitler, but can still take the right path now. All the implications of Galileo's scientific pioneerhood are seen as relevant to the present; the bourgeois revolt against feudalism as a positive historical parallel to the proletarian revolt against capitalism, the temporary setback of the former in the play as a precursor of the latter's embarrassment at a time when Hitler's misleading ideas of what is progressive seem to be winning (with the Munich agreement and Franco's victory in Spain – see the *Foreword* of 1939: 17, 1103–6; *Mat. G.*, 7–10; *G.*, 5–7).

Galileo is however a questionable model of a resistance worker. He does not plan his actions, and his behaviour before the Inquisition is so unworthy, his reaction to danger so timid, as to vitiate the theme.[8] By the time Brecht came to revise the play in 1944, this interpretation was in any case inopportune. The time for exhorting German intellectuals to cheat Hitler was past. And another aspect of Galileo's work had occurred to Brecht in 1939 with the news of the splitting of the uranium atom by Hahn and Strassmann:

Knowledge of the nature of things, so greatly and so ingeniously deepened and widened, is incapable, unless joined by knowledge of the nature of man and of human society in its entirety, of making supremacy over nature a source of happiness for mankind (15, 295: *Über experimentelles Theater*).

The addition he at first made to the text was an optimistic one, referring to 'the greatest discoveries, which must increase the prosperity of mankind immeasurably'.[9] But it was increasingly obvious that modern science, of which Galileo with his insistence on experimentation and evidence was a father, had become mainly a weapon of war. Even in 1939 chain reactions which could destroy the world were becoming thinkable. Instead of being accepted unexamined as a progressive force, science is in the second version critically looked at. News of the first use of the atomic bomb, arriving after completion of the provisional second version, gave the expression of disquiet greater urgency. 'Overnight the biography of the founder of the new system of physics read differently' (17, 1106; *G.*, 8; *Mat. G.*, 10). By 1952, the date of the first hydrogen bomb, the threat was much clearer and the end of the world as a result of the conflict of the capitalist democracies and the U.S.S.R. seemed likely. Such events as the hearings in the case of J. Robert Oppenheimer, declared a security risk in the U.S. because of his scruples about developing nuclear weapons (1953), proved to Brecht that *Galileo* was topical and led him to work on the third version and staging of the play.

The textual references to the atom are easily overlooked, though they can be clarified in production and are present in the introductory verse to scene 15 (used in production as an epilogue to the whole play) and the poems *Prolog zur amerikanischen Aufführung* ('Prologue to the American Production', 10, 936) and *Epilog der Wissenschaftler* ('Epilogue of the Scientists', 10, 937): 'For they dedicate their findings / to the fleecing of mankind / till their last one turns the tables / till the gnomic / white atomic / one finishes you and us and the world.' Brecht was not so simple as to make the play depend on one topical message. That this is possible was shown later by Heinar Kipphardt's documentary play *In der Sache J. Robert Oppenheimer*, with its single, hard-hitting message about the bomb. Brecht's plays are rarely like that (perhaps *Señora Carrar's Rifles* is closest to it). The final version of Galileo still contains passages which can be taken to restate the moral of the first version – propaganda for thinking is always good – or to support quite different lessons. Andrea is allowed to state that Galileo's self-analysis will not be the last word (1342; 119; 14).

In the later versions Brecht grafts on to the parallels between 1633 and 1933, seen in the first version, a different concept: the atomic bomb is one of the logical destructive results of a capitalist era which (as in the meantime Brecht had shown in *Mother Courage*) makes no qualitative distinction between peace and war – both states of Darwinian competition; and the failure to make such distinctions, the readiness of the potentially independent individual to sell out to the powers-that-be and further their aggressive intentions, goes right back to the beginning of the bourgeois era and Galileo's betrayal – as Brecht sees it –

of social progress. In this sense Galileo's new age is to be seen more than critically: the bourgeois age has merely added fresh horrors to the feudalist system's existing iniquities. The sketches for a foreword to the play shed much light on the theme of the beginning and the end of the bourgeois era as seen in the aspect of science and in the model case of Galileo. The main arguments are. these. The bourgeoisie exploits Galileo's objective reason and isolates the world of 'pure' science in order to incorporate it better with bourgeois politics, economics, ideology. Galileo develops the productive ideas which are the germ of the English and Dutch Industrial Revolutions, but on the social front he betrays their productive aspect (17, 1133; *Mat. G.*, 36). Pure science produces the equation $E=mc^2$; others derive from it the destruction of Hiroshima. War encourages science – but how? Hitler's prisons provide experimental material for doctors. In the Second World War scientists get their hands on the means of production – and they produce destruction, till it threatens to engulf them along with everyone else. Hitler was perhaps an excrescence of capitalism – but capitalism was, in that case, a system that lent itself to making excrescences (17, 1112–5; *Mat. G.* 16–20). The whole era of the bourgeois contained from its beginning the seeds both of the Hitlerian excesses and of the atomic bomb, and the false relationship of science and authority is an important problem.

Brecht does not claim that it is the sole problem, but that once the challenge to the Church's feudal authority has been made in the scientific field and to the benefit of the rising bourgeoisie, the Church's victory over Galileo is a catastrophe which distorts the whole following historical development. The hold of the feudalists on power is strengthened just when it could perhaps have been broken. Had Galileo kept quiet like Copernicus until his death, or had he like Giordano Bruno remained steadfast, this distortion would not have taken place; the development of science might have been delayed, but the precedent for its betrayal to feudalism by a great thinker would not have been given, there would have been no threat of a 'race of inventive dwarfs who can be hired for anything' (1341; 118; 14; cf. *Mat. G.*, 61). Galileo has had a warning of the threat in the behaviour of Mucius, whom he and Federzoni found dangerous precisely because having heard Galileo's teachings he had denied them, so that people said 'he's heard everything that Galilei teaches and he has to admit that it's all false' (1300; 81; 9): not knowing the truth is stupid, knowingly denying it criminal. Galileo, devoted to scientific truth, reminds Mucius that he did not let the plague interrupt his work. Mucius says 'the plague is not the worst thing' (ibid.); and indeed, Galileo crumbles at the sight of the instruments. Andrea now takes over as the proponent of the duty of truth, reminding us (1326; 105; 13) of Galileo's reproach to Mucius. In scene 14 Andrea revises his view of Galileo's recantation, making it the basis of a new ethics (1338; 115) in which one is allowed to run away from a hopeless political struggle in order to guarantee the continuation of scientific progress. Andrea builds up theories to suit his professional interests whilst disregarding the interests of the masses; he is the first inventive dwarf. 'Science knows only one commandment: contribute to science', he says, to Galileo's disgust (1339; 116). Even in the first version Galileo rejects any idea that he recanted in order to work on: contributions to science can be made by anyone, physics is not served by one person's survival. When Andrea in one speech approves of Galileo's popularising science by bowing to Cosimo, in the next dismisses the recantation as affecting merely 'a popular point in your teachings' (1338; 116), his contempt of the non-scientist and disregard of social needs are apparent.[10] Any advances in science he and his successors bring about will play into the hands of the rulers. The opportunity to make the course of history more humane has been lost. The scientist's two responsibilities, to the work alone (a pure scientist's view analogous to *l'art pour l'art* in culture[11]) and to all mankind, are sometimes congruent, sometimes not, and it is illicit for Andrea to make the former into an absolute ideal. Galileo represents, at least potentially, a more promising tradition. Scientific advances, water pumps for example (1296; 78), can further the better society which would foster positive virtues; but only if the inventor does not let the selfish classes exploit his work. To avoid this error Galileo–Brecht suggests the scientist's Hippocratic oath (1341; 118; 14) – hopelessly idealistic, yet the only hopeful solution. The scientist – most topically, in Brecht's day, the nuclear physicist – must see his work as a partial process in society, not as 'pure' or value-free. Brecht thought the sentence 'I maintain that the only purpose of science is to ease the hardship of human existence' (1340; 118) was 300 years ahead of its time.[12] He must have forgotten his use of points of contact with the seventeenth century in progressive Holland and England. He mentions Holland, and gives Galileo statements borrowed or adapted from Bacon and Hobbes.[13] Bacon is the source for views on supposed riches meaning real poverty, on science as work against infinite error rather than towards infinite truth – and, importantly, on science as a means to further man's enjoyment of life. Korsch thought Bacon did for natural science what Marx did for social science;[14] Schumacher (pp. 42ff.) thinks him just as important as Galileo for the philosophy of the play; and Brecht's notes include reference to Bacon's venality – a counterpart to the sensuality with which he endows Galileo (17, 1112f.; *Mat. G.*, 16).

By concentrating such wide-ranging thoughts on the use and misuse of science, and about the whole power-structure of our era, around the figure of Galileo, Brecht lays himself open to the reproach at least of an un-Marxist cult of personality – as if Galileo could have altered history single-handed; at most, of a gross unfairness to Galileo, who had not even invented a destructive weapon. The first criticism – Harold Hobson's 'God that failed' thesis[15] – has some justification. It is *a priori* unlikely that a single act of one man could change three centuries of history, historically false to suggest that Galileo held the balance of power in 1633, and perverse to disregard the example of Giordano Bruno, which shows that martydrom at that time for that cause was useless. On the other hand, Brecht believed that individual decisions have a real effect, and he has a right to teach (here as in *Mother Courage*) that the personal decisions of people who do not claim to be politicians or public leaders can be very important. The more serious criticism of unfairness to Galileo, propounded notably by Ernst Busch in discussions before the first Berlin performance, is a misunderstanding: what Brecht wants to emphasise is that even apparently useful technological innovations do no good if they are taken over by the ruling classes and do not improve the lot of the peasants. Galileo's social betrayal is the catastrophe – not the nature of his scientific work as such. Capitalist peace production and capitalist war production are linked for the Marxist. Thus Galileo becomes the anti-hero and in his last scene is no longer seen co-operating with the proletariat, but meekly supplying arguments for the authorities in their dispute with the workers. It is lip-service – but still service – to feudalism.

Yet Brecht writes, '*The Life of Galileo* is not a Tragedy' (*G.*, 10; 17, 1109; *Mat. G.*, 13).[16] The new age described in scene 1 does exist despite setbacks. The final scene – though never performed – still stands in the book, propagating the thought 'Bespattered don't mean tattered' (1343; 120): the catastrophe is not as final as Galileo makes out. This is admittedly contrary to Brecht's personal view towards the end of his life (17, 1133; *Mat. G.*, 37), when in the light of the atom bomb his verdict on science in the bourgeois era was the one we have just sketched; but Brecht considers dealing with inconsistencies the reader's job, not his own. Galileo does not give in inwardly to obscurantism: he dictates a clearly satirical passage in his servile letter (1333; 111; 14), though he then has it struck out. More forward-looking is the riposte to Andrea in scene 13: 'No. Unhappy is the land that is in need of heroes' (1329; 108). As in *Fear and Misery of the Third Reich* a rainy day is an immediate catastrophe (one's son may get bored and go and denounce one to the Nazis), but the underlying catastrophe is fascism, so here the recantation is in the foreground, but the real catastrophe is any system which makes too great demands on human nature. Mother Courage gives the theme earthier expression, Shen Teh more poetic; but Galileo has the greatest dialectical neatness.

There are three autobiographical glosses on the play. In one, Brecht in the U.S., before the Committee on Un-American Activities, denied his Communism (a recantation), then fled the country to continue the struggle against capitalist warmongers. In another, Brecht in East Germany compromised with the régime for selfish reasons and, despite private qualms, publicly supported its repressions (particularly in 1953). These two do shed a little light on the way Brecht moulded some aspects of his behaviour on models, but should be taken with salt.[17] A third interpretation has Galileo as an anti-Brecht who goes to totalitarian Florence, whereas Brecht in the thirties had refused to settle in totalitarian Russia.[18]

(III) GALILEO: SPLIT CHARACTER

Comic elements provide an important key to Galileo. He is an intellectual Falstaff, a man of superabundant energy and overflowing physicality. He is a compulsive teacher; and a fool who demands proof of any scientific doctrine but embarks on the study of sunspots with no evidence at all that it is safe to do so. He plays with fire and brings about the situations of the play by rashness, most of all when he refuses Vanni's help to escape the Inquisition although he has himself anticipated the situation and has a getaway vehicle of his own. He is the activator who carries the plot forward, from the plagiarism of the telescope on; the hero who dominates the stage, not least with the breathtaking scope of his scientific inquiries; the *raisonneur* who keeps the audience informed of the intellectual issues; the clown who keeps us laughing. Like a comic servant he tricks the Curator with the telescope to get his pay rise; and Brecht pushes the Curator into the role of the pompous, self-righteous master who is the butt and victim of the sly servant. Brecht is concerned to keep the comic element under control – to exaggerate it would minimise the moral import of Galileo's dishonesty. But Brecht has to admit the claim to have based the invention on 'Christian principles' (1246; 33) is amusingly provocative (*Mat. G.*, 54). Comic effects are useful in preventing too serious an empathy with the figure. Brecht at first wanted to use controlled self-identification with the hero, since the audience would then have to identify with Galileo's self-condemnation too (*Aj.*, 1, 35: 23.11.38). But this is hard in practice, and later on Brecht stresses Galileo's failures and finds it necessary to warn that his self-reproaches should not be used to produce pity for him. Then identification and distance are better balanced: his vitality is that of an alien phenomenon, like Richard III (*Mat. G.*, 47). The interpretation of the role of Galileo depends on this balance. His failures must be stressed as they occur, or the self-condemnation will come as a surprise and puzzle the audience. Brecht aids this by some of the other characters' dialogue. Disappointment at his recantation for instance, is emphasised by Andrea's reminder that Galileo condemned Mucius for denying the truth. And in scene 13 Galileo (in Laughton's interpretation) comes on grinning and infantile, lacking in self-discipline – an easy victim for threats of force. His character falls short of his intellect – the intellect which allows him with the neat riposte to Andrea to shift the blame on to the country he lives in (1329; 108; 13).

It is important that he is shown as a gourmet. His weakness for food is brought into parallel not only with his all-too-vivid sensual ideas of what instruments of torture can do, but with his weakness for experiment and innovation (132f.; 103; 12). He pursues the fleshpots in a society which, whilst still dominated by powers inimical to innovations, yet has its progressive forces. The same contradictions and problems are thus at work in Galileo's personality and in his situation. His sensuality now furthers, now hinders progress; now he espouses the progressive cause, now be blinds himself to the evils of the existing system. Society now accepts the results of his work, now persecutes him for its principles.

After the Inquisition's condemnation of Copernican theory he believes he has a balanced relationship with the Church. The Jesuits after all praised him (1289; 72; 7); the Church lets him keep his authority on condition he does not use it aggressively. He thinks he has fulfilled the pact by sticking to its letter, presenting Copernican theory in a dialogue and giving the last word to faith and Aristotle (1324; 103; 12); he publicly rejects the popular interpretation of his theories as encouraging anarchy (1319; 98; 11) and thinks his position secure: 'They praised me so highly that now they must accept me as I am' (1320; 99; 11). But the over-popularity of the anarchistic interpretation of his work leads him into renewed conflict with the Church and catastrophe. And when he works on after his condemnation and lets Andrea take his results away he is knowingly working into the hands of the ruling class, by delivering knowledge into a world so arranged that knowledge is a means of oppression,[19] as much as when he recanted out of fear of torture. He regrets his urge to get his work published – but he yields to it (*Mat. G.*, 71 and 73). He has always gone his own ways – sometimes, as in the telescope episode, crooked ones – to reach his aims: sensual and scientific gratification. 'To an old wine or a new idea, he cannot say no' (1324; 103; 12). He cannot resist working on sunspots as soon as he has the faintest idea that a new Pope may countenance the publication of his findings (1307f.; 88; 9). In the last scene, it is goose-livers he cannot refuse – an unheroic touch to counter any admiration the audience may feel for him, an undignified overfed old man who laughs unkindly at the misery his downfall has caused Federzoni (1335; 113; 14; see *Mat. G.*, 69f.). In seeking his own ends he is a bourgeois individualist just as is Vanni with his 'liberty to make money' (1318; 97; 11). The telescope presents itself to him in just this light. A poor man, dejected when told he cannot have more salary, he sees it as a way of making money at the price of interrupting his real work (*Mat. G.*, 53). But then if he were not the great sensualist he would not be the genius he is either. Sensuality is basically positive: Ziffel defends good living in a section of the *Refugees' Conversations* called *On low Materialism* (14, 1392f.) and complains in *Thought as an Enjoyment* that thinking, which should be a pleasure, is spoilt like other pleasures by being yoked into the money nexus (14, 1482f.). Brecht sees Galileo's demands for physical comforts as justified; he furnished his own rooms with solid comfortable furniture and insisted on plenty of space to work. Galileo is conceived by Brecht (who complained at the German mistrust of the sensual and corporeal: 'our heroes engage in conviviality, but do not eat' – *Aj.*, 1, 19; 12.8.38) from the beginning as a man who loves physics as he loves food, not ethereal but 'a noisy, full-blooded man with humour, the type of the new physicist, earthly, a great teacher. Favourite posture: belly forwards, two hands on his two buttocks, head back, always gesticulating – though not with sweeping movements – with one fleshy hand . . .' (*Mat. G.*, 27). Such sexual adventures as occurred to Brecht for him – notably an affair with Andrea's sister[20] – are moved for the sake of economy, though there are hints that Galileo and Signora Sarti are closer than they admit.[21] When excited, she relapses from the formal mode of address into the familiar 'du' (1308, cf. 1306f.; 88, 'Galileo', cf. 87, 'Signor Galilei'; 9). In scene 5, when he refuses to leave Florence, she transfers to the familiar form in the middle of an exclamation: 'Herr Galilei! Komm sofort mit! Du bist wahnsinnig' (1273). When the coach has gone without them both she recovers her composure and formality, while it is his turn to relapse (as he often does when they are alone) into familiarity and colloquialism.

Galileo's general culture is not without its sex-bound side, as when he quotes a Priapic passage from Horace (1297; 78; 8. Horace, *Satires I*, viii, 1–3). But generally sex is underplayed in favour of greed. Love of food is emphasised as a danger – that is, a vice in given social circumstances.

> No one's virtue is complete:
> Great Galileo likes to eat. (1246; 32; 2)

Such is Brecht's explanation of the deception with the telescope. And in a magnificent duality in scene 9, Galileo interrupts a conversation with Ludovico about the pleasures of wine – 'I enjoy the consolations of the flesh . . . I say: enjoyment is an accomplishment' (1306; 87) – to tell Andrea to move the apparatus of the floating body experiments: he is about to enjoy working on sunspots again. At the beginning of the play he delivers his great monologue while Andrea rubs his back: his production of ideas is directly dependent on animal pleasure, 'he would have to stop thinking if Andrea stopped rubbing his back' (17, 1128; *Mat. G.*, 31). And when society stops giving him sensual gratification, why should he not betray it?

Galileo is not pulled between idea and reality like some classical hero: he is attracted by two mutually exclusive realities. One of the two connected facets of his character makes him a man of public importance; the other stops him from using this position responsibly in the face of social pressures. He produces the ideas on which a social revolution could be based, he knows it, and he betrays the idea of the revolution. He is a genuine hero who becomes a genuine criminal, a fallen man;[22] a born teacher whose example ruins his best pupil; a philanthropist of brutal egoism. He, and reason and progress with him, triumphs and fails – part of the dialectic of intellectual and social history seen through one man. Brecht saw the same contrasts in Faust, enlightened intellectual and social criminal.[23] Eisler compares his vacillations to those of Hamlet and of Schiller's Wallenstein.[24] Even during his last scene he changes his attitude and contradicts himself several times.

He is aware of conflicting demands made on him by the powers-that-be and by the rising classes. In scene 4 he defends Federzoni's right to hear scientific arguments in the vernacular (1266; 51); in scene 8 he is interested in the social dimension of science, arguing against the thesis of the necessity of poverty the view that there are virtues stemming from prosperity and happiness, preferable to those necessary to bear misery (1296; 77f.). But after his talk with Vanni he short-sightedly denies any interest in the consequences of his science.[25] After his recantation he works on, and even lets Andrea take his results, contrary to his better insight that publication of the 'Discorsi' will only be a further step in the subjection of science (17, 1130–2; *Mat. G.*, 33–5). Precisely this work on mechanics begins the scientific development which will eventually bring about the Industrial Revolution, as Brecht knew; the threat in Galileo's self-accusation 'your machines will represent nothing but new means of oppression' (1340; 118; 14) refers to this. In fact while making him act in a reactionary manner and play into the hands of the oppressors, Brecht puts the positive message of the play into his mouth. The passage culminating 'The fight over the measurability of the heavens has been won by doubt; but the fight of the Roman housewife for milk is ever and again lost through faith' (1340; 117f.; 14) is a poetic version of ideas of Einstein's which Brecht quotes in *Über experimentelles Theater*: that progress in natural science has outstripped the progress of economic security and the moral development of mankind (15, 296). Galileo reproaches himself for not standing up against the Church when there was time, astronomy was topical and he was as strong as the authorities (1341; 118), and echoes Einstein's proposal to take the argument about warfare and the atom out on to the market-places of the U.S.[26] Thus he becomes his own judge, unmasks himself as contemptible – but also rises in our esteem because he sees so clearly the grounds for despising himself. The audience can, whatever Brecht intended, identify with him to some extent even at the end.[27] The alternative is to see Galileo very much as the *raisonneur*, stepping out of his role when he delivers his lessons.

In *Refugees' Conversations* Brecht mentions the political 'heroic age' of Hitler as making life harder for the average man, just when technology seemed to be making life easier (14, 1497). Similarly Galileo is an average-to-cowardly man in a heroic age, and his forgivable weakness decrees that science, instead of putting technological advance at the disposal of the forces of liberation, and bringing a critical attitude to bear on the Church, shall sell out to the powers-that-be. The play opens up the perspective of a rational, egalitarian society – culminating in the overt revolutionary message of the carnival scene; and then shows how this end is frustrated by human weakness. Truth depends on Galileo (1297; 79; 8), and he betrays it. Truth here is a social value, science and society are dialectically related, and unless the scientist has social integrity and the idea of a social aim to be served by his work, the work is harmful. Perhaps the main tragedy of Galileo is not the over-whelming effect of fate or even of circumstances, nor the tragic flaw of character leading to his recantation, but a wrong decision blindly made, when Galileo, not knowing his friends from his enemies, refuses Vanni's help and relies instead on Cosimo's protection. Brecht saw this as a re-cantation more serious than that before the Inquisition (*Mat. G.*, 65). Galileo's downfall is due at least as much to this misjudgment made while he is still free to act as to the physical cowardice which affects him when he is a prisoner.[28] And as well as ruining Galileo it must weaken Vanni's position: Vanni, like everyone else in the play, is let down by Galileo.

(IV) THE SOCIAL WORLD OF THE PLAY

Of our four plays, *Galileo* relies most on historical fact. Brecht admitted it might be treated as a conventional costume drama. Some parts of the text, such as the servile letter to Florence and the formula of recanta-tion, are taken from the historical sources.[29] But the historical element in this sense is only skin-deep. Brecht has no wish to show the past for its own sake, or to demonstrate timeless patterns of human behaviour in a strange setting. It is typical that Brecht uses only indirectly (1306; 87; 9; spoken by Andrea) Galileo's best-known statement, *eppur si muove*, his muttered denial of the forced recantation; and symptomatic that

Galileo measures in cubic millimetres (1269; cf. 54, 'a fraction'; 4). The game of chess, again, had been stabilised since the early sixteenth century, and to have the secretaries playing the old game is a considerable freedom (1284; 68; 7). Similarly Brecht takes liberties with Galileo's biography and character. He did indeed write in the vernacular for a wide public, as Brecht mentions (1310; 90; 9); but basically he sold his ideas in the dearest market, had only eclectic political ideas, remained uncomprehended by the masses and put his hopes in the prince, was a loyal son of the Church tormented by the heretical implications of his discoveries, was unable to count on any such support from the middle class as Brecht depicts in the figure of Vanni, and recanted – as was generally understood at the time – when faced by overwhelming and growing forces.[30] There is no evidence that he had particularly strong feelings of living in a new age. He had no opportunity of showing bravery in the plague in about 1616, since it did not reach Tuscany till 1632.[31] The severity of his surveillance in house-arrest is much overstated by Brecht; for some time his works were freely sent to Paris and elsewhere for publication, and the Holy Office did nothing even when copies appeared in Rome.[32] Brecht does not try to make the major preoccupations of the historical Galileo major themes of his play.[33] Yet the alterations he makes to history are less grave than those sanctified by the past masters of German historical drama – in Schiller, Joan of Arc dies on the battlefield!

Occasionally Brecht's portrayal of the social situation touches reality: Galileo's freedom of thought in Venice accompanied by poverty (1241f.; 28f.; 1), a historical reason for his move to Florence; the mercantile spirit of Venice; the arguments used against Galileo by Aristotelians; the pleasure-loving life of the high ecclesiastics. But basically, this version of Galileo's age is meant as a thought-provoking foil to the twentieth century. Two ways of provoking thought are used: an analogy between the eras concerned, and an examination of how events of Galileo's time are only now showing their full consequences.

Historically, the bourgeoisie in seventeenth-century Italy was stagnant and conservative, the Church in the full flower of the Counter-Reformation, the nobility gaining in influence. But Brecht depicts a time of social progress; Church and feudal aristocracy are in decline, desperately holding on to power, but having increasing difficulty in dealing with each fresh manifestation of independence of spirit. Whilst still wielding great power, the Church is bound to the nobility (1708; 88; 9) and thus, in the long run, condemned to decline. Already it is not monolithic, as differences between Barberini, Bellarmin and the Inquisitor show. Barberini hints to Galileo that he does not believe in his religion but sees God as a social necessity, borrowing the Voltairean statement 'if there were no God, one would have to invent one' (1290; 72f.; 7). The new science, with the rise of the merchant class, is putting the Church in a false position of having to compromise with heresy and allow the new astronomical charts for navigation (1323; 102; 12), while the dual basis of the papacy in belief and in politics is leading to a dangerous split, as the Pope allies himself with the Protestants in the Thirty Years' War to weaken the Catholic Emperor (1322; 101; 12). A similar gap was discovered in the bourgeois society of his own day by Brecht. The courts are unwilling, whatever the legal grounds, to reach judgments interfering with financiers' return on capital. The rift between codified law and practice is the sign of an ageing ideology (18, 193f.: *Dreigroschenprozess*).

In 1938 Brecht was interested in unstable authoritarian societies: Rome in Caesar's time, where the effort to keep down the slaves in fact enslaved everyone else, depriving political and financial leaders of initiative (*Aj.*, 11; 23.7.38); and of course Nazi Germany, whose ideology is in his view secondary to the aim of exploiting the proletariat (*Aj.*, 1, 10; 22.7.38). In the play he constructs a model of such a society: the prelates are no more free than the peasants and their ideology is only a means of social domination. The social forces are structured *a priori*. His use of the Church to represent the feudal order, and the opposition to it of science and the rising bourgeoisie, are in line with Engels' presentation of the broad movement of history (*Socialism, Utopian and Scientific*, Special Introduction to the English Edition of 1892); Engels, wisely, does not refer to Italy to prove his point. For Brecht the attack on the Church is a social matter: '. . . it would be highly dangerous, particularly nowadays, to treat a matter like Galileo's fight for freedom of research as a religious one; for thereby attention would be most unhappily deflected from present-day reactionary authorities of a totally unecclesiastical kind' (17, 1111f.; *Mat. G.*, 15; *G.*, 12). In scene 7 Bellarmin explains the Church's strategy: to place responsibility for the horrors of life on a higher Being with a great plan which He is pursuing through them (1287; 71). A similar divine plan is mentioned in *The Good Person*, as being beyond Shen Teh's power to execute. There as here, religion is to be seen as meaning conservative and oppressive ideology. The attack on religions goes through all the great plays in this form, based on Marx's *Theses on Feuerbach*, IV: the appearance of an independent religious realm is a sign of something contradictory in society. Against the external religious realm (heaven) Galileo sets up the religious realm immanent to man and within the individual's control: God is 'in us or nowhere' (1255; 41; 3). When he helps the Church in scene 14, it is not out of belief: 'He merely tries to make his peace with the powers-that-be' (17, 1132; *Mat. G.*, 36). Therefore, though with tongue in cheek, he defends charity against social justice, impenetrable divine wisdom against lay curiosity (1332f.; 111; 14). One is at liberty to decide for oneself what powers there are in our century that have treated serious scientific views as treasonable heresies.

Church and nobility stick together. Cosimo (historically older than Brecht implies; and by scene 11 Ferdinand II had succeeded, but Brecht prefers continuity to historicity) passes Galileo on to Rome: first his ideas to the Jesuits, later (though with some embarrassment) his person to the Inquisition. Ludovico sees two proofs that he and Galileo cannot inhabit the same social world: Galileo's godlessness, and his willingness to undermine the landowners' position by writing for the masses. Virginia is doubly involved: a faithful daughter of the Church (perhaps partly because Galileo does not take her potential interest in the telescope seriously) and betrothed to a member of the nobility. Not by chance does she oversee his writing to Carpula in the final scene: she wants him to help the powers-that-be because she believes in their ideology.

In the first version, where Galileo's fight against the régime is automatically a good thing for the masses, only a rudimentary idea of class is required. The tiler is more symbolic of the workers than representative of them; and the noble Ludovico has little more than an episodic function (the student in scene 1 is one Doppone; Ludovico appears in scene 7). In the second and third versions the social structure is given much more attention; Ludovico becomes, largely at the instigation of Charles Laughton (Aj., 2, 767; 10.12.45), a feudalist in a socially motivated conflict with Galileo, potential creator of unrest (1309f.; 89f.; 9). The nature of the unrest is shown in scene 10, where the potential social effect of ideas which destroy the heavenly hierarchy and man's place in it is brought out. Many critics find this scene weak because it shows anarchy and chaos as the consequence of ideas Brecht approve of. This is a superficial reading: except for the farmer who 'kicks the landlord' (1314; 94 – the attack with the scythe only appears in the English version; 10), no one behaves violently in this state of chaos. This anarchy leads to no brigandage or disorder; it is a state in which man no longer has to exploit or be cruel to man. Such a state is for Brecht connected with the future perfecting of Communism, as is best seen in *The Caucasian Chalk Circle*. Here it springs directly out of the seventeenth century, as if the millenium could have been reached without the intervening bourgeois era and its failings. Brecht short-circuits the history of the proletarian idea. In history, according to Korsch, 'every revolutionary movement of the bourgeoisie bred, as an undercurrent, independent stirrings of that class which was . . . the undeveloped predecessor of the modern proletariat.'[34] These stirrings here lead straight to Utopia. But the statement of the potential of equality can only be tentative: in the seventeenth century, and in Italy above all, the rise of the proletariat is impossible. Only with the *Communist Manifesto* does the proletariat reach the stage at which it could pursue its interests independently of the bourgeoisie.

Vanni stands for something historically more definable, the rising bourgeois class; he shows more dignity than Galileo, is not afraid to talk loudly in the palace of Medici (1318: 'Ihre Stimme trägt' – 'Your voice carries'; cf. 97, 'Your opinion carries weight'). He wants freedom in all progressive endeavours, especially money-making (ibid.). He has more all-round intelligence than any other character, assesses the power-structure much better than the naïve Galileo and sees the connections of belief, science, technology, individualism and capitalism. Sagredo, of the same class, is more aware of the dangers of moving too fast – he finds Galileo's abolition of heaven 'appalling' (1250; 37; 3).

Federzoni represents – from the second version of the play on – the urban artisan, standing behind science and progress but sent back to the workshop by Galileo's recantation (1335; 113; 14). Andrea, son of a servant, starts out as a lowly helper, tidying up at the beginning of scene 4, before his symbolic fight with Cosimo during which the Ptolemaic model of the universe is broken: the struggle of Ptolemy and Copernicus is really the struggle of the Grand Duke and the servant. But he becomes a teacher; and, as a scientist and the first 'inventive dwarf', producing knowledge for a world still dominated by its Grand Dukes, he is implicitly seen as representing the emergent bourgeois' meek acceptance of the continuing power of feudalism throughout the bourgeois era (a historical phenomenon particularly apparent in Germany). As a young scientist, he is given, instead of an example of the responsible use of the power bestowed by knowledge, Galileo's recantation to mull over. His incorrect interpretation of its motives does not equip him to face the problems which beset the scientist in the new age: for he thinks Galileo can do no wrong and Galileo recanted on purpose so as to be able to work on. So he copies Galileo's irresponsibility.

The little monk Fulganzio speaks for the peasantry; but as a priest he also represents power; as an astronomer, the new strivings. Persuaded by Galileo in scene 8 to espouse social commitment, he resolutely abandons the ecclesiastical order – but has to creep back to it when let down by Galileo's recantation (1335; 113; 14).

(v) THE STRUCTURE AND ARTISTRY OF THE PLAY

The play follows as its central subject Galileo's work on the Copernican universe. Each scene adds further to our picture of the scientist and gives us material evidence to use in coming to a judgment at the end, when he and Andrea offer explanations of his conduct. Brecht first occupied himself with the subject in connection with a plan to dramatise great trials of world history.[35] The theme of the social value of a heroic act, performed or left unperformed, may come from his thought on Joan of Arc – herself the victim of a great trial.[36] Just as Shakespeare in his historical plays imposes on his potentially formless and discursive material a central subject and theme, and ties in the inevitable episodic elements, so Brecht discerns patterns in Galileo's life which lend themselves to dramatic formation. In the abstract, the procedure displeased Brecht: 'in formal matters i do not defend the play particularly hard' (*Aj.*, 2, 747: 30.7.45). He contrasts the play with others, here lumped together as parables: 'in them ideas are given body, here a material gives birth to certain ideas' (ibid.). In fact a historical subject is intractable material for demonstrative, model-based theatre. Brecht is suspicious of its atmosphere, its cosiness.

The repetition structure is the basis of the play. In the second half (scenes 9–14) the events of the first half (scenes 1–7) are replayed after an eight-year interval and with a different twist. In scene 1 Galileo demonstrates the movement of the earth round the sun, in scene 9 the floating of a needle. In scene 7 his work is condemned, in scene 14 he himself ruined.[37] Such a structure is a good epic vehicle to show human nature. Already in the *Threepenny Opera* Macheath was (almost) ruined, not by going to a brothel, but by going once too often to the same one. Here the hero, though his work is once placed on the Index, disregards the warning and involves himself in a more serious situation. Between the parallel actions Brecht places scene 8, the conversation with the little monk, which faces in two directions: it sums up the positive and socially-orientated aspects of science, Galileo arguing in favour of technical progress and against the superstitions which keep the peasants of the Campagna subordinated to the Church and the lords; and it prefigures the negative aspects of science, the monk throwing himself on Galileo's papers heedless of the consequences, just as Galileo is now to go on with his work regardless. The monk, caught between commitment to the peasant class he springs from and his support of the Church, which acts to oppress that class, reflects Galileo's dilemma between the demands of progress and the constraints of the given political situation. Scene 8, set in Rome and yet in a sense in Florence, provides the ideological superstructure of the play in the clash of these complex attitudes.

But the action also has another structure in the form of a single arc of action following Galileo's occupation with Copernican theory from the 'invention' of the telescope, enabling Copernicus' views to be proved, through to the completion of the 'Discorsi'.[38] This structure is underlined by the parallels between scenes 1 and 14 (which is the last scene, scenes 5 and 15 never being performed): morning and evening, the bed made up after the night and the bed prepared ready for night (by Virginia during the last few sentences, a piece of business arranged by

Brecht at one of his last rehearsals[39]), the speech welcoming the new age and that showing how the new age has been and will be a disappointment. Within this there are correspondences of various scenes: the two carnivals (scenes 7 and 10) are a study in contrast, and the pure dialogue of scene 8 is balanced by the demonstrations and experimentation of the next scene.[40]

The element of dialectics in the play means, at its simplest structural level, the building of contentual contrasts: of Venice, where Galileo is free but short of time and money, with Florence, where he has plently of both but is subject to the Inquisition; between Jesuits and Inquisition in their attitude to Galileo's findings; between the people's recognition of Galileo and his being cut by the Grand Duke; between Galileo's courage in the plague and his cowardice faced with torture. Or the reappearance of things in different contexts gives a shock of recognition: Galileo needs instruments for his work of enlightenment, the Church has instruments of torture.[41]

Variation of elements within the play is much stressed. Each gestic section of scene 1 – dialogue with Andrea, monologue on the new age, interview with Ludovico, and so on – shows Galileo in a different light: as the quasi-paternal teacher, the visionary, the academic in need of extra cash. Brecht is more concerned to keep the dialogue graceful and memorable than to construct realistic scenes. Thus in scene 2 it is improbable that Galileo explains his discoveries to Sagredo rather than giving his attention to his employers, the Venetian magistrates. But this arrangement shows up some of the inherent contradictions in him and the society of his age. The great man cheats – the society employing him practically forces him to, to live decently. He is careless of his employers; he does not realise they are better employers than the one he is about to join, the proponent of a social order which his discoveries will undermine. In an elegant ceremony, all is hypocrisy. Galileo talks of science and means money. The senators are concerned with food and the threat of peeping Toms; but in fact love of food is a disturbing characteristic of Galileo himself,[42] and in the next scene the connection of genius and sensuality is the theme: both the telescope and the move to Florence mean to him discoveries, money, the fleshpots. In scene 4 the consequences become clear: he gets what he wants, but not recognition. In scene 5 his bravery puts Signora Sarti and Andrea in danger – and so on through a series of demonstrations of attitudes and their consequences. In the recantation scene, Brecht decides to show the attitudes of Virginia and the pupils, rather than Galileo's own torments – a procedure which scarcely makes the spectator less involved, but does give him a wider view of what is going on.

The invariable omission of scenes 5 and 15 in performance alters the impact of the play. Without the demonstration of Galileo's bravery in the plague, the disappointment caused by his cowardice before the Inquisition is less keen: his actions seem more predictably unheroic. And without the demonstration of how to smuggle manuscripts across frontiers, one is less likely to indulge in believing that Galileo's work has positive value after all. In general, the performed text is poorer in dialectical contradictions than the printed one.[43]

Motifs hold the levels of the play together. The salient example is the motif of milk (and cheese). Galileo, in reply to Andrea's message that the milkman must be paid, takes the opportunity for a lesson in terminology: if he doesn't get his money, the milkman will *describe* a circle round the house (1231; 19; 1). Insistence on scientific terms for everyday phenomena underlines the social theme: science as the means of mastering the problems of everyday life. That it does not do so directly is mentioned in scene 4: Jupiter's moons don't cheapen milk, but their discovery does imply that the man in the street can see much if he opens his eyes (1270; 54). And at the end, the application of doubt to astronomical matters is contrasted with the blind belief which keeps the Roman housewife short of milk (1340; 117f.; 14). The motif of the unpaid milkman is the occasion for contrasting Galileo, who would rather buy books (1235; 22; 1), with Signora Sarti, whose first question about the new age is whether the milkman can be paid (1236; 23; 1): to her the good opinion of her fellow-citizens is important, and the milkman stands for them in scene 4 (1262; 47). In scene 15 Andrea puts milk outside the door of an old woman shunned by the pious (1343f.; 120f.), just as in scene 5 Galileo was shunned when an old woman left some milk at his door (1276, 1278; 60f.). Generosity with milk is also mentioned in connection with the she-wolf suckling the founders of Rome – but today, in the official view, children must pay Rome for their milk (1286; 69; 7). Myth and business are both part of the general world-order upheld by Church and feudalists: by Fulganzio's mention of his parents eating a cheese dish (1294; 76; 8) and by Ludovico's unjustified complaint that Galileo doesn't appreciate his cheese (1309; 90; 9). The warder-monk of scene 14 too appreciates cheese, which lures him away (1335; 113) from spying on Galileo and Andrea. Finally, Galileo turns the telescope on the Milky Way (1248; 34; 2, and 1253; 39; 3). So the milk motif contains the whole theme of the play – science and social justice – and hints of Brecht's hopes for the future of mankind.

(VI) LANGUAGE

In this play language is first and foremost a means of characterisation. Intellectuals tend to express themselves in metaphors which may be very forced, like the Curator in scene 1: 'the whips of bondage under which learning groans in certain places – whips which the authorities have cut from their old leather folios' (1243; 29). The cliché of the whip comes first, but when it is reinforced by the reference to old folios (Aristotle), the result does not convince. More enjoyable, though more hostile to Galileo, are the neat sentences with which the philosopher and the mathematician needle Galileo in scene 4:

> GALILEO: Are you accusing me of fraud?
> THE PHILOSOPHER: But how could we? In the presence of his Highness!
> THE MATHEMATICIAN: Your instrument – whether one calls it your child or your pupil [*Zögling*] – is certainly most cleverly made, no doubt about that!
> THE PHILOSOPHER: And we are entirely convinced, Signor Galilei, that neither you nor anyone else would dare to bestow the illustrious name of our ruling house on stars whose existence was not beyond all possible doubt. (1267f.; 53)

Having passed off the telescope in Venice as his own child, which it was not (perhaps 'stepchild' would come closer to the spirit of *Zögling*), Galileo may well be deceiving them now. A scandal involving the Medicis threatens. The ruling house serves as a particularly elegant reason for not putting the accusation in so many words; but also the references to it and to Cosimo are put in the hieratic terms which remind one that in defending the highly complex Ptolemaic universe they are also upholding (without hypocrisy) a highly schematised social order. For them Galileo is a dubious interloper.[44] Elsewhere Brecht satirises the existing order, most effectively in the figure of the aged Cardinal, who makes a speech full of first-person pronouns on Man's place in the universe (1282; 65; 6) before symbolically collapsing. In the same scene Galileo is attacked with cheap puns: 'Schwindel im Collegium Romanum' (1279; cf. 63, 'Giddiness') is either dizziness caused by the earth's spinning or a swindle perpetrated by Galileo.

A subtler attack on the language of the established order – so subtle that it is rarely noticed – is contained in the celebrated argument in biblical quotations (1286; 69; 7) between Barberini and Galileo. Galileo's citations are correct, whereas Barberini's are largely made up. Galileo's 'He that withholdeth corn, the people shall curse him' is *Proverbs* 11, 26; but Barberini is tendentious in his alteration of *Proverbs* 12, 23 (a fact clearer in the original where Luther has 'Ein verständiger Mann trägt nicht Klugheit zur Schau', making it clear that modesty, not secretiveness, is the virtue aimed at; whereas the New English Bible agrees with Barberini). So Galileo is better able to quote scripture to his purpose than the Cardinal.[45]

The language of Galileo's opponents is generally shown up as in some way false. He. on the other hand, speaks in terms borrowed from reality, some of them of the force of proverbs or pithy sayings: 'I know they call a donkey a horse when they want to sell, and a horse a donkey when they want to buy' (1256; 42; 3). But all the time he builds them into rhetorical forms. Around the sentence just quoted are two statements which define it as a description of 'cunning'. The rest of the speech is given to 'reason', and consists of three everyday examples of the rational behaviour, followed by a two-pronged conclusion: 'they are my hope – they all listen to reason' (ibid.), a statement of belief about the power of reason, three statements about the irresistibility of logic for the human mind – of which the middle one is reinforced by Galileo's typical gesture of dropping a stone to prove the point: nobody would say it fell up! – and three general statements of which two exploit a paradox, the 'temptation' (ibid). of a proof (as often in Brecht there is the implication that to embrace what is good in the long run brings short-term disadvantages); whilst the third turns the paradox round and describes thinking as a pleasure (opening up the whole theme of Galileo's genius and sensuality and their disadvantages). The concrete examples take up about half the speech, the abstract lessons about half. The examples themselves, however, are given with careful pedantic or poetic touches. The old woman gives her mule hay with a 'horny' hand; the sailor *gedenkt* of the calms, the child covers his head *wenn ihm bewiesen wurde* (both poetic or pretentious turns of phrase, lost in the English) that it may rain. They are not examples naïvely taken from the fulness of experience; they are worked-over, finished products. Similarly his great monologue in scene 14 is an exercise in chiasmus, the juxtaposition of opposites in mirror-image form.[46] If such things impress, they also detract from Galileo's social claims. His mentions of artisans and common people are often more beautiful than true; and this is to be connected with his failure to recognise his (class) interests at decisive moments: he does not have genuine feelings of affinity with the lower orders.

There is perhaps empty pedantry in his use of words such as *diesbezüglich* (1339; 117, 'In this respect'; 14). But some less obtrusive turns of phrase have philosophical weight, stamping his thought as realistic in contrast to established dogmas. Thus the demonstrative, introductory *da*, followed by forms of the verb *sein*, echoes *Dasein*, existence seen ontologically, and is used (1253f., scene 3) successively to point to realities which are observable (Jupiter and its moons), and to philosophical figments which are not (the crystal spheres of Ptolemy). The phrase is odd: 'Da ist keine Stütze im Himmel . . .' The English (39f.) 'There is . . .' cannot give such effects.

Brecht originally used much material from Galileo's *Discorsi* and steeped himself in Galileo's tone. The reading after scene 13 (1330; 108) gives an idea of this basis: rhetorical, persuasive grouping of concrete examples leading to a succinct conclusion. But the speeches of Galileo in the play are much more Brecht, and perhaps also more Laughton, than Galileo – Laughton's knowledge of the Bible and Shakespeare having been an important element in the compilation of the second version. When Galileo is quoted, it is usually in a compressed form and with stress on the theatrical elements Brecht needs. Andrea reads from the *Discorsi*: 'My project is to establish an entirely new science dealing with a very old subject – Motion' (1337; 115; 14). Here Brecht has added the subjective, energetic start and the repetition of *sehr* (the 'entirely . . . very' of the English), but about halved the length of the original.[47] Whereas the historical Galileo, on the other hand, was prone to emotional outbursts in private life, Brecht keeps his language cool, expressing emotion rather by taciturnity, as when he replies to Signora Sarti's long warning against working on sunspots in three words whose disregard of all her arguments implies a deadly insult (1308; 89; 9). Only once, just before his self-analysis, does he give way: 'Welcome to the gutter . . .' (1339; 117f.; 14), ironically identifying himself with the Jewish fishmonger who had so little self-respect that in his endeavour to persuade people his fish was not high he attributed the stench surrounding him to himself.

The Inquisitor is also a rhetorician; his speech in its whole structure, employment of real and invented quotations, careful construction of climaxes and use of vulgarity is fitted to the hearer, the Pope – but also to the audience. When he asks rhetorical questions, we have already heard the answer from Galileo. Are we to found society on doubt instead of faith, is it not indifferent how heavenly bodies move, what wonders will come about through machinery? We know! In each case, put in a different social perspective, the subject looks different; the spectator is invited to compare the Inquisitor's arguments with Galileo's. When the Inquisitor says everyone, even the stable-boys, 'chatters about the phases of Venus' because of Galileo's bad example (1323; 101; 12), he has said nothing vulgar: but we remember that Galileo mentions the phases of Venus in connection with his Priapic poem (1297; 78; 8) and with Virginia's behind (1307; 87, 'her curves', is euphemistic; 9) – so the Inquisitor is gently mocked. Also earthy is Federzoni, who turns the lady-in-waiting's silly remark into a vulgar joke: 'all sorts of things on the Bull' (1268; 53; 4), and cuts through the courtesies of discussion about divine Aristotle: 'But the man had no telescope!' (1269; 54; in many editions erroneously attributed to Galileo). Signora Sarti, finally, is down-to-earth in her evocation of the churchmen as horse-doctors trying to bring Galileo round: 'Die höchsten Kardinäle haben in dich hineingeredet wie in ein krankes Ross' (1308; the English, 88f., cannot catch the tone; 9).

(VII) THE PLAY ON THE STAGE

Through Galileo the play has what may be called the gestus of scientific demonstration. As the play sets out to demonstrate certain truths, so does he. He drops a stone (1281; 64; 6, etc.) to show that no one can stand the nonsense of saying it fell *up*; he makes experiments on stage which spread the ambiguous aura of wonderment and satisfaction because they are deceptively simple (1304; 85; 9). Simplicity does not mean ease of execution. Brecht demands that the actor show particular skill in such things as floating a needle on water; this is an early work-play. In the gracefulness of the demonstrations, mind shows its mastery over matter (only to lose it with Galileo's fear of torture). Similar elegance is shown by the progression of dominant colours in the costumes for various scenes, arranged for the 1947 production with Laughton – Brecht's first chance to see in practice some of the ideas on theatre he had worked out in the previous decade. Joseph Losey's film sticks closely to this scheme and its reflection of the changing moods of the play: morning tones of white, yellow and grey for scene 1, Ludovico's deep aristocratic blue, dark green for the Venetians in scene 2, increasing elegance of silver and pearl grey in scene 4, scene 6 as a *notturno* in brown and black, the two carnivals as high-points of colour and spectacle, and a descent into dull greys at the end.[48] The paintings of Bruegel the Elder did good service in suggesting costumes; Brecht was also glad to find visual evidence that trousers were known in the seventeenth century, so that he could avoid 'what our age finds dressed-up' (17, 1122; *Mat. G.*, 44).

Settings used by Brecht are cool and matter-of-fact, non-representational (Brecht was suspicious of anything that might make the atmosphere domestic) and dominated by the model of the Galilean universe (flown) and other pictorial evidence with a Renaissance and technical flavour. A half-curtain is drawn across the stage between scenes. Laughton as Galileo, drawn from the body of the stage at the end of scene 4 by the need to follow the courtiers out, stood in front of this curtain, pondering the appeal to Rome just announced to him, waiting for scene 6 and establishing the connection between the scenes (scene 5 was of course omitted), playing with the stones he uses to demonstrate the charms of visual proof (*Mat. G.*, 58). The play depends much on tableaux. In scene 9, for instance, the dangerous change in the direction of Galileo's research is made obvious when a carefully arranged grouping (1305; 86, 'All settle round the table', lacks the formality) is destroyed, and revealed as having been ironic all along, by the setting up of the apparatus for research on sunspots (1307f.; 87f.), whilst at the same time the social implications become clear in the quarrel with Ludovico: and at the moment the mirror is finally adjusted and the image of the sun flares on to the stage, Virginia arrives in the wedding-dress she will never use: the first victim of Galileo's thirst for truth at all costs (1311; 91f.). In scene 12, the robing of the Pope which proceeds through the scene turns him not only visually but psychologically from the mathematician Barberini into the Pope who must act to defend his Church; but his unhappiness is betrayed by his helpless eyes. Half the point of this scene is expressed visually and would be lost in a radio performance, a good example of Brecht's technical concentratedness.[49] For Galileo's self-analysis in scene 14 Brecht had Virginia and Andrea on either side, Galileo in the middle: between goose-liver and the *Discorsi*, sensuality and science.[50]

Brecht favoured the translation of all feelings into actions as a step towards interpreting psychology in social terms. There are for instance manifold variations of the act of bowing, reaching in scene 4 from the ceremonial bow of Andrea and Cosimo at the outset (1263; 47), a prelude to their fight, through the formal bows with which Cosimo favours his subjects and dependants (1265; 50), to desperate manifestations of servility from Galileo as Cosimo leaves. In Berlin, Ekkehard Schall, rehearsing the role of Andrea in scene 14, introduced an imitation of Galileo's bow at the point where he talks about it (1338; 116), thus making its ridiculousness belatedly even more obvious.[51]

Speeches too are to be interpreted in social contexts. When Galileo demonstrates the satellites of Jupiter to Cosimo and his experts, he is talking to people who are intelligent, but uninterested if not hostile. He runs quickly through his introduction (1265; 50): a formal speech, not an attempt to put facts across. The demonstration of the earth's movement for Andrea in scene 1 too can be played offhand, as an interruption – albeit a pleasurable one – of Galileo's real work (*Mat. G.*, 51). Similarly at the beginning of scene 3 Galileo turns away from the telescope and relaxes (*G.*, cover photo), trusting Sagredo to observe and draw his own conclusions. Laughton kept tense observation of the skies for when Priuli arrived – so as not to have to look the victim of his deception in the face (*Mat. G.*, 55). In scene 7 Barberini warns the clerks not to take down the 'scientific conversation between friends' (1287; 71). But they do carefully record what Galileo was saying at that point: 'the bit where he says that he believes in reason' (1290; 73). Have they disobeyed the Cardinal in the interests of the Inquisition, or were his words intended as an indirect warning to Galileo to be more circumspect where there are spies about?

Eisler's music takes an independent role, attempting to show underlying strengths and weaknesses – the self-confidence of the revolutionary world in scene 10, for instance – rather than to depict individual occasions. The introductory verses to scenes are lightly scored (three boys' voices, flute, clarinet, harpsichord) but written in a kind of brutalised recitative.

Joseph Losey, the director of the American première, has also filmed the play. This mid-Atlantic product has two main weaknesses: astronomical material is not put visually (why should we see Sagredo looking through a telescope and not see what he sees?), and Topol's comic genius in the title role does not assert itself against rather portentous and heavy directing. Brecht once intended to film the subject on location in Italy[52] – a promising idea, which could be especially interesting if no attempt were made to restore the locations to their seventeenth-century condition.

5 Mother Courage and her Children

The play was written from September to November 1939 in Sweden, the name and some atmosphere coming from Grimmelshausen's seventeenth-century novel *Die Landstörtzerin Courasche*, the figure of an indomitable camp-follower suggested by the poem *Lotta Svärd* by the Swedish author Johan Ludvig Runeberg.[1] The first performance was in Zurich on 19 April 1941 with Therese Giehse as Mother Courage and music by Paul Burkhard. The music now used was written by Paul Dessau, mainly in 1946. On 11 January Brecht and Helene Weigel introduced the play to Berlin, in the *Deutsches Theater*; on 8 October 1950 Brecht produced it in Munich, again with Therese Giehse. In 1960 a film was made of the (by then revised) Berlin production. At the end of his life Brecht wrote a film script under the same title, which is however for all practical purposes a different work.

(I) THE PLOT

Scene 1: The businesswoman Anna Fierling, known by the name of Courage, joins with the Swedish army. Road outside a town in Dalarne.
(*a*) 'Recruiters searching the country for cannon-fodder.'[2] A recruiting officer and a sergeant discuss how there is no organisation in life except in war.
(*b*) 'Courage presents to a sergeant her diverse family, products of various theatres of war': Mother Courage rolls on on a wagon drawn by her two sons Eilif and Swiss Cheese; her dumb daughter Kattrin sits on it, and it is full of sutler's wares to sell to the soldiers. The sergeant demands papers and names, but is merely confused by the comic account which Courage gives of her children after singing the 'Courage Song' which introduces her and her trade.
(*c*) The sergeant and recruiting officer want to enlist the boys, but she is having none of it, drawing her knife on the sergeant. He objects that if she wants to make a living from the war she must give something.
(*d*) She counters by saying that he is a potential corpse, tears a sheet

of paper across to show the fate of those who get too involved in war, and has him draw lots to show him that he is doomed. The boys, however, still want to join up.

(e) To frighten them away from the war she puts more pieces of paper in the helmet from which the sergeant has drawn his fate; all three of her children draw black crosses, which she says means they will die if they involve themselves in war.

(f) 'Because of a little deal she yet loses her brave son': to move things their way the recruiters decide to involve Courage in a business deal. The sergeant takes a belt behind the wagon to examine, on the pretext that there is less wind there. Meanwhile the recruiting officer promises Eilif advance pay and takes him away to join up. Kattrin tries to raise the alarm, but her mother is not listening. The sergeant pays for the belt; she returns to find Eilif gone.

(g) 'Now the sergeant has his turn to make a prophecy to Courage: those who want to live off war must give it something.'

Scene 2: Mother Courage meets her brave son again before Wallhof Castle. Swedish commander's tent.

(a) 'Mother Courage profiteers with provisions in the Swedish camp', to the background of cannonfire and with her own humorous sales talk.

(b) 'In the course of tough bargaining about a capon she makes the acquaintance of an army cook who is to play a part in her life.' He prefers to cook stinking beef rather than pay her price for the bird she is trying to sell.

(c) 'The Swedish commander brings a young soldier into his tent and honours him for his bravery': with a chaplain, they enter the other part of the tent and start drinking.

(d) When the young soldier speaks Courage recognises his voice – Eilif.

(e) 'In view of the honouring of Eilif she is able to sell her capon more dearly': the commander demands food for his party; she trebles the price of the capon and plucks it for the cook.

(f) Eilif describes to the commander how he carried off a number of oxen (which will not reach the camp for a day or two). Meanwhile Mother Courage shows that a stupid general who leads his soldiers into a bad situation (such as they are in at the moment) demands the virtue of bravery; well-regulated states demand no virtues from their subjects.

(g) Eilif entertains the commander with the 'Song of the Fishwife and the Soldier', performing a sword dance to it. At the third verse, Courage joins in from the kitchen.

(h) Eilif goes in to the kitchen and embraces her. After initial greetings she boxes his ear for having been too brave and not taken care of himself.

Scene 3: Mother Courage transfers from the Lutheran to the Catholic camp and loses her honest son Swiss Cheese. Camp with Courage's wagon.

(a) 'Black market in munitions': Courage buys bullets from an ordnance officer, to resell to another who has no ammunition left. The officer goes off accompanied by Swiss Cheese, who has been made regimental paymaster because he is so honest.

(b) Yvette, the camp prostitute, fallen on hard times because everyone thinks she is infected, drinks to console herself and sings the 'Fraternisa-ation Song' describing how she ran away from home following a soldier for love. But she says she never found him – that was ten years ago, and now she despairs of going on as a whore: she leaves her hat behind. Courage warns Kattrin against love with soldiers.

(c) The chaplain and the cook come, and engage in polite political conversation and flirtation with Courage at one side of the cart over drinks. Meanwhile Kattrin struts about, trying Yvette's hat and sexy walk.

(d) The Catholics attack; the cook rushes off through the fire to get back to the commander, but the chaplain has not the courage, gets Mother Courage to give him a cloak and stays where he is. A soldier tries to move a cannon; Courage gets Yvette's things off Kattrin. Yvette returns in delighted anticipation of being occupied by an army that does not know she is ill. She recovers her hat, but Kattrin hides her boots. Swiss Cheese runs in with the regimental cashbox, which he refuses to throw away because it is a trust. Mother Courage rubs ashes on Kattrin's face to make her unattractive; and runs down the Swedish flag.

(e) 'First lunch in the Catholic camp': three days later. The family eats anxiously, hoping their rather unconvincing pretence of Catholicism will hold out and enable them to live well off the enemy as off the friend previously. There are spies everywhere who would love to discover enemy aliens. Courage goes with the chaplain, who has a good nose for meat, to get supplies – in getting ready she finds Yvette's shoes hidden and berates Kattrin.

(f) Kattrin makes signs, and Swiss Cheese talks, about autumn; then he lays plans to get back to the regiment with the cashbox. He fails to understand Kattrin's warning about a spy and goes off with the box. Kattrin is desperate. Her mother and the chaplain return and gather from her signs that Swiss Cheese has probably been caught. Indeed he is arrested and brought on and confronted with the party; but they all pretend not to know each other, and Swiss Cheese denies having been running around with a bulge under his shirt. He is taken off.

(g) 'Mother Courage pawns her wagon to a camp whore to raise money to free Swiss Cheese': the chaplain sings a song about the Passion to Kattrin. Courage arrives: Swiss Cheese will be killed unless she can raise some money for the sergeant; perhaps Yvette, who has picked up a colonel, will buy the wagon. When the chaplain objects that she would have nothing to live off, Courage tells Yvette, who arrives with her ancient beau, that she wants to pawn, not to sell outright. After some argument Yvette agrees and starts taking an inventory. Mother Courage thinks if she frees Swiss Cheese he will recover the regimental cash and she will claim the expenses from it to redeem the wagon.

(*h*) But Yvette, after going to negotiate with the soldiery, says he has thrown the cashbox into the river. Faced with loss of the wagon Mother Courage is forced to lower her offer for Swish Cheese in order to retain working capital for a fresh start. Yvette goes off with the offer.

(*i*) The others polish knives and glasses. Yvette returns: the soldiers insist on the full original amount. But it is too late: drums roll, Swiss Cheese is condemned. Yvette returns to report his execution and that the body will be brought for a final test of whether Courage did not know him after all.

(*j*) 'Dumb Kattrin comes to her mother's side to await dead Swiss Cheese.'

(*k*) 'In order not to betray herself Courage denies her dead son.'

Scene 4: The Song of the Great Capitulation.

(*a*) 'Mother Courage sits outside the lieutenant's tent to complain about damage to her wagon. A scrivener advises her in vain to pretend it didn't happen.'

(*b*) 'A young soldier comes to complain likewise. She dissuades him': the soldier has been deprived of a reward for saving the colonel's horse, he wants the lieutenant's blood, and he is hungry. Mother Courage points out that he and his comrades trampled down the crops, hence the famine now; and the more he complains, the longer he will be put in the stocks. The scriviner orders the soldier to sit – and promptly he sits.

(*c*) Mother Courage sings the 'Song of the Great Capitulation': one learns to keep in step sooner or later.

(*d*) The soldier leaves without making his complaint; Mother Courage too changes her mind about complaining.

Scene 5: Mother Courage loses four officers' shirts, and dumb Kattrin finds a baby.

(*a*) 'After a battle': the wagon is in a ruined village, soldiers stand around.

(*b*) 'Courage refuses the chaplain her officers' shirts which he wants to bandage wounded peasants with': she says she cannot afford to give anything.

(*c*) 'Dumb Kattrin threatens her mother', and the chaplain bodily sets Courage aside to get at the stock he needs.

(*d*) 'Kattrin saves a baby at the risk of her life' from the ruins, and is happy playing with it whilst the rest go about their everyday activities, arguing and stealing.

Scene 6: Beginning of prosperity, but dumb Kattrin is mutilated.
(a) 'Mother Courage, now a prosperous woman, takes stock' with Kattrin, the chaplain plays a game of draughts with a clerk, soldiers come for drinks, and they discuss the death of the general Tilly.
(b) In her appreciation of Tilly, Courage shows how the plans of the great are always spoilt by those with less ambition.
(c) 'Conversations on the length of the war. The chaplain proves that the war will last a long time.'
(d) Kattrin is shocked at this, as her mother promised her a husband once there was peace. Courage, however, tells her peace will be nicer when they have made a little more money, and sends her to bring some goods from the town.
(e) Left alone with Mother Courage the chaplain flatters her and chops wood for her, whilst complaining that his talents are wasted here and offering her a closer relationship. She insists on keeping things on a business level.
(f) Kattrin returns in a fearful state, with a wound that will leave a permanent scar, but with the goods intact. Her mother fusses over her and gives her Yvette's red boots to comfort her; but when Kattrin goes into the wagon she leaves them outside.
(g) 'Mother Courage curses war', whilst counting the things Kattrin has brought. Kattrin need not hope for a husband in peacetime now.

Scene 7: Mother Courage at the height of her business career.
(a) A prosperous Courage, pulling the wagon with the chaplain and Kattrin, defends war as a good source of income.

Scene 8: A peace threatens to ruin Mother Courage's business. Her brave son does one heroic deed too many and comes to a bad end.
(a) 'Courage and the chaplain hear a rumour that peace has broken out.'
(b) The Swedish commander's cook turns up, and says Eilif will be coming too. He immediately – though penniless – starts trying to take over the chaplain's place.
(c) 'The fight for the place at the trough.' The chaplain reacts too heatedly, argues against all the cook says and becomes desperate when Courage shows more signs of taking the cook's advice.
(d) Yvette, now the wife of a Colonel Starhemberg, comes and recognises in the cook the man who was responsible for her original trouble; she leaves Mother Courage in no doubt of it. She goes off to market with Courage, leaving the chaplain gloating over the sudden reversal of fortune.
(e) Soldiers bring Eilif. He has just robbed a peasant with violence – the

sort of thing for which he was rewarded in wartime – and been condemned to death; and as his mother is away, he cannot even see her one
last time. The chaplain goes with him on his last journey; the cook stands
around apprehensively and tries to beg some food for Kattrin, who is
lying in the wagon skulking.

(*f*) Mother Courage returns, still with the goods. War has restarted. The
cook tells her Eilif and the chaplain are in the town; and as the chaplain
is not there, she asks the cook to stay as her helper. He and Kattrin are
harnessed to the wagon to follow the Swedish army again.

*Scene 9: The war takes an unfortunate course. For the sake of her
daughter Courage refuses a home.*
(*a*) The cook and Mother Courage are now reduced to begging at a
half-ruined parsonage. The cook has had a letter saying he has inherited
an inn in Utrecht, which both find preferable to following a war which
has devastated the country. Mother Courage puts the proposition to
Kattrin.
(*b*) But it is a misunderstanding: the cook has no intention of taking on
a dumb, scarred girl in his inn. Courage protests she cannot be left alone.
(*c*) The cook sings the 'Song of the Vexations of Great Men' in the hope
of earning a bowl of soup: it shows how difficult it is to be virtuous and
survive.
(*d*) While Courage still argues as they go to get the soup at the door,
Kattrin emerges from the wagon with a bundle, leaves a skirt of her
mother's and a pair of trousers in suggestive proximity, and makes to
steal away.
(*e*) 'Mother Courage stops Kattrin's flight and goes on alone with her.'
(*f*) 'The cook goes to Utrecht.'

Scene 10: Still on the road.
(*a*) 'From a farmhouse mother and daughter hear the Song of the Home'.

Scene 11: Dumb Kattrin saves the city of Halle.
(*a*) The wagon is parked near a farmhouse. Soldiers come by night, wake
the peasants and force one to show them the path to Halle which they
are to take by surprise. Mother Courage is in Halle.
(*b*) The old peasants remaining conclude they can do nothing but pray;
they get Kattrin to pray too for the safety of the town.
(*c*) But when she hears that they have grandchildren in the town she is
troubled; she gets a drum, climbs up to a shed roof and starts drumming
to give the alarm to the town.
(*d*) The peasants want her to stop because the soldiers will kill them all.
But she pulls her ladder up on to the roof and goes on drumming. Soldiers
come and try to make her stop by offering to spare her mother when

the town is taken and by threatening her with breaking up the wagon. They also try to make natural noises to drown her drumming, but nothing is any use.
(*e*) They shoot her dead. But the alarm has been raised in the town.

Scene 12: Courage goes on her way.
(*a*) 'Peasants have to convince Courage that Kattrin is dead.'
(*b*) 'Kattrin's lullaby' sung by Mother Courage.
(*c*) 'Mother Courage pays for Kattrin's burial and receives the condolences of the peasants.'
(*d*) 'Mother Courage harnesses herself alone to her empty wagon. Still hoping to get back in the way of trade she follows the ragged soldiery.'

(II) THE CHRONICLE

In many ways the structure of this play is comparable with that of *Galileo*. Both have a dearth of what are usually thought of as epic elements in the text. The distortion of dramatic tempo by the foreshortening of expositions and the dwelling on lyrical elements is absent. The initial exposition is a highly traditional one, using the device of a meeting between Mother Courage and the sentries to give a natural description of what we need to know of her history so far.[3] Despite the apparently episodic and discursive structure, there is a centre of emphasis comparable to that in *Galileo* (his work on the Copernican system): the play opens with the first separation of the heroine from one of her children, and ends when they are all dead.[4] The action is contemporaneous with that of *Galileo*, but the atmosphere different. From a prosperous, peaceful Italy we move to the reign of barbarity in the most destructive war in the history of Germany up to 1939.

It is this war which is responsible for the structural differences between the two plays. Galileo was the initiator of the events which became his fate. Mother Courage is not: the framework of her life, and thus of the action, is supplied by the history of the war. A glance at the scene titles found in the printed text and projected on to the half-curtain before each scene in performance shows this: those in *Mother Courage* describe as much what the war does as what the heroine does; those in *Galileo* are centred on the individual. In the text too private and public action are counterpointed: the chaplain says the burial of Tilly is a historic occasion; Mother Courage ripostes that, for her, having her daughter hit over the head is a historic occasion (1408; 55; 6). For here history is seen not from the viewpoint of leaders of opinion, but from that of the ordinary people. Brecht defines the play as 'gestarium' (Aj., 1, 274: 24.4.41), a collection of instances of human behaviour or attitudes. In keeping with this infinitely extensible structure, the ending is open, as Mother Courage tries to start her business again. The subtle 'chronicle' is intended as an analogy to the 'history' of the Shakespearean stage (*Mat. C.*, 86): it does not mean an account of the war. As Keith A. Dickson has made clear, Mother Courage comes near the centre of historical events only in scenes 5 and 6. Habsburg–Bourbon rivalry, the Dutch problem, Bohemian and Hungarian nationalism, the League and the Union, the policies of Richelieu and the speculations of Wallenstein – none of them are mentioned. Gustav Adolf sets the scene with his preliminary exercises in Poland; but his death changes nothing, except that Eilif is executed in a short-lived peace after it.[5]

The historical setting is chosen partly as a v-effect in its own right, making the audience compare the seventeenth with the twentieth century; partly with an eye to particular topical references – whilst Brecht was writing the play Hitler invaded Poland, and the term 'man, beast and wagon' (1374; 25; 3) echoes a gloating remark of his after the Polish campaign.[6] But major historical parallels are absent. The main point is to show an individual acting in a major war, and in order to retain the balance of protagonist and setting, Brecht plays down the mass brutality which was the Thirty Years War's greatest contribution to historical progress: he does not mention that the siege of Magdeburg, which costs Courage four shirts, cost 25,000 non-combatants their lives.

(III) WAR AND MARXISM

The starkest point of the presentation of war is at the beginning of scene 9. In Pomerania nuns have turned robbers and people have eaten babies; the world is dying out; Mother Courage sees herself going through hell with her wagon selling brimstone (1423; 68). The apocalyptic treatment is to be taken seriously, and its emotional impact is heightened by the scene setting, in which a charred, long-unrepaired crucifix draws ironic attention to the religious wars which rage here so frequently that it is not worth repairing the emblem of religion.[7] This chilling episode is the precondition for the further effects of the play: the irony of the 'Song of the Home' in scene 10, Kattrin's decision that she may as well sacrifice herself in scene 11, the horror of the war going on and on in scene 12. All the last scenes are spine-chilling. Yet the beginning of scene 9 is also only an episode. Once we have seen how horrible and hopeless a life in the war is, and the apparent relief of a home in Utrecht has been dangled before Mother Courage, things change. When she discovers Utrecht is not open to Kattrin, she changes her attitude and faces this hellish war with professional optimism once more: 'This winter'll pass – like all the others' (1428; 72).

Mother Courage stays with the war because no alternative is open to her and Kattrin. Once she has involved herself in the war, she cannot withdraw: she becomes tragic. Brecht's original text, as performed in 1941, also shows her as kindly. She hands out her officers' shirts to help the wounded of her own free will.[8] The Zurich audience consequently saw her as an archetypal victim, a Niobe-figure weeping for her children – even though the part was played by Therese Giehse, who was well known for disencumbering mother-roles of the falsity and overstatement that often attaches to them.[9] This had not been Brecht's intention, and for the Berlin performance he tried to alter the emphasis. In scene 12, for instance, there is plenty to be sentimental about: to bury her last child, whose death leaves her half-demented, Mother Courage uses her last sheet and her last money. But the text of the lullaby shows an important social element: the child of this singer is to have a better life than other children. As this can only be done by depriving others of the scarce means of life, it is a murderous thought. Brecht insists that the lullaby be sung unsentimentally, and in general on 'a mode of acting that does not aim at the identification of the audience with the heroine'; for she learns nothing from her experiences, whereas the spectators are expected to learn (*Mat. C.*, 78). In the same scene, the peasants have their own attitude: they show that they dislike Courage because for them she belongs to the unsettling and hostile elements, the rootless followers of war, and specifically because she went off to make a profit and left her daughter in the lurch. The final text, and its interpretation in the 1949 production, repeatedly shows Brecht trying to emphasise the mercantile against the maternal. She loses each of her children while thinking of money; but when it is put to her as a reproach – 'If you hadn't gone off to the town to get your cut, maybe it wouldn't have happened' (1437; 80; 12) – she 'studiously fails to hear it' (*Mat. C.*, 74). She is a split, perhaps even schizoid character, one half mother, the other half courage; she got the nickname running loaves through gunfire at the siege of Riga to safeguard her profit (1351; 5; 1). Where she is trying to do her best for her children by making money, she is destroying them. Kattrin hates her for her hardness (*Mat. C.*, 126). 'She takes her tradesmanship for motherhood, but it destroys her children one after the other' (*Mat. C.*, 94) and turns her into a pathetic, stunned, mutilated and in no way wiser woman at the end (*Mat. C.*, 126).

She trades unscrupulously. In introducing Eilif she defines intelligence as the quality of being able to 'whip the breeches off a farmer's backside before he could turn round' (1352; 6; 1). The qualities she sets store by are the qualities that make money.[10] Corruption is taken for granted in war. When Swiss Cheese is arrested she puts her faith in bribery – 'Corruption is our only hope' (1388; 38). In scene 1, she and the recruiting officer both want to make deals, and they use trickery: she frightens the sergeant by foretelling his fate, he decoys her away while his colleague negotiates with Eilif. To Brecht, such lack of scruple characterises war and business alike; and Courage sees war as merely business, but with lead instead of cheese (1409; 55; 7). She has come out to find the war, could not wait till it came to Bamberg (1353; 7; 1). She is responsible for her own fate, and for that of her children. Brecht believes in human freedom. 'Even for the petit-bourgeois Courage the decision "To participate or not to participate" was always left open in the play'. (*Mat. C.*, 78). The war that destroys her children is not a natural catastrophe that breaks over her. This is not a pacifist play, but an anti-capitalist play. 'War as business' is the theme: Brecht adapts a famous dictum of Clausewitz to state: 'War is the continuation of business by other means' (*Mat. C.*, 17). That war is of itself evil is obvious; but what keeps war going is love of gain, a motive which will overcome any pacific intention and which must be removed first if war is ever to be abolished. The great, like Tilly when he takes a bribe to spare Magdeburg from plundering (1397; 45; 5), hope to profit from the war; if they were not in it for the money, the little people such as Courage could not hope to make their modest cut from it either (1375; 26; 3). But just as Tilly fails to benefit, dying during the campaign, so Courage makes no profit and loses all her children.

No one helps her: in the war she has decided to join in, we see an extreme case of the 'war of every man against every man'[11] which is capitalism. Man behaves as a wolf to man. At the end, the peasants warn Mother Courage against wolves and, what is worse, marauders. Brecht had shown a woman profiting from war in the Widow Begbick, canteen-keeper to the Indian Army in *Man is Man*. But Begbick was alone in the world; Courage has children, hostages to fortune, to be claimed one by one. The sergeant tells her what she can expect from involvement in war: she will have to give something in return for the expected profit (1355; 8; 1). The following piece of humbug in which she draws death-lots to make her children fear the war produces a true prophecy – though she is never to know it, for she does not hear of Eilif's death. She is very clear that war makes the common people injure each other for nothing (1404; 51; 6), and curses it in scene 6 after Kattrin's injury, but is supporting it again in scene 7 (and it would be wrong to place an interval between the two scenes: the contradiction must be brought out[12]). Brecht gives no dates for scenes 4 to 7: no new external events are needed to accompany the process by which Courage's psychological wounds heal, after Kattrin's disfigurement as after Swiss Cheese's death.[13] In scene 7 she says to go to the wall in war is a sign of weakness which would also be fatal in peacetime; and being rich, she says war feeds one better. Her false consciousness is obvious. She believes in war as right for her; it is a wrong belief. Even when she curses war, she is counting stock

(1408; 55; 6). It is made difficult for the audience to participate in her maternal emotion here; but one is freed by this distancing to feel higher emotions – anger at her blindness, sorrow over those who are mutilated and killed by it.[14] In scene 4, again, she shows a wrong attitude: in the light of the realisation that God does not influence events in this world, she chooses to adapt to the existing order (war) even where it hurts her, rather than to revolt. In scene 7, fleetingly, it rewards her for her adaptation.[15] But by taking her advice and rejecting rebellion, the young soldier is enabled to rise till in scene 11 he reappears as the lieutenant – and murders Kattrin. Courage was wrong to capitulate; Helene Weigel made the gap between herself and the figure clear in scene 4. It would be fatal if the audience were tempted to agree with the lesson of the 'Song of the Great Capitulation' (*Mat. C.*, 45). For that lesson is that in the pseudo-order of wartime – represented by the marching band – there is no overall order within which one could realise useful plans. Proverbs teaching the opposite, that activity to alter life is useful, are blatantly contradicted by other proverbs. The figures in this scene do not oppose war sufficiently to want to abolish it: they hope rather to profit from it.

So one must see both sides of this split character. Mother Courage is a monster who drags her children across battlefield after battlefield; she is also selfless enough to prefer war and Kattrin to peace and the cook. Subjectively, she does her best for her children. Objectively, she could not do worse. The critical arguments over whether Brecht meant to construct a monster but was carried away by love of mother-figures tell us little, except where the arguers, from their varying standpoints, face the problem of the split character as reflecting a split society. Society claims to uphold the values of gentle Jesus and bring truth and salvation; it fulfils this claim by means of one of the most wantonly destructive wars of history. Mother Courage does everything for her children but kills them in the process. Her awareness is determined by her social being; as a historical dialectician, Brecht cannot make her realise her error (*Mat. C.*, 88). She participates in the tragedy of her era in that she does not and cannot know better; but the audience is not in the seventeenth century and must from its superior viewpoint recognise the false logic implicit in the concept of religious war and the idea of doing good to one's family through war. Brecht leaves no doubt that today such a tragedy as hers should only be seen as avoidable.

Another 'Mother Courage' is the heroine of Brecht's next great play. Shen Teh must oppress others in order to guarantee her unborn child a good life. She is not seen in a better light because her maternal instinct works thus: she is simply seen trying to deal with a conflict she alone cannot solve. The defenceless woman becomes the capitalist exploiter – who is not castigated, for he too is part of a society he cannot change. 'My standpoint . . . can less than any other make the individual responsible for relations whose creature he socially remains' (Marx, Preface to *Capital*). Mother Courage is even worse off than Shen Teh: although she limits charity from the outset to her own children, refusing to issue linen from stock to tend the indigent wounded (where Kattrin does not hesitate, and Shen Teh would not have either), she is unable with all her hard-headedness to make a profit from war in the long run, and she loses her children. All her good intentions are vitiated by her basically false approach, her acceptance of war; they become paving-stones on the road to hell. Precisely the gap between intention and effect, the fact that Courage is not all bad, allows the spectator to be shown a contradiction which will set him thinking.

Courage has opportunities for tragic, emotional effects, particularly the death of Swiss Cheese and the episode in which she has to fail to identify his body. Here the mother is given full rein. If in the episodes during which she hopes to ransom him she has painfully to balance the short-term aim of being sure of saving him against the long-term aim of being economically able to continue keeping him and Kattrin afterwards (and not even Kattrin is so naïve as to be against the bargaining – only against the undue delay, *Mat. C.*, 41f.), when he is dead the mercantile element can drop from her temporarily. Helene Weigel exploited the opportunity with the famous silent scream reminiscent of the horse in Picasso's *Guernica*, which George Steiner found classically tragic.[16] It is thought to be based on a wartime news photo entitled 'After the Bombing (Singapore)' (reproduced *Aj.*, 1, 406: 5.4.42). When looking at the body Helene Weigel wore an inimitable fixed smile.[17] Brecht undoubtedly underestimated the effect of this scene, which, together with the death of Kattrin (who, with real dramatic pathos, hears just as she dies that she has succeeded in raising the alarm[18]) has always given the audience its strongest impressions, outdistancing better constructed scenes. One need not agree with Gray (p. 82) that Brecht meant to obviate sympathy for Mother Courage altogether and thus ignore an essential element of drama, but it is true that scene 3 gets its unwarranted attention for a piece of crass improbability. The Catholics have surely no interest in executing Swiss Cheese in such a hurry, even after he has admitted to having thrown the regimental cash where neither he nor they can recover it. The following motif, incidentally, the bringing in of the son's body despite the mother's previous attempt to save him, comes from Synge's *Riders to the Sea* by way of Brecht's *Señora Carrar's Rifles* – both plays in which empathy with the mother is more in order.[19]

Mother Courage moves in a world where the great have the same motives as she has. That she sees through their ideological front comes about because she shares their basic viewpoint; and she cannot do otherwise, she is quite adapted to her environment.[20] No one suggests what else she could do. 'You admit you live off war, what else *could* you live off?', says the sergeant (1355; 8; 1). She, like Galileo, makes her mistakes because the socio-economic situation exerts pressure on her. Eisler (p. 25) points out that the play shows the poverty of the poor rather than their badness – something Johanna Dark (*Saint Joan of the Stockyards*) had already noted about her particular explorations of proletarian life. One could add that the play shows not the great, not those who started the war, but only the insignificant people who will be caught up in it whether they stay in their Bambergs or not. Courage is 'free to be crushed by it, or to support it – and still be crushed by it'.[21] From this point of view it is legitimate to emphasise the tragic elements and reject simplistic efforts to dismiss Courage as a mere class enemy.[22] Indeed, as a small businesswoman she occasionally realises that the defeats of the great may not be bad for her (1379; 29; 3), while their victories are, as at Magdeburg, her defeats – only she does not draw the conclusions.[23] If subjectively she has (in Marxian terms) the false consciousness of the exploiting class, objectively she exists in the alienation of the exploited. The existence of war exploits her, whether she approves or not. Even more exploited than she are her children, and most of all the soldiers. The soldier's song in scene 6 (1402; 49f.) shows that his time is not his own, but the Emperor's. Another image of alienation is Eilif's description of how he made his subordinates aggressive by keeping them short of meat: 'Their mouths'd water at the sound of any word beginning with M, like mother' (1364; 16; 2) clearly refers to Pavlov's experiments with dogs, and Brecht sees the conditioned reflex of behaviourist theory as a particularly striking instance of alienation.[24]

The message that war is a continuation of capitalism by other means was brought into the present in the programme notes of the Berliner Ensemble, which print the relative profits of the Standard Oil Company in peace and in wartime. Brecht has no desire to base pacifism on individual ethical judgments without reference to a social theory of the origin of war or to a political group which could work on a practical level to avoid the conditions which lead to war. Brecht certainly has views on why a Communist pacifism was the only viable pacifism, but they do not appear in the play, whose message thus remains apparently vague. They do appear in an extra strophe and refrain which Brecht wrote but did not intend for inclusion in the play:

> A day will come when things will take a
> New turn for us, it won't be long:
> When we, the people, put an end to
> The great long war of the great men . . .[25]

Brecht rejected the idea of an epilogue pointing the message on stylistic grounds: it could only be a song, and a song could not organically

continue the content of the play.[26] All we have in the text is stray references to, or possibilities of showing the common people as longing for
peace: the resistance that the sergeant says in scene 1 people put up
to getting the war going; the dazed relief of the old woman when peace
breaks out at the beginning of scene 8; the dumb insolence of the
soldiers when Kattrin captures their sympathy in scene 11.

There is however much that hints at possible opinions. Mother Courage's statement about only rotten states needing virtues, for instance
(1365f.; 17; 2), leads one into the thick of Brecht's opposition to Nazism.
Around 1936 he satirises the 'spirit of self-sacrifice' which led the Germans
to submit to the Führer's bestial discipline and participate in the cere-
monies and celebrations he arranged to distract them from their misery
(20, 183: *Unpolitische Briefe*). In *Refugees' Conversations* the theme re-
curs, and Ziffel complains of the number of virtues needed just to survive
in our century (14, 1496f.). In the play the war leaders have no heroic
or admirable points, and in the world they run Mother Courage's children
are ruined by their bravery, honesty, humanity. The order they make is,
as described by the sergeant at the beginning of the play (1349; 3), not
only a topsy-turvy one; it is also a mere power-system with no moral
backing and no conviction – the sergeant who is so eloquent about it
always stays at the rear in safety and sends others forward to earn glory
(1359; 12; 1). The power-system is also a profit-system. The soldier
thieves what and where he can; victory means booty for him, but Mother
Courage is worth a try as well: the soldier in scene 5 wants 'another
victory' when he tries to steal a bottle from her (1399; 47). Courage
ironically says she is sorry for the generals and emperors who know
nothing better than to conquer the world and be commemorated on a
statue, but whose plans are thrown into confusion by the common folk
who just want an evening's drinking. But she wants much more from
war herself. She must think of it as primarily a field for profiteering as
she does in scene 2, making a fast buck. Otherwise we must agree with
Gray (p. 129) that the outbreak of peace would not in fact ruin her:
most if not all of her stock is equally saleable in peace, though perhaps
not for inflated prices. But her profiteering is of no avail, she is poor at
the end. A symbolic aspect becomes apparent – 'the image of germany
looms up, carrying on wars for gain, destroying others and herself, learning nothing from any catastrophe' (*Aj.*, 2, 1004: 12.1.53).

(IV) GOODNESS AND VIRTUE

Each of the children has a virtue in which Mother Courage rests her trust;
each carries it to the point at which it offends the military ethos. Swiss
Cheese is executed because he takes honesty too far in looking after the

regimental cash; Kattrin is shot down trying to save the children of Halle; Eilif carries over his bravery from war into peacetime, when it becomes outlawry and is punished. Each is executed; none dies in battle or accidentally. It is not the unforeseeable chance which dooms some combatants to destruction and spares others that claims them, but military discipline; not the disorder of war, but its order. Each death is foreseeable, if not actually avoidable. Brecht is not concerned to get pathetic effects from death on the battlefield; he wants to show that the killing is no unfortunate accident, but an integral part of the ethos of war (and thus of capitalism).

But in the context of the *gestarium*, it is important to be clear what attitudes one defines as virtuous. Ronald Gray (pp. 130–6) finds Brecht's guidance here unsatisfactory. Indeed, Mother Courage's views on virtues in scene 2, and the cook's song in scene 9, are unhelpful and tend apparently to put Kattrin's selflessness on the same level as Eilif's low cunning. But looking at particular extracts out of context and asking whether Brecht agrees with the speaker takes us only so far. The spectator must be able to stand above what any or all the figures on stage say, and to assess the results of the 'virtuous' actions, considering them in relation to war. Eilif's bravery is only a 'virtue' in that in wartime it furthers the cause of the right side – which of course begs the question of which is the right side. With the coming of peace, even the organs of military discipline quickly repudiate it. Swiss Cheese's honesty, though originally intended by his mother as a counterweight to his stupidity, is turned (thanks to that very stupidity) into a similar military virtue, whose subjective aim is to please Swiss Cheese's superiors by faithfully returning with the cashbox. The beneficiary of these qualities is thus the military order, the exploiters. And these qualities are inculcated by ideologists such as the chaplain in order to make people sacrifice themselves for the rulers. Caesar – the cook's paradigm of boldness in scene 9 – is in Brecht's interpretation (in *Mr. Julius Caesar's Business Deals*) little more than an Eilif, who gets his chance of making history when it suits the bankers.

Kattrin's good-heartedness, on the other hand, is a basically humane urge to help the poor and defenceless. In scene 5 she incurs the odium of unfilial behaviour to do good. In scene 9 she wants to steal away in order to allow her mother to be happy with the cook, whilst the mother in Mother Courage asserts herself touchingly in her refusal to countenance this self-sacrifice. Finally she dies through her selflessness. One could not imagine the cook so far forgetting the instinct of self-preservation, so one sees his song as hypocritical. He is not virtuous. Yet he is to be taken seriously. Confused as it may be, his song does point out that charitable St Martin succeeds merely in bringing both himself and the beggar to their deaths. It is not far-fetched to point out that Kattrin too kills herself and probably does not lessen the total number of deaths in the war. So the cook's song makes us think about the theme in hand and further distinguish between virtue that objectively helps (as Kattrin and the chaplain did in scene 5) and virtue that defeats its own ends. Obnoxious as he is, the cook has a little bit of truth on his side.

And he is in general no warmonger. It is those who make war an article of faith whose descriptions of virtue are always to be taken ironically. They are the strong, cynical, unscrupulous. Over against them the weak represent true, if ineffective, virtue. The epitome of weakness in this sense is Kattrin. She scarcely counts as a person: dumbness makes her an animal (1381: cf. 31 – 'poor thing'; 3), unreceptive to ideology and proof against hypocrisy, knowing only concrete dangers and pleasures. She has no interest in war for profit. Profit is an abstract to her, except when her mother points out that they have to make money for her trousseau (1404; 51; 6). And the trousseau is no use to her without peace, in that Mother Courage 'promised her she'll get a husband – when it's peace' (1403; 50; 6) – so she is angry when the chaplain proves that war can go on indefinitely. She is sexually frustrated because her mother will not let her, like Yvette, sell her body – the only form in which love offers itself during war. When, in defending the goods she associates with a trousseau, she is mutilated so that she has no further chance of a man, she gives up, loses interest in Yvette's sexy red shoes (1408; 54; 6) – her mother, conversely thinks it safe to give her them now, as the scar on her brow will put off any soldier attracted by the message of the red shoes – and becomes a 'beaten animal, not without malevolence' (*Mat. C.*, 82). Her face loses its expressiveness, her body its youthfulness. Yet (one of the contradictions in character Brecht loves) one reason for her wanting a husband is that she is 'so mad about children' (1408; 55; 6); this has been demonstrated at the end of scene 5; it remains in force, and when her weakness for children becomes stronger than her instinct of self-preservation – what has she to live for? – she shows the quality of pure goodness. It is typical of Brecht that such a virtue should proceed from a dialectical development of character, if we are to sympathise with it. The good-humour she shows early in the play – playing a mouth-organ, or discussing the beauty of autumn with Swiss Cheese – is not goodness. To develop goodness she needs to be so maltreated that her own personality is no longer of importance even to her. Then she shows a decisiveness that proves her her mother's daughter: when in scene 11 the peasants, who put their own lives first although they have relatives in the town, have concluded they can do nothing but pray, she contradicts them by deeds, getting the drum to warn the town. She has asserted her freedom from personal ties (a freedom she did not want) to perform a willed moral act in a hostile situation, and we are allowed to share her emotions; but the delineation of her development so far shows how inadequate these emotions and her self-sacrifice are when unaccompanied by any inkling of social mechanisms. When Brecht next shows a girl mad about children, Grusha in the *Chalk Circle*, he gives her more social awareness. Togther with Shen Teh, whose maternal feeling is only part of her general kindliness, these two figures make up Brecht's trilogy of caring feminine characters set in the harsh masculine world of conflict. The real suffering mother-animal in *Mother Courage* is Kattrin, and this was the role written for Helene Weigel (non-speaking so that she could take it in a planned Swedish production[27]), though finally immortalised, like that of Grusha, by Angelika Hurwicz.

Between Kattrin and Courage on a scale of goodness is the chaplain. Whereas Kattrin forswears war and profit and sacrifices herself, her mother embraces war and profit and restricts any goodness to her children. The chaplain is less adapted to war than Courage, but more compromised than Kattrin. His profession, of which he is proud, is to bring religion and war into harmony. His pseudo-theological justification of Eilif's brutality is rightly taken by the commander as the work of a Pharisee (1364; 16; 2). He is servile to the commander, who treats him as a court jester. His job is to get soldiers into a mood to throw away their lives for Christ; to be forced to become an odd-job man is an indignity to him (1405f.; 52f.; 6). He is thus cut out for comic treatment. From scene 3 on he is dependent on Mother Courage, who sometimes makes him feel it; yet in scene 5 he rises above comedy and is the one who gets at the shirts for bandages by simply lifting their owner out of the way (1398; 46), as well as the one who rescues people from the ruins. But unlike Kattrin he restricts himself to help after the event and does not interfere in the business of war. He rises to the insight that guilt in war belongs to those who start wars (1407; 54; 6); he accurately describes Courage as a hyena of the battlefield, a scavenger (1414; 60; 8); he claims to have become a better man and less of a preacher (1416; 61; 8) – but it is as a clergyman that he accompanies Eilif to execution (1419; 64; 8). He may suffer from the war, but he accepts his role in it.[28]

(v) LANGUAGE AND DUMBSHOW

No play of Brecht's uses more paradox and wit – which in keeping with the subject-matter soon turns into black humour, starting with the *dramatis personae* – Swiss Cheese is to earn his name when, in scene 3, he stops eleven bullets.[29] (As a specially macabre note, the New York Performance Group production had an interval after this scene and members of the group served refreshments including Swiss cheese.)

Paradox enters with the opening dialogue on how war alone brings about order. For Brecht order is often associated with war and with exploitation. The subject is discussed at greater length in *Refugees' Conversations* (14, 1383–91). The dialogue in the play ingeniously confuses man, beast and vegetable, as Fuegi (pp. 84–7) points out. He also notes that when the recruiter admires the build of the boys he treats them like horses or oxen – and indeed they are drawing the wagon. Everyone in the play is at some stage a draught animal for the wagon of war. The scene title uses the term *abhanden kommen*, to get mislaid, of Eilif, as if he were some piece of lost property. Man is dehumanised in war.

This opening, as Hans Mayer (pp. 107f.) notes, also abandons surface reality. Presumably middle-ranking soldiers did not talk like this in the seventeenth century; they will have paid lip-service to official ideologies, treated war as an evil necessary for religion and truth, even if in fact they behaved as if they thought war right and natural and used it to cloak their egoism. But here war presents itself without its mask. A comic effect arises from socially unacceptable behaviour: we are tempted to laugh at the soldiers as though they were innocents ignorant of conventions of drawing-room behaviour. But the objective situation overtakes our laughter. Similarly when in scene 3 the chaplain says the religious war is 'pleasing unto God', the cook glosses sarcastically: 'In one sense it's a war because there's firelaying, putting people to the sword, and plundering, not to mention a little raping, but it's different from all other wars because it's a war of religion' (1373; 24, but I have altered the translation). By leaving God out, he reduces war to the level of this world, on which the definition *religious* war is meaningless; his treating rape as scarcely worth mention is a touch of black humour. But the same cook, in scene 8, when peace seems to be going badly for him, will produce the ranting religious tone (1418; 63). Attitudes to religion are a matter of circumstance, not of character.

From Mother Courage's first appearance, the exploitation of the humorous gap between the semblance of logic and the seamy side of reality becomes a standing feature of the play. She produces a whole missal (1351; cf. 5 – 'Bible'; 1), but quickly explains that it is for wrapping cucumbers in. This comic discrepancy is a wry reference on a small scale to the ideology of war: religion is the ostensible matter at stake, but more tangible things really occupy everyone. The ridiculous description of her family with which Courage confuses the soldiers is a prime example of the Bavarian humour Brecht learnt from Karl Valentin, which is turned to serious use later with such statements as that the Poles in Poland should not have interfered in their own affairs, or her reaction to the chaplain's 'We're in God's hands now!' – 'I hope we're not as desperate as *that* . . .' (1378; 29; 3). Hašek's Schweyk is also a model for such humour (*Aj.*, 1, 172: 19.9.40). Zeugma too has a tendentious effect, in 'Do you know what we need in the army? Discipline!' – 'I was going to say sausages' (1352; 6; 1). The description of the Fierling–Noyocki–Haupt family, incidentally, anticipates a theme of *The Caucasian Chalk Circle*, in that Swiss Cheese is described as taking after the Hungarian to whom he owes the name Feyos, who didn't mind him but was not his father (1353; 7). Heredity is of less importance in determining his honesty than a sort of imprinting from the honest Hungarian. Similarly Grusha will set out to make the Governor's son into a worker by force of example and education.

Not only comic dialogue, but also lack of dialogue, is used to good effect in the play. In scene 10 two figures appear on the stage, but remain silent and do not express their feelings by gestures either. 'What is going on in them is not to be shown; the audience can think it out for itself' (*Mat. C.*, 65). And one major character is dumb. Brecht uses various theatrical techniques to allow her to be understood: her gestures, her irrepressible activity where it is a matter of children or sex. The sounds she makes are also meaningful; the actress should in rehearsal first put in words what Kattrin is trying to say, then gradually reduce it to the inadequate word-substitutes of the mute (*Mat. C.*, 106f.). But there are also literary ways of dealing with the problem of comprehending her: comments on her by her mother.[30] What Mother Courage says about Kattrin turns out to be true: 'you have a good heart' (1358; 11; 1); 'The war frightens her' (1424; 69; 9). In a sense Mother Courage acts as her interpreter, though she has to admit there are limits even to her understanding of her daughter (1408; 55; 6). She also interprets the boys, not letting them speak for themselves. In scene 1, where she is trying to keep the recruiting officer away from them, this is particularly obvious. Sometimes what she says is obviously untrue, but at other times she functions as a narrator, reminding the audience of what has already been said in dialogue (1369; 21; 3 – Swiss Cheese's honesty). Thus she imposes herself as a central figure, but also to some extent (giving up her own character) as a commentator and mediator between stage and audience. She in turn is the object of expositionary comments by others: Swiss Cheese explains, when in the heat of argument she has no time to, 'She can look into the future. Everyone says so' (1356; 9; 1). The descriptive note thus given to the play is an epic element.

Difficulties of communication affect others besides Kattrin. The cook, a Dutchman, was endowed by Ernst Busch (Berlin 1951) with a practically incomprehensible Dutch accent. A strong South German tinge is suggested for Mother Courage and the boys by textual features: mutations diverge from standard German (missing or introduced *Umlaut*), final -e is elided, a redundant -s added to plural verb forms – 'Nehmts mich mit' (1438; 12) – the conjunction 'vor' used instead of 'bevor', 'nix' and 'bissel' preferred to 'nichts' and 'bisschen', the interpolated 'halt' frequent, ambiguous forms of 'mögen' substituted for the flat-footed future tense. Brecht also encouraged actors to use their native dialects in rehearsal.[31] Furthermore, the syntax is broken up, word-order and agreement often unconventional and expressive: 'Die zahlen nicht, warum, die haben nix' (1397; cf. 45, 'They have nothing and they pay nothing'; 5). Such sentences expressing reasons are particularly prone to this emphasis – Brecht, as always, stressing logic and decision-making, even if their processes go sadly wrong in Courage's case; her wrongness is expressed by false logic in little comic interpolations: 'I call him Swiss Cheese. Why? Because he's good at pulling wagons' (1353; 7; 1).[32]

Dialect serves Brecht as a way to shake the rigidity of the standard-ised diction. *Bühnendeutsch*, of which the German stage used to be proud (16, 731: *Aus einem Brief an einen Schauspieler*), and which he thought bloodless, 'a thin shorthand without undertones or over-tones' (*Aj.*, 2, 916: 5.3.50). The seventeenth-century setting also comes to his aid. Eisler (p. 57) remarks of Brecht's language that he starts not from Lessing or Goethe, but from Luther. Luther's Bible and Grim-melshausen's novels of the Thirty Years War period represent for Brecht a stage at which German is unified – Luther had written his Bible in the dialect of German which would be most readily understandable over a wide area – but not forced into all-too-decorous standardisation, still earthy and direct. Some archaisms ('allewege' and 'allhier') are taken from Grimmelshausen; occasionally the Bible is quoted, usually against the grain, as when the chaplain refuses to risk going through enemy fire and says 'Blessed are the peacemakers' (1376; 26; 3) – not a text he would choose for one of his pre-battle sermons. The German language's stock of proverbs is drawn on particularly in the 'Song of the Great Capitulation', both to spice the argument and – in accordance with the tendency of the scene – to be held up as false wisdom. 'Der Mensch denkt: Gott lenkt – / Keine Red davon!' (1395; not trans-lated; 4) alters the sense of the original ('Man proposes, God disposes') radically ('Man thinks God is in charge') by changing the usual punctu-ation, then demolishes the proverb's and religion's claims by straight negation.[33]

Brecht likes to change the level of language too. 'Unhappy mother that I am, rich only in a mother's sorrows! He dies. In the springtime of his life, he must go. If he's a soldier, he must bite the dust, that's clear' (1357; 10; 1 – the German echoes Goethe's *Faust* before reach-ing the Western imagery). There is no attempt to reproduce outer reality or to write within a convention; a sort of comic inconsequentiality is aimed at. At one point Brecht intended the opening dialogue to be in *Knittelvers*, a doggerel-like rhymed form with irregular rhythm which flowered in the sixteenth century and gives the modern ear an impression of naïve clumsiness.[34] Perhaps this struck him finally as too comic for the serious subject: the contentual paradoxes make their mark without help from verse form.

(VI) THE SONGS

In performance the 'Courage Song', which in the text appears within scene 1, was used by the Berliner Ensemble as a prelude: on to the empty stage the wagon is pulled and the family sing the song before leaving again. This alteration (Helene Weigel's idea – *Mat. C.*, 18) transforms the song from a conventionally operatic song self-introduction (like 'I am the very model of a modern major-general') into a preface to the whole play. It is used ironically. If here at the outset Mother Courage is happy for the soldiers to be led into the jaws of hell (1351; not translated) once she has sold them sausages and wine, she is not so happy for her Eilif to be one of them. In scene 7 a new verse of the song – an answer to arguments of the chaplain's which must be inferred as brought forward before the scene begins – refers to soldiers' deaths in callous terms; in scene 8 Eilif will die and she will not know about it. In scene 12 the final verse is sung by soldiers off stage: chillingly, with the cheerful marching rhythm set against the bleakness of the general situation and Courage's particular situation, it summarises the objective misery of the war and the subjective illusion – 'Jedoch vielleicht geschehn noch Wunder: / Der Feldzug ist noch nicht zu End!' (1438; reversed in the translation, 'miracles have had their day', 81). Brecht wrote the words to the tune of an old French song which he had also set his *Ballad of the Pirates* to; he insisted on Dessau using this melody, but Dessau altered the metric arrangements to give it more decisiveness and less grace; whilst strident subdominant chords in the accompaniment make a suggestion of falsity and tell the listener to be critical of the sentiments expressed. In general Dessau likes to start from folk material and to enrich it with harmonic and rhythmic variations.

The songs have very various functions. There are some approaches to operatic treatment, as when Yvette explains in the 'Fraternization Song' how she came to have her first lover and thus reached her present situation. This song derives, by a long process of adaptation, from Kipling's 'Mary, pity women!'[35] The 'Song of the Great Capitulation' (scene 4) is part of an episodic sub-plot and carries it forward. Or a song has ironical function, as when in the 'Song of the Vexations of Great Men' (scene 9) – largely borrowed from the *Threepenny Opera*, and given a new setting with harmonium, flute and trumpet accompaniment – the cook implies that he shares the virtues he sings about, which he does not; Mother Courage's children have them, but break into song less. When

Eilif does sing, the 'Song of the Fishwife and the Soldier' (scene 2), he proves if anything that he has the virtue of bravery despite his mother's lessons: he knows the song she taught him, but has disregarded its moral and acted foolhardily.[36] The song is accompanied by dance and comic acting – he caricatures the fishwife when he reports her words; but she triumphs in the last stanza. In the 'Song of the Hours' (scene 3) the chaplin, like the cook in scene 9, invokes a great parallel, of Christ and Swiss Cheese. Again the lesson must be thought out by the audience. Brecht borrowed the song with its bitter accusing tone from Christian Weise (1642–1708), though there are parallels to a hymn of 1531 by Michael Weisse too.[37] The songs thus all mean different things to the singer, the hearers on stage and the audience.

Dessau's music adds its own touches. Just as Brecht's whole production of the play was drab but elegant, so the music suggests a good represenation of a shabby reality. The overture expresses by sparse instrumentation and paratactic themes an inadequate attempt to introduce a vast panorama of war: the attempt to be solemn being cut across by lack of practised musicians. Themes from the overture are repeated – right through to the finale, at Brecht's suggestion. Brecht is also thought to have suggested to Dessau an innovation used here which then became one of Dessau's hallmarks: the 'Gitarrenklavier', a piano whose sound is made like that of a guitar by pressing drawing-pins into the felt of the hammers. This instrument can also produce an approximation to the harpischord, useful for the 'Fraternization Song', where the main parts of each stanza are in the genteel style of the period, with *Volkslied* elements modified by fiorituri, and with keyboard accompaniment, whilst a heavier and less sensitive harmony emphasises the vulgarity between the lines towards the end of the stanzas. The music to the 'Song of the Great Capitulation' expresses by dissonances – a motif in parallel ninths – Dessau's disagreement with the sentiments of the close. The 'Song of the Fishwife and the Soldier', a Kipling adaptation incidentally, set in free rondo form, has similar dubiety expressed by unexpected modulations. The 'Song of the Hours' has a concealed canon in the strophe, and an introduction borrowed from an ancient source. The 'Song of the Home' (scene 10) has folk-song character. Part of the Luther hymn, 'A mighty fortress is our God', is sung in scene 3 (omitted in the German text, but the place is after 'in Ihrem Gesicht', 1374; in the English text, 25) to its usual melody unaccompanied (*Mat. C.*, 39). In the 1951 reprise in the Berliner Ensemble, a Dutch song in praise of pipe-smoking is sung by the cook to Mother Courage whilst they haggle over the capon; their intimacy thus starts earlier. The other music of the play consists of marches off (using three march themes, variously interwoven in the course of the play), used to give v-effects, for instance by contrasting with the on-stage tableau at the end of scene 5.[38]

(VII) THE SCENIC INTERPRETATION OF THE PLAY

The 1949 Berlin production, taken into the Berliner Ensemble repertoire, reached 405 performances. Each scene is introduced by summaries or commentaries projected on to a half-curtain. These texts anticipate the action or the gestus of the scene and may also provide historical information not found in the dialogue. That for scene 1 supplies the thought that Eilif is only one of many men being recruited; that for scene 5 connects Mother Courage's journeyings with the course of the war.[39] As inscriptions, the scene headings speak as it were over the head of the dialogic and scenic presentation straight to the audience's intelligence, and put across the scale of the war – which the stage could not convey directly – and the lessons of the play. In scene 6 the title scarcely goes beyond the content of the scene, for here Courage is allowed to put the moral in words: 'Curse the war!' (1408; 55); but in all the following scenes, when she has forgotten that flash of insight, the headings insist ironically on the destructiveness of war.

The stage is bare at beginning and end. From nothing Mother Courage's mercantile enterprises start; in nothing they end. The ground-tone of the production is drab, and Wekwerth (pp. 279f.) dates from it the 'grey period' of Brecht-theatre, a stage at which Brecht attempts to shock by the painful contrast with the colourful, empty spectacles provided by Nazism: hard-bitten sobriety against perverted belief and daemonic intoxication. The wagon enters – 'a hybrid of military vehicle and market stall' (*Mat. C.*, 17), almost an actor in its own right: now smartly painted and festooned with wares, later shabby and empty; now pulled on by two strong youths, eventually pulled off by the owner alone. Its single shaft has a crossbar near the front, which those pulling the wagon hold to steer. Fuegi (pp. 88–90) draws attention to the symbolic cross thus formed, which is of visual significance at various points of the action. Perhaps he over-interprets; but certainly when Kattrin prepares to leave her mother free to go with the cook, the raised shaft forms a cross dominating the display of trousers and skirt and corresponding to the crucifix specified in the setting for the scene – whose theme is virtue, claimed and real. So the subject of Christianity's relationship with war and commerce is, literally, never lost sight of. The wagon moves mainly round the outer edge of the stage turntable; such trips are established in the course of the play as showing the covering of ever greater distances, so that at the end a circuit of the stage, ending with the wagon upstage and about to start a second circuit, signifies the indefinite prolongation of Courage's wanderings.[40] Another speaking prop is the drum which is among the goods for which Kattrin suffers her wound in scene 6; it awakes the town of Halle in scene 11, and in an early production in Rotterdam was the only item of stock hanging from the wagon as Courage departs in scene 12 (*Mat. C.*, 110) – a touch of masterly irony thought up by Ruth Berlau.

For the songs a flown 'music emblem', an illuminated swag of seventeenth-century musical and martial attributes, is displayed. Whereas everything practical – props, the roof for Kattrin's death – is realistic and heavy, the guns perhaps real museum pieces, what is not to be used – drops representing housefronts and so on – is merely sketched with attention to line but no claim to realism. A few tufts of grass signify a roadside. Courage has on her the attributes of her profession, notably the short knife with which she discourages attackers; the cook too shows his calling by a knife, Yvette hers with large hat and red boots; whilst the costume designer Kurt Palm had the idea of dressing Eilif shabbily at first, but in costly black armour by the time he is executed: he has enriched himself in war, but pays with his life (16, 768: *Palm*). The chaplain wears an exaggerated Roman nose. Costumes are drab and undifferentiated, warm and practical clothing which has seen too much use.

The play is carefully analysed into small gestic units. In scene 2 a basic gestus of 'profiteering with food' (*Aj.*, 1, 206: 9.12.40), cut across by joy at Eilif's appearance, soon swings back as she raises the price of the capon: everything she touches becomes mercantile, her reaction to an event shows her attitudes. But directer characterisation is used too. In scene 1 Swiss Cheese, ineffectual and simple as he is, is trying to look warlike; Eilif too would obviously rather fight than pull the cart. What their mother does in scene 1 is a reaction to their wish to join up – although Swiss Cheese never puts it in words. Nor is Kattrin purely happy – even at the beginning she does not intend to spend her life sitting on her mother's cart. Mother Courage's jauntiness is matter for a grin, rather than a smile: something is discordant inside her too. The happy family is full of tensions even before the dialogue begins.[41]

Each gestic section is the basis for a grouping of figures on stage, usually in an obvious manner: opponents opposite one another, allies side by side. But the cook and chaplain, when they argue, may face away from each other.[42] The wagon is often used to divide the stage, as in scene 1, where Courage moves away from Eilif and busies herself at one side of it, whilst the recruiting officer strikes his bargain with Eilif on the other side. Her movement turns out to have been symbolic of her whole erroneous attitude: neglecting her children's true interests for the sake of business.[43] No one moves on stage without a reason; at the beginning, for example, sergeant and recruiting officer stay together at one side of the stage until the wagon appears. After such a static period as the beginning of scene 3, with Mother Courage unhurriedly mending Swiss Cheese's underpants – she is scarcely ever idle – and chatting comfortably with Yvette at the cask which serves as a table, then taking her visitor over to the other side of the wagon for a political talk, the panic at the sudden attack when she rushes from one side of the stage to the other in her haste to pack up and escape is all the more impressive. Not that she has lost her head; Weigel gives a virtuoso performance of lightning packing – Mother Courage is used to alarms. And the public according to Brecht has come to the theatre – *inter alia* – to see familiar actions performed with unwonted skill. Meanwhile, as everyone rushes about, the chaplain stands still and is in everyone's way: one of the gratuitous comic effects Brecht the director loves (*Mat. C.*, 34). Also dependent on movement effects is scene 5, where Mother Courage drinks to keep her spirits up, thus motivating her bad-tempered, tigerish activity during the scene, from defence of the cart and its contents against the chaplain and Kattrin, to the counter-attack on the thieving soldier. Having sacrificed Swiss Cheese to the wagon in scene 3, she has become more attached to it and to money – it was because she could not be open-handed with money that she could not save him. The chaplain's movements are, as always when he has something physical to do, clumsy; and opposing the woman who after all feeds him is difficult; yet he has a certain residual dignity, that of the clergyman giving a moral lead (*Mat. C.*, 48). Another instance of clumsiness is Eilif's sword dance in scene 2, taken with an appearance of strain and over-concentration as if he had difficulty in remembering the steps; this particular martial art does not come easy to him. In general, however, any point of the text where business is indicated is an occasion for graceful movement or skilful technique. In scene 2 the cook fishes mouldy meat out of the rubbish and carries it to his chopping-board ceremoniously on the point of a knife; and he prepares the capon with a dash, to impress his new lady-friend (*Mat. C.*, 29).

Much business can be added to elucidate the interworkings of society and character. Thus in scene 6 Mother Courage's speech on Tilly is easier to deliver if she is being watched by the scrivener, on the watch for subversive statements she does not quite make (*Mat. C.*, 52f.). Weigel added the aside 'Lord, worms have got into the biscuits' (not in the German text, but *Mat. C.*, 53: 'Jesses, in den Zwieback sind mir die Würmer gekommen'; 48) and laughed at it, thus freeing the amusement she felt at teasing the scrivener (a rare borrowing by Brecht of an idea from Freud). The soldier's song following is accompanied by a little flirtation with Kattrin – the last reminder before her mutilation of her potential for love (*Mat. C.*, 53). The chaplain's role in this scene was greatly built up in the 1951 reprise of the Berlin production. After losing money gaming with the scrivener, he is sad, and tries to improve his finances by rubbing a chalk mark off his debt record on Courage's slate; then he sees how unworthy this is, prays silently, and is thus prepared to make himself popular with her by woodcutting – the closer their relations, the less she will remember his debts. But he drags the axe to the block and works with as little effort as possible, emphasising that he still sees himself as an intellectual, misused as a manual worker.[44] Courage, prosperous in this scene, is a little softer; he is encouraged to propose marriage, but she prefers a helper under her control to a husband. She also speaks more warmly than she need of the cook; so when the latter arrives in scene 8, though he and she only talk of ruin, we hear the affection between the lines better (*Mat. C.*, 58). Kattrin, hurt in scene 6, is bandaged in scene 7. In scene 8 the scar is shown, and when the cook sees her he is taken aback for a moment; in scene 9 the scar makes him decide not to offer her a home in Utrecht.[45]

In accordance with Brecht's requirements of reading the text against the grain, some parts of the dialogue can be undermined by reinterpretation. The commander in scene 2 for instance will stand playing as an absent-minded, effete aristocrat who goes without any conviction through the routine of praising one of his soldiers and talking like a regular fellow (*Mat. C.*, 30). Such an interpretation strengthens the theme of social class, not overtly developed in the text in this play. And Wekwerth notes disarmingly that in the 1951 revision they discovered that Eilif's similarity to the king, mentioned by the commander (1365; 17), is supposed to consist of a liking for drink! So they gave him something bigger to drink from (*Mat. C.*, 115). Some speeches which are likely to arouse the spectator's sympathy are given in super-cooled style: the peasants of scene 11 plead for their animals to be spared in the tone of people to whom such crises are familiar, who have a form of words ready. Such threats of destruction have become the norm. 'It pays to give up the "direct impression" of the apparently unique, real horror, in order to reach deeper layers of terror where frequent ever-recurring misfortune has already forced people into making their gestures of self-defence a ceremonial – which yet can never help them to avoid the actual real fear' (*Mat. C.*, 70). Absence of dialogue is taken as a hint. In scene 11 there is a point where the soldiers stop making suggestions as to how to stop Kattrin, and there may be some satisfaction in the first soldier's closing line, 'She did it' (1436; 80). In between, the soldiers can show apathy or bloody-mindedness, carry out orders only just fast enough to avoid disciplinary action, and grin behind the officer's back (*Mat. C.*, 73).

Tempo is in general not forced. Details are to be taken one at a time, Brecht stresses (*Mat. C.*, 25). Helene Weigel after each monetary transaction closed her leather purse with an audible snap before proceeding. Running time is about 168 minutes, plus scene changes of never more than two minutes and a single interval after scene 7.

After Weigel in Berlin, Brecht directed Therese Giehse in the part of Mother Courage in Munich in 1950. Giehse's ideas included an ill-tempered reception for Eilif in scene 2 even before the slap; in the scene over Swiss Cheese's body, on the other hand, she preferred a direct change of mood, inspecting the corpse as if insulted by the idea she might have known such a criminal, then suddenly collapsing forwards from her stool after it was carried out. In scene 7 she staggered and swung a bottle, so that drunkenness would forestall any empathy with her view on war expressed here. In scene 9 – where Weigel introduced the idea of feeding Kattrin the soup she brings (1428; 72) with a spoon – Giehse also returned the soup-dish to the parsonage with deep bowings and scrapings which show how far down the social scale she has sunk – and also how old and stiff she is getting, too old to refuse easily the cook's offer of a home.[46] Weigel took this up. In the same episode Giehse's treatment of the word 'wagon' showed that she was trying to avoid making Kattrin grateful to her. Yet at the end when Courage has thrown the cook's things out of the wagon, both Weigel and Giehse reached out for Kattrin's bundle to put into the wagon: Giehse with obvious tenderness, but Weigel this time disguising her love of Kattrin behind a show of impatience.[47] A good example of differing interpretations not interfering with the dramatic function of an episode is afforded by the beginning of scene 3: Weigel gestures to Swiss Cheese not to listen to her illegal dealings with the officer, then tells him to be honest; Giehse allows Swiss Cheese to listen to the talk despite the officer's misgivings, then tells him to be honest! (16, 754: *Über den Gestus*).

In the Berliner Ensemble, three young actresses were faced with the task of playing old women: Carola Braunbock as the peasant woman in scenes 11 and 12, Regine Lutz as Yvette, Käthe Reichel as the old woman in scene 8. In each case Brecht declares against stock characterisations of age by voice and movement, and insists that the individual mode of the character's ageing be analysed. The peasant woman, about forty, is aged by miscarriages and the loss of children, physical maltreatment by parents and husband, spiritual brutalisation by pastors, and the necessity of taking up servile attitudes in order to survive in wartime. Thus she kneels to pray carefully, one knee at a time, and she prays in a practised and formal manner, at the same time trying to involve Kattrin, who seems to her to have been brought up in irreligious ideas; by this and by the fact that, despite her life-weariness, the fate of her relatives in the town does in fact touch her, she seems to become more sincere as the prayer goes on. Yvette ages in a more comfortable manner, deformed by the twin pleasures she can indulge in as the wife of an ancient colonel: eating and giving orders. She comes on padded and powdered and snaps with stupid arrogance, the corners of her mouth turned down, yet still has remnants of charm. The woman in scene 8 is less characterised by the text: the interpretation chosen was to make her appear turned in on herself, unable immediately to take in the meaning and importance of the news of peace: she cups her ear with her hand as if mentally deaf (*Mat. C.*, 70–2).

The play has supported many divergent interpretations. One, strange to thé European eye, is a thoroughgoing adaptation by Nick Wilkinson, set in Africa and suited to local ideas of performance, which made some of the audience think afresh about the Biafran war.[48] Another radical departure is a New York Performance Group production: the play was chosen mainly to provide the group with rewarding female roles. With apparently unconscious Brechtianism Joan MacIntosh (Mother Courage) says 'I'm obviously not 50 years old, so there was no way to act that I was 50, or to pretend that I was a mother. I did not want to get into acting old age. I decided it would have to be me the performer, telling the story about this other person.' The part of the commander was also taken in a similar spirit by a woman. Perhaps further from Brecht was the repeated use of a system of pulleys and harness for representing the deaths of Swiss Cheese and Kattrin by dropping them violently to the ground: it threatens the takeover of technology, a mistake Brecht saw in Piscator's work. The decision to dispense with a movable wagon also limits the possible effects. An interesting final touch: Courage strips the clothing off her dead daughter before leaving to take up business again.[49]

6 The Good Person of Szechwan

Brecht started work on the play in Denmark in March 1939 on the basis of an earlier sketch *Die Ware Liebe* (1930), but stopped in Sweden in September. Completed in Finland, May–August 1940, the play was worked over again in January 1941. 'it gave me more trouble than any other play ever did' (*Aj.*, 1, 120: 29.6.40). The first performance was in Zurich on 4 February 1943. Music by Paul Dessau was written in 1947–8 and first used in an American performance in 1948.[1] The Berliner Ensemble production by Benno Besson with Katrin Reichel in the lead opened on 5 October 1957.

(I) THE PLOT

Prologue: 'Difficulties of a Believer in Getting Satisfaction for his Gods.'[2] A street. Wang, a water-seller in the capital of poverty-stricken Szechwan province, introduces himself to the audience and looks out for the three high gods whose arrival has been adumbrated to him by a cattle-dealer. They arrive, glad to see such a faithful believer, and ask him to find them somewhere to stay. At the houses of the well-to-do he is refused or given only grudging offers. The gods become despondent, having already visited two provinces without finding a good person able to live decently. Even Wang has a water measure with a false bottom. He runs himself off his feet to find hospitality for them before thinking of the prostitute Shen Te (Shen Teh in the English translation), who is incapable of saying no. Despite ill-health and the need to make some money that night to pay her rent, she agrees to take the gods in, which after a few complications is accomplished.

In the morning they emerge, thankful to have found a good person; Shen Teh's doubts about her morality they dismiss shortly; but when she is finally driven to hinting about her money problems, they give her something as payment for their lodging.

Scene 1: 'Quick Ruin of a Livelihood by Goodness.' A small tobacconist's. In the three days since the gods went, leaving a thousand silver dollars,

Shen Teh has bought herself this business with which she hopes to be able to give her penchant for doing good free reign, with doles of rice for such people as Mrs Shin, the former owner of the shop, an intolerable moaner and parasite; and her one-time landlord and his family, who threw Shen Teh out when she was penniless, and now that they are poor come demanding her charity. Shen Teh is unable to say no to them. She even gives a cigarette to a passer-by who asks for it. The others, unwilling to share their source of handouts, suggest Shen Teh should refuse such people on the pretext that the shop is not hers but belongs to a relative who demands exact bookkeeping. A carpenter comes and makes a scene about the shelves, which, he claims, Mrs Shin has not paid for. Shen Teh recognises his claim but needs time to pay; she allows the parasites to persuade him to write out a bill to her non-existent cousin, the fictive owner of the business. The landlady of the building, Mrs Mi Tzu, comes with a form of agreement regarding the lease of the shop; she wants personal references which the ex-prostitute cannot of course provide. So Shen Teh unwillingly uses the name of her cousin, Shui Ta, in Shung. Meanwhile various arrivals have swollen the number of the parasite family to eight, and they all smoke and drink and sing a song to entertain the hostess. They fight and demolish the shelving, and even more of them arrive outside demanding entrance. Shen Teh sees her dinghy pulled down by the hands of too many drowning people.

Interlude: Under a bridge. The gods appear to Wang in a dream and ask him to watch the progress of Shen Teh's charity while they are looking elsewhere for more good people.

Scene 2: 'Quick Rebuilding of a Livelihood by Hardness.' The Tobacconist's. The parasites are roused from sleep by a knocking, and let in a young gentleman who introduces himself as the cousin Shui Ta. Shen Teh, he says, is detained elsewhere and can do nothing for them any more. They respond by planning a theft of cakes from the local baker and a search party for Shen Teh to come and restrain Shui Ta. Shui Ta merely reflects that no one person can help all the poor in the town, and sets about dealing with the carpenter; since the shelves are made to measure and it is no use taking them away, the carpenter has to accept a fifth of the price he demanded. In order to get rid of the parasites, Shui Ta then starts a leisurely conversation with the local policeman, which he prolongs until the cake thief returns and is thus caught red-handed. The parasites are led off. Next the landlady: Shui Ta uses all his powers of persuasion without getting her to revise her demand for six months' rent in advance. The policeman, worried lest he lose such an excellent supporter of authority as Shui Ta, helps him to think how to raise the sum: marry Shen Teh off to some well-to-do man, to be found by a newspaper advertisement which the policeman drafts for the relieved and grateful cousin.

Scene 3: 'The Good Person, looking for one to help her, finds one whom she can help.' Evening in a public park. Two prostitutes are waiting, without much hope in view of the rainy weather, for customers, as Shen Teh passes through on the way to meet a widower whom she hopes to marry. She notices Yang Sun, a trained pilot who is looking for somewhere to hang himself because he cannot find a flying job. She stays with him in order to stop his suicide, the immediate cause of which she sees in the bad weather – the last straw to one who is so miserable. As her sentimentality leads quickly to tears, it is soon unclear who is trying to cheer whom up. They like each other. Shen Teh shows her good mood by buying water from Wang although it is raining and she could have it free.

Interlude: Wang's sleeping-place under a culvert. Wang tells the gods, who appear to him in a dream, of Shen Teh's progress. They are not dissatisfied with her charity but discontent that she has failed to pay the carpenter: she must fulfil the letter of the law, and to see that episode as regrettably necessary business ethics does not appeal to them either; they are in an intolerant mood because they are finding no good people anywhere.

Scene 4: 'Unfortunately only the cousin can help the beloved.' Square in front of Shen Teh's shop. Shen Teh's neighbour, the stout barber Shu Fu, chases Wang – whose water-vending he finds importunate – out of his salon and hits him over the hand with a pair of curling tongs. Mrs Shin and others, who are waiting for Shen Teh – who has been out all night – commiserate. Shen Teh arrives with a lyrical monologue on the beauties of the town in the morning, and goes into a neighbouring carpet shop to buy a shawl. Shu Fu admires her beauty. Shen Teh discusses with the old couple who own the carpet shop the necessity of raising a half-year's rent; for the man she loves has no capital. The wife offers to lend her the money, since they are favourably impressed by her charitableness. But when Shen Teh comes across and has Wang's injured hand pointed out to her, her happiness is dissipated. Everybody present agrees that Wang can sue Shu Fu for damages, but none of them want anything to do with the courts as witnesses. Such lack of solidarity shocks Shen Teh, who determines to go to court herself and say she saw the incident, rather than leave Wang in the lurch.

Mrs Yang, Sun's mother, runs up. Sun has the chance of a job in Peking but needs 500 dollars to clinch it. Shen Teh, clear that a pilot must be given the chance to fly, immediately hands over the 200 dollars the old couple have given her, and decides she will have to call on Shui Ta again to raise the rest.

Interlude: Shen Teh dresses as Shui Ta whilst singing the 'Song of the Defencelessness of the Good and the Gods'.

Scene 5: 'But the cousin discovers the badness of the beloved. This, admittedly, does nothing to help the woman in love.' The tobacconist's. Shui Ta is reading the paper and not listening to Mrs Shin's attempts to marry Shen Teh off to Shu Fu. Sun arrives to see about his 300 dollars; Shui Ta is cool and asks what the 500 dollars are needed for. Sun explains he has to induce the superintendent to find a pretext to sack a good pilot. Shui Ta objects that the man could then sell Sun in the same way in a short time; and the proposal means selling the shop. Sun should rather run the shop – a proposal the pilot treats with scorn. Mrs Mi Tzu comes and they try to sell the shop to her – Sun for 300 dollars, Shui Ta for 500 so that he can repay the old couple. But as there is no written agreement with them, Shui Ta is soon persuaded to come down to 300, and provisional agreement is reached. There is however no spare money for the expenses of a move to Peking, and it comes out that Sun intends to go to Peking alone and leave the girl behind to fend for herself. Shui Ta thereon claims the 200 dollars back and says Shen Teh will doubtless not want to sell her shop on those terms. Sun disagrees: Shen Teh loves him to distraction and will not listen to Shui Ta's reasonings. After he has gone Shui Ta rants about the power of love which destroys all one's ambitions. Mrs Shin thinks the time ripe for Shu Fu's courtship and brings him. Shui Ta explains to him that Shen Teh has thrown away 200 dollars in one day and the shop is on the brink of ruin. Shu Fu expresses his readiness to help Shen Teh's charitable actions, for instance by lending her empty houses to shelter the homeless in. Wang arrives with the policeman, looking for his witness; Shui Ta gives him Shen Teh's new shawl as a sling for his arm, but says Shen Teh did not witness the incident and has too many troubles of her own to be able to start fresh ones by perjuring herself for Wang; nor will Shui Ta do anything against Shu Fu. Wang has to retreat, Shui Ta agrees to get Shen Teh to meet Shu Fu for a discreet meal, and goes into the back room. Shu Fu congratulates himself on his tact and generosity, and writes off Sun as a rival of no account. Sun returns wanting to know what is going on, but Shu Fu stops him going into the inner room where Shui Ta and Shen Teh are talking. Shen Teh emerges and confirms that she espouses Shui Ta's ideas. Sun however exerts himself, his fascination takes hold and Shen Teh goes off with him.

Interlude: Shen Teh on her way to her wedding with Sun hopes that what Sun said to Shui Ta was merely masculine boastfulness, and that she will be able to persuade Sun to give up his aeronautical ambitions and return the 200 dollars to the old couple, whom she had forgotten in the excitement of the previous scene and who are now worried about the safety of their money.

Scene 6: 'Where Shen Teh goes, Shui Ta cannot go.' Private room in a cheap suburban restaurant. The wedding party is ready to begin, except that Sun will not proceed because Shen Teh refuses to sell the shop for him because of the 200 dollar debt. He has sent for Shui Ta to make it clear to Shen Teh that if she holds out the creditors will seize the shop anyway, so she would be better advised at least to sell it and secure his job with the proceeds. Shen Teh remains unaware of this hitch. Sun tries to pass the time with jokes, while the priest gets impatient. Mrs Yang too is worried because the little wine they have ordered is running out. Eventually they tell Shen Teh they are waiting for Shui Ta, and she realises it is because of the 300 dollars; but Sun refuses to talk business with her, he insists on seeing Shui Ta. Shen Teh says he cannot come. Sun on the other hand is convinced he will and will bring the money. Shen Teh says he will not, because he thinks Sun is going to abandon her. Sun shows her two pieces of paper – two tickets to Peking! Shen Teh is very tempted to throw caution to the winds, but still remembers that if she completes the 500 for the job it can only be by robbing the old couple – to say nothing of an innocent pilot in Peking who has to lose his job. The guests are by now all aware that something is wrong; the priest goes and the guests follow. Sun sees his ambitions thwarted.

Interlude: Wang's sleeping-place. In a dream Wang expresses to the gods his fear that Shen Teh is too good for this world, that even the repeated appearance of the hard-hearted cousin cannot save the shop. The gods refuse to help: the good person is best shown by and in adversity – though so far they have not found any good people living decently . . .

Scene 7: 'To help Shen Teh's little son, Shui Ta has to sacrifice the little sons of many people.' Yard behind Shen Teh's shop. Shen Teh faces ruin, as to raise the old couple's money she has to sell out to Mrs Mi Tzu. But Shu Fu arrives, incapable of standing by while her charity comes to such an end, and gives her a blank cheque. Mrs. Shin finds this marvellous, but Shen Teh has no intention of accepting the money. She is pregnant by Sun. In a dramatic monologue she imagines herself with a growing son, a budding aviator and cherry-thief. Wang comes with a little boy, a waif whom he hopes Shen Teh will do something for. Shen Teh thinks of Shu Fu's empty premises. Wang's hand is useless; she gives him things to sell so that he can go to a doctor. Mrs Shin is annoyed that Shen Teh gives away the little she has left. Two of the parasitical family arrive with bales of tobacco they have stolen; they want Shen Teh to take care of them until the police lose the scent, then they want to start a little factory. Shen Teh agrees and they put the bales in the inner room. The orphan meanwhile fishes in the rubbish for something to eat; Shen Teh vows her son shall not have to do that, however hard she has to be to others to guarantee it. She decides to turn into Shui Ta, she hopes for the last time; Mrs Shin sees her going into the inner room and suspects what is going on. Parasites gather, all hoping she will call Shui Ta and save the shop so that they can start living off her again. Shui Ta emerges with plans: they can all live in Shu Fu's warehouses and work – utilising the tobacco Shen Teh has in the inner room. The shop will be kept, the rent being paid by filling in Shu Fu's cheque for 10,000 dollars. The parasites accept their fate with ill grace, the old couple and Wang are disappointed at Shen Teh's disappearance.

Interlude: Wang reports to the gods that Shen Teh is unable to bear the burden of so many commandments; but they do not agree with his suggestions for reducing it.

Scene 8: 'What Shen Teh has promised is kept by Shui Ta.' Shui Ta's tobacco factory. In Shu Fu's premises a number of poor families, very crowded, are working. Mrs Yang comes to the front of the stage to report how Sun has got on in Shui Ta's factory. The episodes of this story are dramatised. First Mrs Yang goes to see Shui Ta, who had filed a writ alleging breach of promise and fraud to the extent of 200 dollars. Sun has of course spent the money. Shui Ta offers him the chance to pay it off by working in the new tobacco factory. Soon Sun distinguishes himself in Shui Ta's eyes by carrying three bales of tobacco at once to help an aged colleague; Shui Ta sees this and orders the old worker too to take three. On pay day Sun refuses a day's pay which is credited to him by the foreman – who likes to make mistakes in the pay for the employees' benefit. Shui Ta thus becomes aware of this deception and Sun gets the foreman's job. Instead of rising literally as a pilot, he rises in his career on the earth, by insisting on hard work from all.

Scene 9: 'Has Shui Ta murdered his cousin Shen Teh?' Shen Teh's shop, now a counting-house. The old couple have had a letter containing their money, but Shui Ta cannot tell them where Shen Teh is. He is very fat – seven months gone, and relying on Mrs Shin's well-paid discretion and care. Sun comes with a briefcase and tries to get Shui Ta, who he thinks has been slipping recently, to take some interest in the details of the business. He attributes Shui Ta's vagueness and irritability to rumours coursing in the area, and to rainy weather, which always makes Shui Ta melancholy. Wang, outside, laments the loss of the good Shen Teh who always bought water from him even in the rain, and who entered this house months ago never to emerge. He comes in to ask Shui Ta for information, and in the course of talk lets drop that he knows she was pregnant when she disappeared. He goes and Shui Ta retires to the inner room. Sun is suddenly interested in Shen Teh again now that he sees himself as a potential father; he hears sobbing within and suspects Shui Ta is merely hiding Shen Teh. When Shui Ta returns Sun attempts to blackmail him on this basis, threatening to join forces with Wang and the police in searching for Shen Teh. When he has gone Shui Ta brings out objects belonging to Shen Teh, but hides them under the table as he hears steps: Mrs Mi Tzu and Shu Fu, with whom he is negotiating plans to extend the tobacco manufactory and establish a chain of shops. Sun and Wang return with the policeman. They find that there is no one in the inner room, but a bundle of Shen Teh's things under the table; Shui Ta goes to assist the police with their inquiries.

Interlude: Wang tells the gods of Shen Teh's disappearance and Shui Ta's arrest. Since they have found no good people, but only war and misery, and are on the point of having to admit that their moral system places too great demands on people, they take a keen interest in Shen Teh and decide she must be found.

Scene 10: 'The gods interrogate the murderer of their good person.' Courtroom. The group of poor people despair of getting justice from the trial, as Shui Ta has friends in common with the judge and has bribed him. But instead of the judge the three gods appear. Shui Ta faints but recovers. The gods hear the policeman, Shu Fu and Mrs Mi Tzu in favour of Shui Ta; the poor on the other hand list Shui Ta's misdeeds. Shui Ta defends himself: he only came to do the dirty work necessary for the popular Shen Teh to keep her shop, so he is hated. In a fast-moving argument Shui Ta's business and personal dealings are summarised. He insists throughout that all he did was intended to save Shen Teh from being ruined by the excessive demands made on her charity, but eventually, worn down by the attacks, agrees to make a confession to the judges alone. The court is cleared and Shui Ta unmasks himself. Shen Teh describes her feelings and the difficulty of loving according to their commandments: she was too small for their great plans. The first god interrupts her, says they can be satisfied that there is someone bearing the lantern of goodness in the world, and gives signs for a pink cloud to collect them and return them to the higher regions. Shen Teh cannot see how she is supposed to go on, among people she has disappointed, pregnant, caught between Sun and Shu Fu. The witnesses re-enter to see the disappearance of the gods, who allow Shen Teh to call in her cousin not more than once a month and are deaf to her pleas that this is not enough to help her.

Epilogue. An actor regrets the bitter ending of the play and invites the audience to think of a solution: there must be a good one!

(II) THE PARABLE PLAY

The appearance of the gods attaches this play to an old theatrical tradition which reached its apogee in Raimund's Viennese magic-plays of the last century where the juxtaposition of the human (all-too-human) and divine worlds is used comically, satirically but still not without some remnant of naïve wonderment. The subject of a divine visitation is of course one of the oldest in world literature. Reinhold Grimm speculates that Brecht based his plot on the destruction of Sodom and Gomorrha (Genesis 19): as Lot took in the two angels and was the only good person of his town, so is Shen Teh in hers. The motif of the world or town being saved if there are enough good people is shared.[3] The rest of the story, admittedly, is radically altered. Esslin finds the first germ of the subject in Brecht's biography in an incident of 1926 when Brecht, Döblin and Bronnen met with a shabby reception in Dresden; Brecht wrote a poem at the time in which the three writers appear as gods able to threaten rain and flooding (8, 158f.). Finally, the specific element of the prostitute's hospitality to a god is to be found in Goethe's poem *Der Gott und die Bajadere*.

Within this loose framework of tradition and reference, the plot is an invented one, as is that of *The Caucasian Chalk Circle*, in which once again the traditional motif will only be a jumping-off point for Brecht's imagination; and it is invented with a single lesson in mind, which sets it apart from *Galileo* but implies a close relationship with *Mother Courage*: that play proves that war is a continuation of business by other means, *The Good Person* shows that business is a kind of war. But it is a play of obviously much more symbolic type. The symbolic narration pointing to a single lesson is in Brecht's terminology a parable. The characters and situations of the parable are recognisable, logical within themselves so as to be effective in stage terms. Factory workers, a poor self-employed small trader, a prostitute turned shopkeeper, petty landlords, artisans, layabouts — the persons of the play are familiar types generalised enough for Brecht to make their story apply to all societies based on capitalist exploitation.

The stage-directions' evocation of a transitional Szechwan, a province whose sky is alternately occupied by gods and mail-planes, is obviously unrealistic. Hans Mayer has shown that Szechwan is a model, a version of a split pluralistic society reduced to a small scale and with salient features emphasised, like Brecht's Mahagonny before it and Frisch's Andorra and Dürrenmatt's Güllen (in *The Visit*) after it. The model is very complex and fragile: 'interesting how every little error of calculation comes back at one with these thin steel constructions', Brecht notes (*Aj.*, 1, 45: 15.3.39). There are elements of massivity: Shen Teh is 'a big strong person'; the town is 'big, dusty, un-livable in' (*Aj.*, 1, 52: May 1939). But they are not very heavy anchors for a structure which has nothing to spare, from the very formal exposition at the beginning leading into the gods' arrival, to the verse epilogue at the end after their final departure: elements of circularity. Brecht uses the sequence of gestic elements and controls the tempo with particular care, introducing short lyrical interludes in Chinese style to add to the play's charm and a comic scene when Sun and the wedding party wait in vain for the impossible. The parable play supports better than other types straight apostrophes to the public, the sheer fantasy of Wang's reports to the gods in his dreams, and songs sticking out of the text. These make a contrast to the more brutal parts of the content, the depiction of exploitation and cruelty (see especially 1531–3: 41f.; opening sections of scene 4), but also loosen the structure, provide something enjoyable and ornamental. 'hard where the aim is rigidly laid down to give the tiny little scenes that element of irresponsibility, chance, that feeling of just scraping through (*dieses . . . passable*) that is called "life"!' (*Aj.*, 1, 144: 9.8.40).

The action proceeds on differing planes. The plane of dramatic action is broken up by the interludes with Wang and the gods, in which the action is commented on, summarised and seen through the gods' eyes. The apostrophes to the audience allow us to judge both of these planes and their relationship, and thus come to a conclusion about the relevance of the gods.[4] The constant reappearance of the gods with no sign that they have power to do anything useful is part of Brecht's message. Nor can he put gods on the stage without parody. Their trio at the end bears echoes of Goethe's *Faust II* and of *A Midsummer Night's Dream* in A. W. Schlegel's translation. Elsewhere too Brecht manages a little literary satire, as when the unemployed man takes a cigarette in order to become 'a new man', the mystically transformed expressionist hero – and goes off coughing (1509; 14; 1). Not that Brecht rejects the idea of a new mankind – the epilogue suggests it; but certainly not through tobacco alone!

The rigid structure itself may be seen from a scheme from Brecht's working notes (Shen Teh and her cousin are referred to by different names at this stage, but the sense remains).

The Good Deeds of Li Gung
(1) sheltering a family
(3) saving a man in despair
(4) false witness for a victim
(5) trust in the beloved
(6) trust is not disappointed
(7) surety for those who want to improve themselves
(8) everything for her child

The Misdeeds of Lao Go
(2) delivering a family into prison
(4) discrediting the victim
(5) abandonment of the guarantors
(6) planning a marriage of convenience
(7) getting cheap premises by misrepresentation
(8) exploiting children
(9) exploiting the beloved (the tobacco queen) (*Mat. S.*, 87)

Another note (*Mat. S.*, 88) consists of a list of bad deeds showing where they are committed in the play.

With its complex action and psychological development, the play tended to grow too long. Brecht seems to have feared it would grow to five hours, and tried to cut it to two-and-a-half (*Aj.*, 1, 54: 15.7.39). The plot has 'three sections chronologically presented and governed by Shen Teh's three goals: to help her neighbors, to love her lover, and to protect her unborn child from want.'[5] Between them, these three sections put the question of why evil flourishes in the world and good has such a difficult time.

This play is more open-ended than any other of Brecht's. Mother Courage went on with her war, but one could say that the loss of her last child had some finality about it; whereas Shen Teh is pregnant and only at the beginning of her troubles. Further sections like those in the play might succeed each other indefinitely. The epilogue draws attention to this lack of an ending and asks the audience to supply it.[6] Thus the communicative elements, the appeal to the recipient and the refernce-back to reality are clearer here than anywhere else in Brecht.

(III) A CHINESE PLAY?

Brecht first took up the theme in a European context; when he took up the Chinese locality he used it with caution. At one point he intended to have the figures eating bread rather than rice – a desperate way of avoiding the kind of local colour which makes the audience think such an exotic play does not concern their own life (*Aj.*, 1, 126: 2.7.40). The play has nothing to do with twentieth-century Chinese developments, not because Brecht had never come across any information or could not have written a topical play had he wanted – he apparently took details such as the name Shu Fu from Friedrich Wolf's topical play *Tai Yang erwacht*, staged by Piscator in 1931 – but because for his purposes he was more interested in the classical Chinese.[7] Most names and quotations are genuine. The poem demanding a blanket to cover the whole city (1512; 23f.; 2) is borrowed from Arthur Waley's anthology *170 Chinese Poems*,[8] the reflection 'To let none go to waste . . .' (1553; 60; Interlude before 6) is 'a reformulation of a saying by Mo Tzu as translated by Alfred Forke'.[9] The dramaturgical techniques of self-presentation and commenting songs have affinities with Chinese theatre; the title role with its 'charade work' (*Aj.*, 1, 45: 15.3.39), changing of clothes on stage, use of a mask, opportunity for an actress to play a man's role with the underlying demonstration of the woman hidden in the man, is inseparable from Brecht's views on Chinese acting. Peach trees, cranes and silver dollars give local colour.

Pseudo-Chinese, on the other hand, is the way in which members of the lower classes are able to quote the classics; so is the gods' view that suffering purifies (1565; 70; Interlude after 6) – a Christian element, for in Chinese thought suffering merely deforms. Brecht's thought here is closer to Chinese models, notably his favourite Mo Tzu (Me-ti), than is the thinking of the gods – it is Shen Teh whose name means 'divine effectiveness'. Antony Tatlow has pointed out also weighty parallels between Brecht and Mencius in the matter of the basic goodness of man perverted by social circumstances, and of the difficulty of being bad, which people only become because of the force of hunger and thirst.[10]

(IV) THE GODS AND THE GOOD

The gods stand for exactly defined moral standards which the individual is expected to reach regardless of his conditions of life. They are seen investigating whether it is in fact possible for anyone to reach the standard of love, justice and honour (Interlude after 7). If one can, they finally say, then all could. Such moral demands made without consideration of each individual's social handicaps are reminiscent of Kant's categorical imperative, which places the onus on each person to behave so that his deeds could be taken as the paradigm of a universal and benevolent law. Such idealism is to Brecht simply the ideological apologia for capitalism, with its stress on individual strivings both in the field of money-making and in the field of moral self-perfection. Brecht wants to examine the Kantian demands against the real background. Idealism explains frustrations met by the individual in the pursuit of goodness by concepts such as that of divine providence testing the individual with a view to reward or punishment hereafter. Shen Teh's peculiarity is that, rather than accepting the well-known paradox of a perfect God (gods) creating an imperfect world, and doing her best in such a world, she expects the gods to share her active, dynamic goodness and back up her single-handed attempt to change the predicament of the inhabitants of Szechwan. Wang, for instance, reconciles himself to his inability to keep all the divine commandments properly; but she does not. In the 'Song of the Defencelessness of the Good and the Gods' (Interlude after scene 4) she asks with increasing force why the gods do not have the armed power to impose goodness on the world, why good is powerless. This demand to know underlies the play – but because she unquestioningly aligns herself with her idea of the gods, Shen Teh cannot perceive the answer, which is that the gods have disqualified themselves from helping.[11] They represent a pantheon which refuses any responsibility for economic affairs, sees earthly life increasingly dominated by economics, and yet would like to cling to the fiction that it is in authority. This declining class, comparable to the Church and the feudalists in *Galileo*, is disunited within itself as to what concessions can be made to economic and technical facts: whether they can admit that floods are due to neglect of dams, not to their wrath (1491; 5; Prologue) – thus implying that men are masters of their own fate; whether they can help Shen Teh along or even compensate her for loss of earnings when she takes them in. They show just that passivity which she does not; in a sarcastic reversal of the classical concept of *deus ex machina*[12] they call on a pink cloud at the end to take them away and save them the embarrassment of trying to regulate her existence. To admit a flaw in the world and envisage changing it (1605; 107; 10) would be to deny their own divinity; they prefer to believe, in the way long since castigated by Wilhelm Busch, that 'nicht sein kann, was nicht sein darf': what does not fit their precepts is *ipso facto* impossible and illusory – a vulgar-idealist error. They disappear into nothingness, the particular end Brecht reserves for what has outlined its historical function and can be forgotten. They are, to paraphrase Engels, 'Supreme Beings shut out from the whole existing world: a contradiction in terms, and an insult to the feelings of religious people'.[13]

So Shen Teh cannot become a saint, the 'Angel to the Slums' (1604; 106; 10); her 'goldene Legende' (1607; 109 – 'golden myth' is not quite the same; Epilogue) cannot be written; what we see is not perfect behaviour, but the only possible behaviour of a potentially good person.[14] Martyrdom too is impossible: unlike Johanna Dark (*Saint Joan of the Stockyards*) Shen Teh is not free to ruin her health in working among the poor and die in a passionate apotheosis. With a child on the way, she must fight on and harden herself to the rest of the world as the price of goodness to her flesh and blood.

Wang, at the beginning, awaits the gods' coming with the religious expectation that they will transform the unholiness of earthly life. For two thousand years the gods have been hearing that life is too hard for their commandments to be fulfilled (1492; 6; Prologue). Brecht shows what can really be expected from the return of the gods.[15] Wang tries to mediate between gods and men, but men have other things to think about. The gods are unable even to find lodgings by themselves, they are quite dependent on man, only as important as men let them be. In fact the presentation of the religious realm accords with Marx's thought (*Theses on Feuerbach*, IV): 'that the secular foundation detaches itself from itself and establishes itself in the clouds as an independent realm is really only to be explained by the self-cleavage and self-contradictoriness of this secular basis. The latter must itself, therefore, first be understood in its contradiction and then, by the removal of the contradiction, revolutionised in practice.' The gods represent a *status quo* and oppose their inertia to any social change. Shen Teh's goodness, useful to them as proof of the thesis that anyone can be good in the world they set up, is also useful to the parasites who feed off Shen Teh. Like the trees Wang mentions (Interlude after 6), she is cut down because she is useful. But she grows again in the form of Shui Ta, becomes a duality, the example of Luther's statement that man is always *simul iustus et peccator*, just and sinful at the same time. In Luther's thought the contradiction is resolved by divine grace, promising redemption from the necessary sinfulness of human life and pardoning the sinner, if not the sin. Shen Teh expects something of the sort from the gods when she admits that she as a poor human was too small for their projects (1604; 106; 10). But they have no grace to bestow.[16] Brecht cannot pardon the sinner: for the total of sinners adds up to bourgeois society, and the individual bourgeois must not be accused and then absolved, but – in the terms of the *Communist Manifesto* – be made impossible.

The gods by their unworldly generosity enable Shen Teh to convert herself from a marginal petit-bourgeois (self-employed with no capital) into a fully-fledged one (capital tied up in trading assets; no employees) and thence – as Shui Ta – into a capitalist (exploiter of wage-labour). But at the same time her natural goodness is codified into virtue[17] – she is supposed to live by the divine precepts in order to leave the divine prejudices unshaken. The dogmatisation of virtue, reaching its apogee with Kant, accompanies the historical development of early capitalism. According to the *Communist Manifesto* the only way to remain an individual is to be a capitalist. Only for the capitalist's benefit is society structured. Thus here in the last scene the policeman introduces Shui Ta as 'a man of principle . . . always on the side of the law' (1598; 100). That he saved Shen Teh from perjuring herself in the case of Wang against Shu Fu is a point in his favour; yet precisely Shen Teh's false evidence would have contributed to getting Wang justice, where all others hesitate to oppose Shu Fu because of his riches and influence.[18] As later in *The Caucasian Chalk Circle*, Brecht is for disregarding the forms and precepts of the law, a law which is an 'outgrowth of the conditions of bourgeois production and bourgeois property' (*Communist Manifesto*) and so *ipso facto* suspect.

Shen Teh's active goodness, the mainspring of the action, shows itself primarily in generosity: the inability to say no. Nature is for Brecht unboundedly generous. In scene 3 the rain symbolises this, water enough to waste – and it puts Wang out of work, as his song (1526f.; 36f.) graphically states.[19] Shen Teh buys water from Wang in the rain to refresh Sun whom she saves from suicide: her bounty, like the rain, falls on the just and the unjust. She fights throughout the play to unleash her affinity with nature itself, to give as freely as the 'great udder of the clouds' (a phrase from the song, 1527, lost in translation), to keep Sun happy, to protect Wang, to feed her parasites, to provide for her baby. Others lack this naturalness, and then she is shocked by their indifference: 'When an injustice takes place in a town there must be an uproar . . .' (1536; 45; 4). They are responsible for their own fates. But Shen Teh too is soon involved in imperfection. When, to secure a basis for her charity, she attempts to make a rich marriage, she is just as much a whore as when she waited in the park for customers. In each case financial relationships intrude on personal ones. When she falls in love with Sun she frees herself from the money nexus – only to fall back into it because he needs her cash for his purposes. When we first see him he is about to hang himself out of a frustrated desire to be a pilot. He is genuine enough, he only wants to realise his talents; but that, in this imperfect world, depends on money. Shen Teh's prosperity comes opportunely for him; he involves her in expense. Love is, as Shui Ta says, a catastrophe – it costs money (1546; 54; 5). And when Shen Teh loves, she moves in a world where she is seen as a sex object. No sooner has she escaped the life of a prostitute than she falls between Sun and Shu Fu, the one of whom wants to get money from her by playing on her feelings, while the other is willing to pay to be allowed to play on her feelings. The transfer from prostitution to love, business to generosity, cannot be made unilaterally. In her love for Sun, Shen Teh wants to provide him with the means to satisfy his ambitions, to gratify her own wish for uncommercial love, and to be fair to others by returning the old couple's 200 dollars on request. The task is hopeless: a penniless lover or husband is something she cannot afford.[20] Later, obsessed by the welfare of her unborn child, she can afford no goodness to anyone else. Her pregnancy paradoxically does more to force her into masculine attitudes than anything else in the play.[21] To assert herself, she has to behave like everyone else: in a man's world, she must be a man.

The old couple lend money with the same self-denying goodness as Shen Teh, and are indeed ruined when Shui Ta does not repay the debt promptly; and they believe in no gods, pure as their goodness is. Unfortunately what they intend for the good Shen Teh becomes an element in the calculations of Shui Ta, who happens to be a capitalist without capital and dependent on money brought in by Shen Teh's reputation – nobody is going to give him money. 'Why bark for him, they say, he's a dog himself!' (*Mat. S.*, 89). The same happens to Shu Fu's blank cheque; but Shu Fu's munificence, coming from riches gained by brutality such as he shows to Wang, is tainted. Giving money is a sign of goodwill, but of limited significance – objectively and subjectively.

A puzzling element in the configuration of the play is the one which corresponds to those who help Shen Teh with money: the parasites who batten on her goodness and take her money. The first to arrive of the family of eight are her former landlord and his wife, who had thrown her out when she was penniless. They are not too soft to make their way in life, and they have, or had, property. Yet here they are, with all the family including a niece who is prostitute, begging. Mrs Shin has just sold the tobacco shop to Shen Teh for a four-figure sum, but immediately she reappears with a rice-bowl, behaving as if Shen Teh had somehow evicted her and left her to starve. Was she so deeply in debt that the price of the shop went on repayments, and was Shen Teh such a bad businesswoman as to buy this highly suspect business completely unexamined? Then in the course of the play the poor who form Shui Ta's workforce are joined by the carpenter and his family; is there not enough work in Szechwan to keep him independent? The stage of economic development at which the play is set is not the one at which manual tradesmen are so easily put out of business, and even if we allow a little licence here, we still have to ask – in vain – what the parade of the utterly shiftless and temperamentally dishonest represented by the family of eight is supposed to prove about economic relationships.

(v) THE SPLIT CHARACTER

Shen Teh/Shui Ta is the most clear-cut of all Brecht's split characters. In the real world – and still more in Szechwan, the exaggerated model of the real world – the prostitute with a heart of gold, that popular literary paradox, has no chance. Brecht allows her to use the invented cousin: not a bad, but a realistic cousin, Mayer (p. 177) suggests. He appears with a theatrical flourish reminiscent of Pirandello; and he is not without his own sense of the precariousness of existence, though it has a social dimension shared by no Pirandello figure. His brutality is explained by his upbringing 'in the gutter' (1546; 54; 5); he is keenly aware of the dangers to the individual's survival which lurk in love and generosity. If Shen Teh represents Brecht's pleasure principle – give freely of yourself – Shui Ta represents his reality principle[22] – charity begins at home. He exerts himself to subjectively good ends: to keep the shop on whose profits Shen Teh's charity depends, to establish a secure future for the child. Shen Teh would like to do these things but lacks the brutality. That she unwillingly adopts the mask of the cousin does not make her completely brutal. Brecht wants not to attack capitalists, but to show what makes a capitalist and how he too is subject to alienation. Other plays have similar themes: Mother Courage sees – or thinks she sees – that only by exploiting others can she do the right thing by her own children. Shen Teh realises that to continue her charity she must exploit others. Mother Courage at the end still hopes to make her fortune from war; Shen Teh still does not realise that the gods, whilst demanding absolute individual goodness, cannot provide her with the means to realise their demand.[23] Yet unlike *Mother Courage* the play has not attracted many un-Marxist or anti-Marxist interpretations: perhaps because the audience is less tempted to empathise with a protagonist who appears for so much of the play in the visually obvious form of an exploiter, rather than claiming always to be the suffering mother-figure as Mother Courage does.

More or less schizophrenic variations in the conduct of the same character are of course nothing new in literature. *Dr. Jekyll and Mr. Hyde* may be said to have set the subject going.[24] Social pressures forcing the meek and kindly individual to adopt an overbearing exterior are seen in comic form in Voigt, the hero of Zuckmayer's *Captain of Köpenick* (1930); unable to get valid personal papers from the bureaucratic system by fair means, he adopts the uniform and bearing of an army officer so that he can trick his way into a passport office (and, a born loser, chooses a town hall without a passport office to raid). In Brecht's work the theme occurs in *Man is Man*. Galy Gay, an ineffectual person who, like Shen Teh, cannot say no, kindly agrees to help a squad of soldiers out by standing in for an absent comrade – and is forcibly converted into a brutal fighting machine. This benefits imperialism and represents a social alienation. Many of Brecht's plays show the impulse to do good coming up against social pressures. In one case, *The Measures Taken*, the pressures are approved of: they are exerted by the Communist party in the interest of the long-term amelioration of working conditions, as against short-term help which alters nothing basic; the young party worker lets his heart rule his head, jeopardises his comrades' work and comes to a bad end. In *Puntila* the landowner is expansive, easy-going and humane when drunk, a cold struggler to keep up his position when sober. Like Shen Teh, he can be humane only by disregarding his alienation in the concrete socio-economic situation.[25] But his case is a comic one: his excesses of humanity do not weaken his socio-economic position.

Shen Teh lives in a world where many people need the generosity of others; she has as the best part of her personality the desire to help them, and (Brecht posits) it is objectively in line with social necessities. But in a town whose systematised misery has dragged on for eleven hundred years (1512; 23; 2) one person cannot help: the dinghy of individual charity is swamped by the numbers of the drowning (1508f.; 20; 1). Shen Teh is thus frustrated in trying to do good, as was Galileo in trying to increase knowledge and ease human life. A society which allows social injustice to go on, and does not even allow the charitable individual to do his best to stop it, is for Brecht one that must be changed. Most of us accustom ourselves to the evils which Shen Teh refuses to treat as inevitable. She is sensitive and open to humane impulses, and to see society through her eyes is a salutary experience for us. For her, goodness – self-sacrifice – is a terrible temptation, a self-indulgence. She is not completely selfless, but a *Mensch*, a human being, first (*Aj.*, 1, 116: 20.6.40). She wants to do good to herself as well as to others (1553; 60; Interlude after 5), indulging in a love for Sun which is economic nonsense when she has a rich widower lined up. Nor is Shui Ta completely egoistic: he returns the 200 dollars of the old couple (though too late); but for most purposes he shows that 'in order to realise his goodness man must renounce his goodness . . . This tragic dilemma is clearly imposed by society.'[26] The most extreme alienation is Shen Teh's alienation from herself, the metamorphosis of the angel of the suburbs into the tobacco king. Charity and exploitation are sides of the same coin. The better any one of us tries to be, the more he is a potential victim of this transformation. We should all like to be good. There is no figure in the play who is purely an exploiter – Brecht removed a tobacco monopolist, Feh Pung, who made things hard for Shen Teh, no doubt partly because trusts and monopolies do not fit the stage of economic development shown in the play, but also in order not to provide an easy target. Rather, the exploiters come from the ranks of the exploited. The dramatic rebuilding of Shen Teh's personality is merely an extreme demonstration of this. Becoming Shui Ta is deeply painful to Shen Teh (1603; 106; 10); for Brecht, to be evil is a hard fate, as the poem *The Mask of Evil* says – a personal counterpart to the question Shen Teh asks the audience: 'To trample on one's fellows / Is surely exhausting? . . .' (1570; 75; 7). Like Galy Gay, Shen Teh is brainwashed into aggressiveness – though with her the process is (apparently) reversible.

When the pregnant Shen Teh, seeing a child fishing in rubbish bins, decides that her child shall not have to do that, she paradoxically needs to be Shui Ta more than ever, to amass money for the child. The woman must complete her armoury by drawing on the resources of the man; the maternal instinct calls forth the paternal instinct. Feminine weaknesses, charity and love, must be limited by masculine hard-headedness and ruthlessness in imposing a system of priorities. Shen Teh becomes more deeply a mixture of the frustrated strivings and uninhibited brutalities of capitalist, charitable *homo sapiens*: masculine and feminine, yin and yang. This development also involves even the spectator who so far has seen Shen Teh's charity as rather unnecessary softness to a set of layabouts. Now, it is seen that even if we believe charity both begins and ends at home, we must still – in the capitalist system – accept that it requires brutality. Shen Teh will stop trying to save everyone else and devote herself to one person and still – indeed more than ever – need Shui Ta (1572; 77; 7). Furthermore, her wish to ensure that her child will never see the odious but necessary Shui Ta threatens to cut him off from true understanding of reality, of how his prosperity is achieved. 'The life and happiness of the new generation is to rest on a fraud', on the myth of a world 'without exploitation, competition and evil'.[27] Shen Teh, who believes in the gods, comes finally to an ideology much like theirs, with its blindness to glaring evils and its trust in pathetically weak manifestations of goodness; and so, though left in the lurch by the gods, she never sees through them.

Where the drama is based so exclusively on one constructed character, what have the rest of the cast to do? It might seem un-Brechtian to suggest that, as in the visionary plays of Strindberg, they are partial reflections of the central figure, yet it could help (as long as we remember that, the central figure standing for certain social facts, her reflections will do so too – not, as in Strindberg, remain quasi-unreal). What they lack is her intensity of character and consequent suffering. She is an extreme of goodness – 'She easily goes too far' (*Mat. S.*, 88). But Wang too exerts himself for the gods and for her so far as he can, and is so conscious of moral demands that he exiles himself from the town when he believes she has let the gods down and so exposed his promises as empty (1509; 21; Interlude after 1). He has not her development, though; he neither claims to live according to all the precepts of virtue, nor becomes a capitalist. His version of the good person's need to be hard in order to survive is the minor deception of a false-bottomed water measure.

Sun is less good, closer perhaps to a reflection of Shui Ta, ready to take money from any source and climb over others. But Shen Teh loves him, whereas she hates the necessity for Shui Ta. So Shui Ta is not so remote from her as her subjective view would suggest. Sun shows the full process of deformation by social pressures, whereas Shui Ta appears fully hardened from the outset. Sun's goodness is gradually squeezed out. As long as he is shown as a keen but frustrated pilot, one can sympathise. Even at the wedding scene, there is no evidence that what he shows Shen Teh is not indeed (contrary to his cynical hints to Shui Ta) two tickets to Peking. But the chaos which reigns in capitalism makes him suicidal by frustrating his talents, when there are more qualified pilots than there are jobs; the attraction of Shen Teh for him becomes confused with the attraction of a source of money; he even abandons marriage to her because it is not accompanied by the extra 300 dollars needed to secure the pilot's job. His hopes thus dashed, he presumably spends the 200 dollars he *has* got from her on drink, and is back in the same hopeless situation as when he tried to hang himself. But this time he is ready to give in and adapt to society – represented by Shui Ta, on whom he is dependent because of the threatened lawsuit over the 200 dollars. At first he is an unwilling worker; but soon his ambition to rise is at work again, diverted into making the best of the given circumstances for himself. Finally he is strong enough to make a bid for control of Shui Ta's business. To underline the change from pure young love to corrupt capitalism in his life, Brecht now brings on Mrs Mi Tzu as the repulsive lecher wanting to buy a fetching young man, just as Shu Fu wants to buy Shen Teh. Shu Fu himself, incidentally, reflects the duality too; the generous capitalist whose generosity depends on his ruthlessness. So all show some version of Shen Teh's polarity, differing according to their social origin. From poor to rich, all are engaged in various stages of the class struggle which rages around and within them.

Brecht is not the first to see the social side of goodness. Goethe had written the purest, least socially orientated drama of pure humanity in *Iphigenie*, but not – as Mayer reminds us – without awareness that the weavers of Apolda were hungry. Even for Goethe, the appeal to classical morality, in isolation, is already a dubious way of dealing with the catastrophic consequences of human frailty. By the 1830s Büchner can show in *Woyzeck* that virtue depends on a certain level of income. Brecht with his dialectical materialism wants to join the tradition of Büchner in opposition to the typically German tradition of Kantian idealism, whose uncritical propagation of the virtue of obedience to the established order played a part in bringing Germany to the militaristic-feudalist débâcle of 1914–18, which sparked off Brecht's revolt.[28]

The play's ending is open, and the epilogue refuses to spell out a lesson. Shen Teh has, however, drawn attention to the general future rather than to her own specific future when she complains of the need and desperation in this arduous world (1603; 105; 10). Brecht really does see the future as open. Obviously a fresh set of gods is the least likely solution. But new people are a possibility – some of the secondary characters in the play could quite easily become less obnoxious by taking lessons in oriental courtesy, without the need for Marxism. A certain progress is seen through the theme of aviation. The sky of the play is occupied alternately by aeroplanes, and by the gods' pink cloud. Whereas the gods do nothing for anyone, the mail-plane brings 'To friends in far countries / The friendly post' (1538; 47; 4) – where 'friendly' has overtones of a superior grace (Bonhoeffer, in one of his letters from prison, uses the word speaking of God). Interpersonal relationships are taking over from the age of belief.

But actually flying the planes is subject to human financial laws. Here Marx comes in. To get a flying job one must, as everywhere in the capitalist economy, be cruel and corrupt and encompass the dismissal of a 'highly conscientious' pilot (1542; 50; 5) in order to replace him. Because Sun has not the money to do this he cannot be a pilot. His personality-distortions thus have their origin in a situation typical of capitalism. Communism, on the other hand, means for Brecht productivity, the freeing of the individual to perform the tasks that most suit him. For Sun, a different society is needed. In the meantime, the potential advances in human relations brought about by technology are rendered impossible. In *Der Lindberghflug* ('Lindbergh's Flight', 1928–9), Brecht had still seen mainly the daring of the aviator and the positive technical advance represented by his crossing the Atlantic. But in successive reworkings of the subject, as Lindbergh became an influential proponent of fascism, Brecht stressed more the arrogance of the pilot, the claims of the masses to consideration in the exploitation of technical advances, the socially retrograde role of the proud pioneer. In the second version of *Galileo* the theme is to return in the form of the fateful consequences of the scientist's cutting himself off from ideas of social advance. Here Sun shows successively the arrogance of the pilot and the arrogance of the foreman (did Brecht know a certain parody of *The Red Flag?*), thus demonstrating Brecht's social point with greater accuracy than in the *Lehrstücke* and perhaps less strain than in *Galileo*.

(VI) EPIC-DRAMATIC TECHNIQUES

A salient feature of the play is little monologues set apart from the action, often in free rhythms or at any rate set out as poems of oriental type in which metrical qualities are less important than the extreme brevity, the recognisable progression of thought and the striking conclusion. Thus in the five lines 'They are bad . . .' (1502; 15; 1) a lesson about badness is presented by a progression from vagueness to a specific accusation in the third line, then the statement of the justification for the vice and a rhetorical question. And the lesson, that the individual is not to blame for his own badness, is obviously relevant to the play. Such passages are in effect little parables within the parable play. The songs are similarly parabolic and contribute to the statement of the play's theme;

they may have much or little to do with the action in which they are embedded. The 'Song of the Eighth Elephant' (1582f.; 87f.; 8) – in a vein influenced by Kipling[29] – has most to do with the action, having a content parallel to the situation in the scene and being intended by the workers to provoke Sun – though he does not rise to the bait. Singing is not enough to make him feel his position is endangered; he even enjoys the manifestation of rebelliousness and encourages it: the workers get rid of their discontent, and rhythmic singing increases the production rate. The 'Song of the Smoke' (1507f.; 19f.; 1), on the other hand, is introduced as entertainment and has a more complex relationship to action and theme of the play. Like the 'Song of the Great Capitulation' in *Mother Courage* it inculcates resignation or inactivity, and just after it Shen Teh seems about to despair. But those who sing it are not themselves resigned or inactive in fact (the same is true of the 'Song of Green Cheese' in scene 6). For most of the figures of the play, despair and activity alternate; they sometimes feel like giving up, as Sun does after scene 6 or Shen Teh after scene 1; then they return to attempts to shape their own fate. The motif of smoke seems to be taken from a poem of Nietzsche's on the fate of the social outcast; and the tone of the whole is asocial, a reflection of Brecht's early nihilism – the song is an adaptation of his *Der Gesang aus der Opiumhöhle* ('Song from the Opium Den', 8, 90f.) of about 1920. The audience has to formulate its own views on the lesson of the song without direct help from the context. In the Wuppertal production of 1955 Shen Teh came forward while it was being sung and drew the audience's attention to the family sitting around motionless.[30] We are intended to start thinking.

The same applies to the epilogue in which a member of the cast admits that the solution to the play's problem has not been found. We have been given enough encouragement to think in terms of social change, but not had specific remedies suggested to us. Furthermore, we are being addressed now not by a figure in the play but by an actor, a member of the same society and a child of the same age as ourselves. Brecht's words are quoted to us as still relevant. When we are directly addressed during the play, we may also be encouraged to be aware that it is an actress who is talking. Then such an aside as that in scene 3: 'In our country / There should be no dreary evenings . . .' takes on shock value: it says that, so many years after Brecht, the country we live in is still a miserable place.

In scene 8 Mrs Yang takes the role of narrator, standing between actors and public to 'describe' (1578; 83) and comment on a series of episodes showing Sun's rise to be Shui Ta's foreman. At the beginning of the scene, without moving, she shifts the setting from an unspecified place to the area in front of Shu Fu's houses: she as it were conjures them up and Shui Ta with them. The whole scene is treated as a short story and we see the events of a three-month period through the first-person narrator.[31] But there again we must think: her attitudes are not to be shared, we should be on our guard against thinking, for instance, that Sun really has bettered himself (1582; 86). The narrator, however, cannot impose herself completely on the story, any more than can the narrator in fiction; the episodes themselves are valid representations of social reality.

Shen Teh's asides to audience too have to be thought about and perhaps taken against the grain. Her lapidary abstractions about the need for patience and forbearance (1503; 15; 1) are all very well, but in the plot context the carpenter points out that as no one is patient with him he cannot be patient with Shen Teh: he needs money to feed his family. A virtue – patience – practised by one person is no virtue.

At least two figures speak to the audience as to a jury which can decide on their claims: in scene 4 Shu Fu announcing his love for Shen Teh (1533; 42) – but his behaviour to Wang just before has shown us what to think of his protestations; in scene 9 Sun showing indignation at the news of Shen Teh's pregnancy having been kept from him – but one realises that he has financial interests rather than pure paternal feelings, he wants a stick to beat Shui Ta with in order to take over the firm himself after a scandal (1588f.; 92). In any case his feelings for others are suspect to us. Thus by being appealed to directly the public is encouraged to form judgments about the behaviour of the characters, rather than sit back and let the plot flow over it.

Less dubious apostrophes to the public explain behaviour, report events or create a mood. Thus in scene 6 Shen Teh reminds us of those who are absent but the thought of whom must help her to resist Sun's attempt to drag her down (1560f.; 66f.). At the outset Wang supplies an exposition; and in scene 1 Shen Teh brings it up to date (1499; 12), with due attention to money. Her summary between scenes 5 and 6 is an instance of events being arbitrarily excluded from the dialogue and reported instead: Brecht accentuates the psychological aspect by having Shen Teh report her emotions at the meeting with the carpet-dealer's wife and superimposing her emotions at the time of reporting. She tries to minimise her shock by optimistic arguments about Sun (1553; 60). In scene 4 we saw the mood for which she reproaches herself: the mood in which love transfigures everything, even the town at dawn, and enables her to forget money (1532f.; 42).

Like other Brecht plays, *The Good Person* often requires reading against the grain or reading between the lines. The old couple smile at each other (1534; 44; 4) when Shen Teh, in thanking them for their help, mentions the gods. A note (*Mat. S.*, 89) shows that they do not believe in the gods and are merely trying not to offend Shen Teh by contradicting her. The gods also help in their own discrediting with their farewell 'mach's gut!' (1605; cf. 107, 'good luck'; 10), a phrase usually equivalent to 'be seeing you', but literally 'do it well'. Brecht takes the debased locution in its stronger sense too: the gods leave Shen Teh to get on with the job, disclaiming responsibility.

Never staged by Brecht, the play has a generally disappointing stage history, perhaps largely because of the difficulty of the leading part. Apart from the first Zurich and Berlin performances, mention should be made of the Synthaxis Theater Company production in Santa Monica with the gods descending on rollerskates and ascending on an escalator,[32] and of the Milan production with sets by Luciano Damiani of fragile lyricism: white backdrops, pastel colours.[33] For Hamburg, Damiani added rubbish and puddles of water on the stage. Other productions have used movable screens. Departing from the principle of full light, Brecht demands pink clouds for the departure of the gods (Schiller had asked for pink light for the transfiguration at the end of *The Maid of Orleans*, an obvious target for Brecht's parody, representing the idealistic tradition in drama[34]). A contrast of setting is formed by the tobacco factory in scene 8; Shu Fu's sheds, too damp for his goods, are good enough for people, the crowding indescribable, the activity with children lugging bales of tobacco and so forth hectic.

(VII) MICROSTRUCTURES

Small touches of humour contrast with but also correspond to the heavy moral theme of the play. Thus Hinck (p. 67) sees in Shu Fu, unpleasant little barber but also rich merchant, ridiculously and unsuccessfully loving a younger woman, alternately calculating and generous, analogies with the Pantaloon of the Commedia dell'arte. But Shu Fu in his self-contradictions is also one of the characters who reflect Shen Teh's split. Another piece of Brechtian humour is that Wang learns of the gods' approach from a cattle-dealer, not an oracle or anything of the sort; and so earthly are these unworldly gods that when they go, one of them is afraid their having given Shen Teh money will be misunderstood.[35]

Brecht echoes things the audience will find familiar. The numbers three and seven, important in Christian imagery, are used repeatedly with no religious implications, simply for their associations. Wang waits three days for the goods; three days later Shen Teh buys her shop: Shui Ta comes thrice, and so on. The number seven occurs in the 'Song of the Eighth Elephant'.[36] More functional is the use of officialese, which as in *Mother Courage* shows the dehumanisation of man, not in war now, but in business.[37] Shui Ta announces his plans in a form all the harsher for its euphemistic tone: 'an unpredictable eventuality, which may have certain consequences . . .' (1591; 94; 9).

Shen Teh's language is carefully worked out. Righteous anger at social wrongs is marked by speeches in free rhythm with an interrogative isolated by a line division: 'How / But for patience could we live together?' (1503; 16; 1). Lyrical expressions of goodness have adjectival phrases as apparent afterthoughts: 'But I want your water, Wang. / Laboriously carried / Exhausting to its bearer . . .' (1527f.; 37; 3). A bald statement, itself proof of goodness, is filled out with words which add grace to the goodness.

Her preceding talk with Sun in the park (1522–6; 32–6) is one of the best passages for exemplifying gestic language. The dialogue proceeds not with the pseudo-logic of much dramatic dialogue, but with the leaps and undertones of real life; its realism is modified by the need to demonstrate, one by one, the stages in this particular model of human relationships; and the progress of the dialogue is dependent on scenic elements. In the first phase Shen Teh seeks an understanding with Sun which he is unwilling to enter into. What he says up to and including his speech on being an unemployed pilot is concerned with himself; yet it opens with a passage of social intent, directly drawing the audience's attenion to the persistence of the prostitutes. Brecht means us to see something Sun has certainly not thought out: that it is the poverty of these women which forces them to work on in the rain. This speech is rhetorical with its threefold repetition of 'selbst' ('even' occurs twice only in the translation) and its biblical parallelisms. In the following dialogue Sun reverts to greater naturalness. He rejects her interest, claiming she has bandy legs in order to alienate her. But even before this the phrase 'einen Becher Wasser kaufen vorher' with its shy reference to his impending suicide (missed in translation) has hinted that his suicide is really meant to draw attention to himself, as many suicide attempts are. And since she – a lovely touch – sets about proving that her legs are not crooked by pulling up her skirt (Brecht typically spares himself the stage direction for something deducible from the dialogue), he very quickly lets her shelter under his 'bloody tree'. His self-presentation, mainly in pilots' jargon and colloquial style, is convincing enough to show Sun's feeling for the work of a pilot. But the sentence 'Das kommt nur in eine Kiste, weil es den Hangarverwalter schmieren kann' deserves extra attention (the English omits the vital *nur*, 'only': 'Gets into a kite by bribing the hangar superintendent'). This is just the way in which Sun a little later hopes to get a job. By the strains of the socio-economic system he is immediately reduced to the level of the pilots he despises. The full import of this sentnce is only apparent later: it is a copybook example of dramatic irony, an age-old technique which Brecht takes up with a new function. Whereas traditional dramatic irony points to the workings of inscrutable fate cutting across human plans and resolutions, Brecht's points to the workings of the economic system: something made by man and in due course alterable by men. And when men have altered it, then it will be possible for a Sun to be happy that he knows his flying manuals, instead of worrying about that page which says 'Airmen Not Wanted'.

As Sun's long speech has issued in generalisations (allowing the recurrence of rhetorical parallelisms and other similar techniques), so Shen Teh's story of the crane, marking the new section of dialogue, is of parabolic nature. The crane at once *represents* and *symbolises* the aviator. The restlessness of the crane when its fellows migrate recalls Sun's watching a plane just before Shen Teh sees him. But in this form the story of the frustrated flier take on a wider symbolic significance and we see that Sun himself too is symbolic – of all those who are prevented from living as nature intended; and Shen Teh is half laughing, half crying because whilst the crane could not be helped, she is full of confidence that Sun can be helped. As yet (dramatic irony again) she does not know the trouble helping Sun is going to make for her.

When the female takes the lead in a relationship the male is the apparently active party. So now, disarmed by her story and her tears, Sun takes an interest in her which is the sign of his return to life, and when she remains silent he insists on filling the silence with talk. Brecht helps the dialogue over this embarrassing stage in a budding affair by giving Shen Teh her monologue-poem on the danger of dreary evenings and high bridges: the last straws in a country so miserable. But the gestus is not so simple as that. To Sun, Shen Teh optimistically says the dreariness of the evening was the sole cause of his suicidal mood. To the audience she admits the truth: that poverty and wretchedness are at the root of the trouble. Shen Teh next has to describe her life. Compared with Sun's life-story hers is lacking in brilliance and verve and Sun continually has to keep her going. But her factuality and painful honesty hint that Sun may be rather hypocritical with his smooth tongue. Yet there is more. She imitates a masculine voice not in deadly seriousness, as when she takes the role of Shui Ta, but for entertainment. And she couches her feelings at being able to give up prostitution in a short poem which has its social barb too: it is a topsy-turvy situation in which a woman can be glad to look forward to a year with no man.

The next paradox follows quickly and leads into the third phase of the dialogue, in which Sun has the initiative. Now the social truth too can be expressed by Sun: 'Easily satisfied, you are. God, what a town' is his variant on her poem about dreary evenings. If a little suffices to make Sun suicidal, a little suffices to make Shen Teh happy. Shen Teh's attempt to moralise after this sounds too eager, too naïve. It seems dramaturgically false that in this over-bright speech she should introduce some of Brecht's favourite ideas: the generosity of the poor, the basic kindliness of productive activities of all kinds. Sun effortlessly re-establishes his mastery of the situation afterwards by teasing Shen Teh a little; and although they have now established a personal relationship he still calls her 'sister' as if she were any old prostitute. She needs him, already, more than he needs her.

A hight point of the play's lyricism is Shen Teh's long monologue on the town in the early morning as seen through the eyes of one in love (1532f.; 42; 4). Brecht takes up the tradition by which the lover sees nature in a more friendly light; but the nature he invokes is the townscape – and not with the scene transfigured by being still asleep and not showing the signs of vulgar human activity, as in Wordsworth's sonnet on Westminster Bridge, but in the process of awakening and going about its business. Not only is work Shen Teh has actually seen going on described, but the city is compared to an old artisan – a comparison which lends both the town and the worker a dignity they rarely find in literature. Brecht's ways of celebrating the working class are subtle. The workers should be allowed to enter into all the sophistications and traditions hitherto reserved for the cultivated classes. Being the second term of a comparison is one of the least obvious of those enjoyments.

(VIII) THE MUSIC

Dessau's music[38] begins with an overture introducing a motif also used to underline central points of the play, sometimes even as an interjection in spoken dialogue. Another motif from the gods' trio deploring men's lack of faith emphasises points where the conflict of moral demands with reality is acute. The 'Song of Green Cheese' is treated as a parody of an operetta number, and in the Berliner Ensemble Ekkehard Schall built his performance of it on this, making the falsity of the optimism apparent and bringing together the unmasking of cheap art and the unmasking of religious hopes. Multiple dissonances in the accompaniment to the words 'Sankt Nimmerleinstag' ('When the moon is green cheese') symbolise pain at unrealised hopes. The 'Song of the Eighth Elephant' uses jazz techniques and ends with sixteen bars for percussion *ad lib.* and a jazz parody: the 'hot' music corresponds to the overheated demands of the capitalist system, here represented by Sun, on the workers. There are two versions of the close: in one the text is spoken but given a dissonant musical accompaniment; in the other the gods' final words are set to the melody of the 'Song of the Smoke' and thus associated with the nihilism of the parasites early in the play; but the instrumentation (with harps and Glockenspiel) is given a touch of saccharine – the fine words of the gods are illusory and deceptive. Similarly the trio in which the gods tell Wang to have more faith parodies operatic *parlando*, and Dessau suggests accompaniment by a musical box to show the mechanical and inhumane nature of the text.

Dessau set the short lyrical reflections in the text to music and demanded that they should be strongly distinguished from the spoken text; but the music generally consists of interjections and the text is still spoken. Texts dealing with love are given Chinese atmosphere; those of accusing content a hard percussive tone.

7 *The Caucasian Chalk Circle*

This reworking of the traditional Chalk Circle theme was written in March to June 1944 in Santa Monica, California, with a New York production in mind: the actress Luise Rainer had been instrumental in getting Brecht a contract with a Broadway theatre. Alterations were made in July and August, the prologue was recast in September. The first performance was however not until 1948, when a student production took place in Northfield, Minnesota; the first professional performance was on 7 October 1954, when Brecht, assisted by Manfred Wekwerth, put it on in the Berliner Ensemble. Angelika Hurwicz played Grusha, Ernst Busch the Singer and Azdak, Helene Weigel the Governor's Wife. Exported to Paris in 1955, London in 1956, and Moscow in 1957, this production played a major part in establishing Brecht's reputation abroad. Both Hanns Eisler and Paul Dessau have written music for the play; Dessau's (1953–4) is that used by the Berliner Ensemble. This is the most-performed Brecht play in Great Britain (443 productions up to October 1976).[1]

(I) THE PLOT

The 1954 production being the last that Brecht completed of any play, our summary gives prominence to the scenic effects, as Brecht's last word.[2]

1. The Struggle for the Valley. In the ruins of a village in the Caucasus, immediately after the Second World War, the members of two colchos villages, a fruit-growing and a goat-breeding collective, sit smoking and drinking wine: women, old men, soldiers. The grouping and attitudes show that their argument is a friendly one. An expert from the capital is in attendance. Members of the fruit-growing colchos have worked out a plan for irrigating the valley for their purposes; as the plan lies on the ground, one of the goat-breeders – they held the valley before the war – is impressed by it, others are sceptical or angry. But soon they are convinced that the fruit-growers have a better use for their valley than they themselves have; it is to be assumed that they are willing to stay further east, where they were evacuated to on Hitler's advance. To celebrate the agreement, the fruit-growers announce a theatrical performance: an old story from the Chinese. A celebrated singer has been engaged to be compère and is ready, book in hand and glasses on nose. He has three assistants, and almost every member of the collective has some part in the play he will narrate. After a meal they start:

2. *The Noble Child.* The singers describe the lavish court of the Governor of a city in Grusinia. This ruler and his retinue appear on their way to church and are delayed by a crowd of petitioners, showing how many people are reduced to misery under this régime. They block the narrow gateway, fighting amongst themselves for the best place. A few coins and many strokes of the whip are distributed to them. The Adjutant is behind the Governor's wife, and a very tall male nurse holds the Governor's son, Michel (Michael in the English), a baby, well up and in view. Two doctors are constantly in attendance on the child. The Fat Prince Kazbeki, a conspirator, hypocritically greets Governor Abashvili and his wife. His small nephew keeps behind him but turns an attentive ear to the ambiguous conversation. The lazy Governor refuses to listen to talk of the current Persian war going badly. The court enters the church in procession.

Grusche (in translation Grusha), a kitchen maid, hurrying across the courtyard with a goose for the Easter feast, is stopped by an acquaintance of hers, Simon Chachava, the soldier on duty, who teases her; she is too simple to recognise the meaning between his lines.

On the return from the Church the Adjutant in vain tries to get the Governor to receive the latest report on the Persian war; the Governor has eyes only for his peevish wife, who complains that his new building is done with Michael in mind, not her. The Governor has suspicions of the Fat Prince but does not follow them up. He goes in to eat, leaving two Ironshirts (armoured cavalry, but we never see them mounted) on guard. The Adjutant receives some architects, but the guards refuse to let him into the palace without a struggle, and instead of joining the Governor the architects think that if the Fat Prince's conspiracy is starting to act they should get out of the way.

The fall of the Governor is told in a mime sequence commented on by the Singer: the Governor is pulled on on a great rope by two heavily armed soldiers, despite his attempts to hold fast to the palace gate; he falls and has a spear thrust at his back; he is pulled across the stage, still looking back at what he possessed: his last visible attitude suggests a hanged man.

Attention is turned to the chaos among the lesser folk. The shocked servants watch a fight between the doctors, who both claim it is their day off because neither wants to stay with the Governor's son; one of them has already packed his bag. Grusha says a comet of ill omen has been seen. Other servants say the Persian war is lost, all the princes are in revolt, the Grand Duke has fled and all his governors are to be hanged, but the poor have nothing to fear. Simon is loyal and is to be among the guard of the Governor's wife, Natella Abashvili, who is going to flee. Grusha too is in a hurry, she must help to pack the lady's belongings. But they take time for a ceremonious betrothal – it becomes apparent that Grusha has noticed him before, after all; they keep a formal distance of two yards between them and Grusha ends their talk with a song describing how faithfully she intends to wait while he is away at the war.

The Adjutant orders Simon off. The servants come, busily preparing the Governor's wife's luggage; the lady herself casually sits on the back of a crouching maid to give orders. The servants show an increasingly rebellious mood, standing up straighter than usual and even contradicting their mistress. The Adjutant presses her to hurry, but she cannot separate herself from any of her rich clothes and acts coquettishly, used to having plenty of time and all her whims attended to. Only the sight of the city, off, burning brings her to her senses, and she flees leaving everything. The nurse – a woman this time – whom she had sent to fetch something returns and realises her mistress has left Michael. She gives the child to Grusha to hold 'for a moment', but she has no intention of returning. Other servants stand around close by and watch while Grusha with her stupid conscientiousness has the Governor's heir planted on her. The cook tries to persuade Grusha to leave Michael and flee; reluctantly Grusha puts the baby down, covers him, and goes to get her things, ready to go off to her brother's in the mountains.

The Fat Prince, elegant fan in one hand, sabre in the other, appears with Ironshirts, one of whom has the Governor's head on a lance; it is nailed to the gate. The Fat Prince orders Grusinia to be searched for the Governor's child: reward 1000 piastres.

As they leave, Grusha reappears with her bundle. She has heard the order. She is running off when she thinks of the child and stops. The scene is mimed and commented on by the Singer from this point; Grusha's face expresses horror at what she is doing, never goodness. She seems to hear the child telling her that one who refuses help to fellow-human will never rest content again. She stays near the child. Night falls. She gets a lamp and some milk which she warms over the lamp, hastily, as if she must be off. But she stays, and she covers the child better. Finally she sighs, picks up child and bundle and sneaks furtively off.

3. The Flight into the Northern Mountains. Grusha walks through a changing landscape, carrying the blanket she will need later when it becomes cold. A peasant's hut appears, the first stage and first difficulty of the journey. Grusha needs milk, and her surprise at the price named sends one hand to her purse and the other to her ear. It is not the peasant's fault: in the war situation he must sell what little he can sell dearly. She tries to deceive the child by giving it her dry breast, looking daggers at the hut meanwhile; but she has to give in and buy milk. Showing the first signs of tiredness, she goes on.

(In a scene cut in performance, Grusha pretends to be a rich lady in order to be able to share a room at a caravanserai with two ladies who are fleeing; but her skill at making the best of a poor room, and her chapped hands, give her away as a member of the lower orders and thus a potential thief, and she has to leave precipitately. She is followed by two Ironshirts. The one in charge, the corporal, has sold their horses, so the trooper is limping, and the corporal complains of his lack of devotion to duty.)

Grusha, having no nappies, feels it is time to find a home for Michael and turn back to the town to await Simon's return. Seeing a peasant woman carrying big milk-jugs into a farmhouse, she decides that is the place, lays the child at the door, knocks, and – conscientious to the last – hides behind a tree to see what happens. The peasant woman is willing to take the child in, despite her husband's ill-temper. Grusha sets off happily but also sadly back to the town.

She runs into the two Ironshirts who are looking for the child, and her horrified gesture gives her away. When they question her about a noble child she breaks loose and runs to the cottage. She tries to get the woman to hide the child or say with some conviction that it is hers. But when the Ironshirts catch up, the woman gives the game away. The corporal gets the trooper to take the woman outside while he examines the child. Grusha seizes a log of wood and hits him over the head with it as he bends over. Climbing over his stunned form, she escapes through the window with Michael – but without her bundle.

Having cost her so much, the child is now dear to her. She removes its fine linen and wraps it in her blanket. A stunted tree shows the nearness of the mountains. A wind rises and Grusha comes to a half-collapsed bridge over a glacier. Merchants are trying to recover a fallen rope to make it safer, but with the Ironshirts following her Grusha cannot wait: she would rather risk the two thousand-foot drop. Just as she has got over the bridge the corporal, his head bandaged, wearing a fur jacket, reaches it and it collapses. Grusha goes on through the snow.

4. In the Northern Mountains. Whilst the musicians narrate Grusha's feelings about the welcome she hopes for from her brother, she goes on in increasing exhaustion and fever. Finally a stableman has to lead her into her brother's house. Brother and sister-in-law, eating from a common dish, are not pleasantly surprised; the pious sister-in-law immediately wants to know whether Grusha's fever is catching and how she came by a child, and the brother is unable to assert his kinder feelings – he married for money, is ashamed of his wife and subservient to her. He claims the child is Grusha's and she has a husband with a farm who is at present away at the war. Grusha is accommodated in a scullery until spring. She makes herself useful by weaving at a large loom and sings to Michael, who remains wrapped up: it is cold in the room (and Michael has to grow rather fast without the audience noticing).

Grusha's brother comes and, standing behind her – he cannot look her in the face – makes it clear to her that the thaw is coming and he – or rather his wife – wants Grusha out of the house before her pursuers are able to arrive and before gossip about an unmarried mother starts. He has a solution: he has found a woman who, for a fee, will let Grusha marry her dying son Jussup (in English, Yussup) and so become a widow with papers to prove it.

So they go to the dying peasant. Grusha's prospective mother-in-law is in a hurry to get the ceremony over before her son dies, but bargains for a bigger fee in respect of the shame of taking an illegitimate child into the house. She tells Grusha to hide the child when the monk is fetched to perform the ceremony. The monk has spread the word, and the neighbours crowd in, to the mother-in-law's annoyance. As Grusha says her 'yes' she looks at Michael, for whom she is doing it. The monk wants to administer Extreme Unction, but the mother-in-law finds this too expensive. The bed-curtains are drawn to show the nearness of death, and Grusha's brother pays and leaves. In the living-room the wedding/funeral guests mill about, pray and joke, and are introduced to Grusha. In the bedroom the mother-in-law and Grusha break cake into small pieces. The monk makes an obscene speech. Musicians arrive, one of them with a gigantic trumpet: they too want to make money out of the wedding. An old woman stuffs on a large piece of cake, a drunkard has to be thrown out. To cover the embarrassed pause guests start talking of the latest news: the return of the Grand Duke, and peace in the land. Grusha smiles as she thinks of Simon's return. But news of peace also brings the dying bridegroom to his feet: he has only been shamming to evade military service. Haggard in his white nightshirt, he rises like a ghost. Grusha drops the tray of cakes she was about to hand round. Stuffing last morsels of cake into their mouths, the guests flee; the last to go are the monk and a couple of old ladies, who attempt an exorcism in vain.

A series of tableaux show Grusha's married life. She spends much time with Michael and gives him simple tasks – her mode of education. Yussup calls Grusha to scrub his back as he sits in the bathtub. Her sleeveless dress excites him: he complains that, though she must have seen a naked man before, she refuses herself to him. Grusha washes clothes in the stream and watches the local children, including Michael, playing Heads-off, a game in which the death of the Governor is re-enacted (and the audience prepared for the next act, which starts again from that event). Simon reappears, in a shabby uniform and with a saddle but no horse, on the other side of the stream. They shout happy greetings across it, but Grusha is unable to shout the explanation for her apparent faithlessness across the stream, and Simon does not think it worth going to the bridge to hear a set of excuses. As he turns away the Ironshirts finally catch up with her: the children have gone off playing, and now Michael reappears led by a trooper with an official order to take him to the city for investigation of the suspicion that he is the child of the late Governor. Grusha says he is her child, thus putting the seal on Simon's alienation. Michael is led away, Grusha follows to try and save the child for herself.

5. *The Story of the Judge.* The judge of Grusha's case is to be Azdak, and the Singer introduces his story. On the day of the revolt Azdak, a village clerk (his hut is strewn with paper and pens) with a demanding palate (a hare hangs prominently in the foreground), finds a fugitive in the woods, a man whose face and hands show he is used to prosperity. When Azdak gives him cheese the careless way he eats it also betrays that he is not used to defending every crumb he can get. He offers 150,000 piastres for a night's lodging. Azdak is about to refuse when the village policeman Schauwa (Shauva in translation) comes to make enquiries about a stolen hare. Superior to Azdak in the disciplinary structure, and sure Azdak is the offender, he is yet overawed by the intellectual superiority which allows Azdak casually to pull the wool over his eyes. He leaves. How could Azdak turn anyone in to such a policeman?

But when Azdak discovers the fugitive was the arch-criminal, the Grand Duke, he gives himself up to Shauva, has himself bound and taken into Nukha on a charge of abetting his escape; for he is under the impression that the Princes' revolt is a workers' revolution. At the court they find the Ironshirts swaggering and drinking and the judge hanged. Azdak garrulously describes the revolution in Persia forty years before, when the peasants and workers took over because there had been too long a war and no justice. When he has shown enough delight in the revolution the Ironshirts move in: there was indeed a revolt of the weavers in the town, and they strung up the judge, but Prince Kazbeki has paid the Ironshirts to suppress them (and a carpet lying around shows that they looted as well). Azdak is depressed, and the Ironshirts pretend to be about to hang him but suddenly stop and burst into laughter, in which Azdak hysterically joins. The merriment is interrupted by the Fat Prince, who comes with his nephew. The nephew is to be the new judge, but the Fat Prince is not sure enough of his power to simply impose him on his executive, so suggests the Ironshirts should elect the judge. Had the Grand Duke been caught the Fat Prince would have been more secure: thanks to the clerk Azdak, the Ironshirts hold some temporary power. He suggests testing the nephew's aptitude for the job: he himself will act the part of a defendant. Shauva meanwhile gets hold of some wine. The nephew takes the seat of judgment and Azdak imitates the Grand Duke – accused of losing the war but blaming the Princes for the corruption and slackness which led to defeat. The nephew is no match for his arguments, which culminate in the proof that Grusinia may have lost the war, but the profiteer Princes have not. So the Ironshirts physically remove the nephew from the judgment seat and install the unwilling Azdak on it. The Fat Prince picks up his nephew – but they are only momentarily on the ground, symbolically as well as physically. The soldiers dress Azdak in the judge's robe and carry him off in the hammock-like chair, introducing his peripatetic administration of justice seen in the following scenes.

Azdak's ragged clothing remains visible under the robe throughout. He receives bribes openly at the beginning of his cases, which he generally takes two at a time whilst nonchalantly peeling apples and drinking. He uses inattention as the cover for punishing the guilty but well-defended for crimes they have not committed and not giving the rich satisfaction when they have been duped or robbed. A comic procession of witnesses, plaintiffs and defendants passes before him: the doctor who amputated the wrong leg; the doctor's patron who had a stroke when he heard that the doctor had treated a patient without first receiving the fee, and is pushed on in a wheelchair; the patient who now has rheumatism in one leg and the other leg amputated. (The doctor is sentenced to amputate the patron's leg free should he have another stroke.) A case of rape interests him – and the Ironshirts who form his retinue – more; they listen to the victim's well-rehearsed tale, and then Azdak gets her to demonstrate how she walks and bends, and finds her guilty of rape – assaulting the stableman with a dangerous weapon, her bottom. Then he goes off with her to examine the seat of the crime. In a further case, a landowner's cows were killed after he asked an old peasant woman to pay the rent for a field. She is also in receipt of a ham and a cow brought to her by St Banditus, alias the robber Irakli, who appears in court heavily armed, claiming to be an old hermit. The landowners are powerless against him, and Azdak blesses the alliance of the poor and the violent by symbolically putting the old woman on his seat of judgment and adoring her as the personification of long-suffering Grusinia. The landowners present are fined for atheism in that they do not believe in the miracles of St Banditus.

But when the Grand Duke returns fear seizes Azdak. The time of disorder, in which a judge could perform such travesties of legality unobserved, will be over. Back in Nukha, Azdak mends a shoe whilst the Fat Prince's head is carried by on a lance, and regrets that the times described in the old Song of Chaos, which he sings elegiacally, have not yet come. He takes the law book, which so far he has only used as a cushion, to see what punishment is in store for him and to give the impression of being a pedantic judge, but a wine-jug stands near him too. The Governor's wife comes; she does not like him, but she needs a judge who will find in her favour and get Michael returned to her. Azdak, already without his robe as he was about to flee, promises to do as required; and when his noble visitor leaves, he runs for it.

6. *The Chalk Circle*. The parties to the case assemble in Court. Grusha is accompanied by the cook, who is willing to swear that the child is Grusha's, and hopes Azdak will be drunk and deliver one of his freak judgments. Simon comes too: though still unable to understand Grusha's marriage, he is ready to swear he is the child's father. Ironshirts get worried because Azdak is missing. One of them is the one Grusha hit over the head, but he cannot settle the score with her without admitting that he was pursuing the child to kill it. The Governor's wife arrives with the Adjutant and two lawyers; they are glad most of the common people are prevented from attending the trial by rioting going on in the town. The lawyers have been trying to get the Grand Duke to nominate a new judge in place of Azdak. Ironshirts drag in Azdak – who has been denounced by some landowners – and Shauva, tied up, and want to hang Azdak. The Governor's wife applauds hysterically. Azdak, cornered, reviles the Ironshirts. At this moment a rider brings a despatch containing the nomination of the new judge: Azdak, who saved the Grand Duke's life. Hurriedly the Ironshirts cut Azdak down. He is dressed in the the judge's robe, orders wine to cure his shock and the law book to sit on, and takes bribes from the lawyers, who give more when he remarks that Grusha is attractive. He interrupts a lawyer's poetic praise of motherhood to hear Grusha's case, which is mainly that she has done her best for the child. The Governor's wife, prompted by the lawyer, says a few words; but the second lawyer lets slip that not love of the child, but desire to enter into the revenues of her late husband's estate – which is tied to the son – is the moving force in the case. Azdak takes note of this and listens summarily to the lies of Grusha and her witnesses. He wants to cut the case short. Grusha says there is no wonder, he has got his money. The cook tries to restrain her, Simon argues with Azdak and is fined for indecent language, and the Governor's wife supports herself on the shoulder of her indispensable Adjutant. Grusha delivers a denunciation of Azdak, which he listens to with increasing pleasure, fining her thirty piastres for contempt of court. Then he interrupts the case to hear an old couple who want a divorce and who stand back to back, but very close to each

other: they have been married forty years. Grusha has an argument with the Governor's wife, ending when Azdak says he has reached no conclusion from the evidence and must proceed to the Chalk Circle test. Michael is put in a circle drawn on the floor and the true mother will be the one who can pull the child out of the circle. Grusha in her simplicity is so overjoyed when she touches Michael again after so long that she forgets to pull. As the real mother pulls Michael out of the circle she reaches after him. Azdak decides to repeat the test; the lawyer, leafing through his law book, objects, and Shauva is inclined to listen, but the test takes place. This time Grusha pulls, and she is stronger than the Governor's wife: but in order not to tear the child in two she lets go. Azdak starts to take his robe off: he wants to get away quickly after the verdict, which is in favour of Grusha. The Abashvili estates fall to the city to be made a playground named after Azdak. He signs a divorce, but it turns out to be in favour of Grusha rather than of the old couple. Simon and Grusha are both looking at Michael rather than at each other; when she gets her divorce Grusha kisses Azdak, but means Simon. Azdak collects the fines from them. Simon takes Michael on his shoulders so that they can get out of town quickly. The lawyers desert the Governor's wife, who is not in a position to pay their fees. She leaves in the Adjutant's arms. The Fat Prince's head is still stuck over the gateway as the less involved characters carry out a leisurely and joyful exit. The Singer ends the story: Azdak disappeared, but the moral is that things should belong to those who are good for them.

(II) FORERUNNERS

The motif of the chalk circle is ancient and widely known.[3] The quarrel of two women before a wise judge over which is the true mother of a child goes back to the judgment of Solomon (I Kings 3, 16–28); in the *Hui Lan Chi* ('Chalk Circle') of the Chinese author Li Hsing-dao (or Li Hsing Tao, thirteenth century), the motif of personal enrichment is already present: the real object of the court case is the inheritance which is bound to the child. Hai Tang, the (socially inferior) second wife of the rich man Ma, has borne him an heir, endangering the first wife's primacy. Mrs Ma murders the husband in order to enjoy life with her lover Tschao, accuses Hai Tang of the crime, and claims the child (and the estate) as her own. She tries to kill Hai Tang, who escapes by chance. A bribed judge finds in her favour, but by pure chance an appeal judge is incorruptible and determines maternity by the chalk circle test: the child is put in a circle, the claimants are directed to pull him out, and the one who lets go because she does not want to hurt him is the true mother. The child and the estate are adjudged to her, Mrs Ma punished.

In a way the story might appeal to Brecht, with its clear social bias; dramaturgically, it has instances of self-introduction and sung inter- polations which would interest him;[4] and that Hai Tang only by very good luck survives and gets justice is perhaps an element in Brecht's conception of Grusha's vicissitudes.

In 1925 Max Reinhardt put on a lyrical and fantastic adaptation of the play by the poet Klabund (Alfred Henschke). Brecht's interest in this version was reinforced after Klabund's death: his widow, Carola Neher, was one of Brecht's actresses. The play was a success in London, and was produced by Piscator in New York in 1940–1. Another precursor to be mentioned is a celebrated German enlightenment play on parenthood, Lessing's *Nathan the Wise*: as Ritchie (pp. 50f.) reminds us, looking after the child is here set alongside the ties of blood, and Nathan, after being established as a good foster-father, is revealed as the real father too.

Brecht's first treatment of the theme was perhaps a parody of Klabund – the interlude 'The Elephant Calf' in *Man is Man*.[5] In 1940 a short story, *Der Augsburger Kreidekreis* ('The Augsburg Chalk Circle'), transfers the theme into the world of *Mother Courage* and radically re-evaluates it. In a Catholic attack on Augsburg during the Thirty Years War, a rich dyer is killed; his wife flees, leaving their child behind. A maid Anna takes the child to her brother's; he has married a strict and well-to-do Catholic who would not take in a Protestant child, so Anna claims it is hers. When no father turns up, the sister-in-law is dubious. By marrying a man apparently at death's door Anna regularises her position; the man does not die, but she gets used to life with him. At last the dyer's wife comes to claim her child. Anna appeals to the judge Dollinger, famed for his fairness. She is suspected in court of wanting the inheritance, but insists she does not care about that, only about the child. The chalk circle test proves she is the true mother; she keeps the child. It was of this story that Brecht thought when the chance of writing a play for Broadway was offered him. To it he adds the Azdak plot. The figure may owe some- thing to Haitang's brother in Klabund, a revolutionary student who be- comes a judge, and to the stories of a historical figure, the magistrate Pao or Bau Dschöng, best known to us as the Judge Dee stories.[6]

(III) THE DEMONSTRATION PLAY

The play is hard to classify. Brecht denied that it was a parable appar- ently because the argument of act 1 is resolved before the main action, the Grusha and Azak plots, starts; the main action is thus not used to help in solving any present-day problem. In early drafts, admittedly, and in later summaries, Brecht defers the decision about the valley to the day after the performance of the main action (17, 1203; *Mat. K.*, 16). Walter Hinck points out a more basic consideration, that the main action concerns a child, the opening action land; it would thus be incommen- are to reduce the main action to a mere backing-up of the conclusions reached in act 1. But Hinck (pp. 35f.) concludes that the first act is thus merely accidental and dispensable, a conclusion too often reached also by directors wanting to shorten the running time, and even by Harry Buckwitz in the Frankfurt production of 1955.[7] Omitting act 1 reduces the play to an interesting anecdote in which an improbable happy end- ing is wrung from a continuingly hostile historical situation, and to exactly the kind of play Brecht objected to when he met it on the natural- ist stage: one in which there is no criticism of the idea that social catas- trophes happen by fate, no perspective towards a different, less alienatory social world. Brecht says the prologue is necessary to motivate his changes of the Chalk Circle theme; only the setting in the Soviet Union explains the whole play (*Mat. K.*, 28). Grusha and Azdak work illegally to do good in an unalterably unpromising state of affairs. The peasants of act 1 are able to do good, by considering in a spirit of amity and fairness the use of their valley, without fear of bad laws. Where the social situation is right, people can be helpful to each other without bringing trouble on themselves – and only then. The two problems – valley and child – are in some ways analogous, in others not; and whilst the finding is the same, that things should and can be entrusted to those who make the most of them and care for them best, the social worlds in which the verdict is reached are crassly contrasted. (The finding was applied by Brecht to the eastern areas of Germany arbitrarily transferred to Poland at the end of the war, *Aj.*, 2, 749: 3.8.45; but that he was thinking of them in writing the play[8] is a chronological impossibility.)

The various elements (commune plot, Grusha plot, Azdak plot) use widely differing tones and conventions. Act 1 is apparently set in a particular place and time, but cannot really claim such closeness to real- ity. The time of the other acts is left vague, and for all it means to the Western audience, the place (Nukha, a city of Soviet Azerbaijan some 200 km east of Tiflis) might just as well be vague too. Brecht uses the unfamiliar name 'Grusinia' for Georgia; Georgian names were substituted at a late stage for Russian ones.[9] The Azdak plot is very discursive. The Grusha plot, on the other hand, despite (or because of) its episodic struc- ture is firmly based on traditional dramatic tension, and the whole Azdak plot, interpolated by a bold stroke of disregard of dramatic chronology exactly at the point where we are most tense about the fate of Michael, is a retarding element of the first water. The stories of Grusha and of Azdak are set off by the same event, the Easter rising (2065; 61; 5), but Brecht chooses to start them separately and only bring them together with the event which ends them both.

Critical controversy rages around all these breaks. Peter Leiser finds the question of a mother for a child qualitatively so different from the question of use of a tract of land that he feels Brecht has lost track of his criteria of proportion.[10] Fuegi (p. 145) on the other hand makes out a case for act 1 as 'a kind of decompression chamber as we step from the here and now into the never-never': contemporary farmers lead us carefully into the stylised presentation of the ancient tale.

According to Brecht the Grusha and Azdak plots show to the colchos spectators 'a particular kind of wisdom, an attitude which may be exemplary in the case of their topical dispute', thus giving a background demonstration of the practicability of this kind of wisdom and some idea of its historical origins (17, 1205; *Mat. K.*, 18). Grusha and Azdak are pioneers of what will in the fulness of time become habitual attitudes. The communes have already in act 1 shown what can be done by reason. The argument about the valley is doomed, by any conventional knowledge about human behaviour, to end in deadlock and to have to be decided by higher authority or by force. But Brecht shows it being amicably settled, thanks to the secure social situation in which the goat-keepers have an alternative tract of land and can count on the same state support wherever they are. To envisage such a situation is an act, if not of faith, at any rate of optimism. The dramaturgical equivalent of a mood of optimism is a *comédie*, in the sense of a non-tragic play which may have more or fewer overt comic elements.

In line with the attitude thus imposed by the optimistic perspective, the pioneers of modern attitudes are made the protagonists of plots in which, despite the barbarous conditions of their past era, a happy ending can be salvaged. Grusha enters of her free will into a situation which by normal ideas of human nature is hopeless. A defenceless girl moving across country in time of war and rebellion, clutching a child with a price on his head – it is a hopeless endeavour. When she allows herself to be married off it seems to put an end to hopes of a happy ending to her love for Simon. A villager hurrying to accuse himself of crimes against the people, only to find that the people is no more in power than it ever was – the wonder is that he does not end on the gallows.

But the Soviet citizens of the communes are to be entertained, not saddened, by the fate of their ancestors. Mayer (p. 243) describes the conception of the Grusha and Azdak plots as 'fairy-tale material'; indeed the saving of a happy ending from such vicissitudes is typical of fairy-tale – and also of sensational 'cliff-hanger' films, comic strips and stage comedy. So is the relationship of character and plot: 'the poor simple person despised by the rich proves helpful and resourceful and overcomes all obstacles to win the prize in the end.'[11] Brecht goes deeper than most such literature. But he also includes more overtly comic elements. Azdak is a comedy figure of vitality and cunning; his virtuoso performances of judging two cases at once are given a serious function in the plot when he bungles a divorce and so frees Grusha to marry Simon. The Ironshirts who pursue Grusha, cavalry on foot, trudging against the stage turntable, are figures of fun, but their pursuit forces Grusha to retain the baby and thus keeps the plot moving. The scene of Grusha's marriage, for which the monk with sarcastic glee demands 'a hushed Wedding March or a gay Funeral Dance' (2055; 52; 4), is ended by the resurrection of the bridegroom, resulting in the comic exodus of the wedding guests but an unwelcome turn in Grusha's fortunes. The comic may be the final and true perspective on human life, but has to assert itself against the decidedly tragic: Brecht's optimism is not Panglossian. In act 1 the tragic is represented by the destruction in the war against fascism, in the main actions by the oppression and insecurity inherent in the feudal system; in each case it is overcome but not negated. A Hegelian synthesis, combining its elements yet not superseding them, is a possible analogy; closer is perhaps the thought of Brecht's favourite Mo Tzu on the two aspects of the universe – yang the masculine, the sunny side, the active; yin the converse; both intertwined, each a valid and necessary part of a universe in which the higher element and the guarantee of the meaningfulness of the whole is however represented by yang. Such oriental serenity on Brecht's part has led to a comparison with Shakespeare's last plays.[12]

(IV)   NARRATION

The Singer, a 'summing up and extension'[13] of all Brecht's narrative devices – placards, choruses, apostrophes to audience, scene titles, introductory verses – has affinities to the Aeschylean chorus. These appear particularly in his sententious commentaries: 'Oh blindness of the great! They walk like gods . . .' (2015; 15; 2). Here he stands above time and place and delivers general truths on the possibilities of change in human affairs. But from such a commentary he can move straight into issuing orders to the actors: 'walk even now with head up' (2015; 16). These orders are obeyed – in the Berliner Ensemble, the Governor responds marionette-like to the Singer's words. Similarly he says what Grusha is to do: 'Run, kind heart! The killers are coming!' (2037; 36; 3). So he exercises a direct control. Being in charge of the book he is also responsible for the division of the story into two chronologically concurrent halves in defiance of dramatic convention.[14] He selects parts of the story to tell, aided by slips of paper he has placed in the book (2008; not in the translation; 2). He passes over long periods of time, both between and within the acts, with a few words. In fact he is the sovereign narrator of a story, and the scenes of the Grusha plot in particular merely body forth his conceptions.[15] He stands between the action and the public. Brecht placed him with his musicians in front of and in a stage-side box, a visual indicator of their function. The Singer asserts himself as the real reality we are to hold on to, and relativises the dramatic reality – a necessary counterpoise to the emotional tendencies of the Grusha plot. He is always there, and sometimes when he opens his mouth we are reminded that the action is in the past, and supplied with hints as to how to think about it, which modify our emotional response. He also plays directly with the audience, raising political hopes – 'Oh, Wheel of Fortune! Hope of the people!' only to dash them: 'When the houses of the great collapse / Many little people are slain' (2015; 15f.; 2).

The most daring aspect of the Singer's work is however that he is made to speak the thoughts of Grusha when she would otherwise have to remain silent or engage in monologue: the equivalent of voice-over narration in film, this is a specifically epic procedure.[16] While the Singer holds the stage aurally, Grusha (and at the end of act 5 Simon) mimes the emotions concerned. Distancing of the words is sufficient for Brecht, the emotions need not be underplayed too. These songs do not interrupt the action in the way that songs generally do in Brecht, but transfer it temporarily from the social to the psychological level, encouraging the spectator to assess character for its own sake as well as in its social context. In a sense Brecht thus turns the wheel full circle: just where he insists most strongly on the privileged position of the Singer-narrator, emphasises the epic element and thus (theoretically) the primacy of plot over character – the greatest degree of opposition to naturalist theatre, in which character and situation often took precedence over plot – he smuggles back the drama of character, the self-revelation of the individual figure taking priority over the forcing of the pace of the action.

The musicians supporting the Singer fulfil *ad hoc* functions. Sometimes they act as representatives of the audience, asking questions full of dramatic tension: 'How will the merciful escape the merciless / The bloodhounds, the trappers?' (2026; 26; 3). Sometimes they supply lyrical generalisations on the basis of Grusha's plight (2035; 34; 3) – what in *The Good Person* Shen Teh had to do for herself. Once in a short interlude they even take the words of Grusha (2036; 35; 3); the Berliner Ensemble played this sense before an empty road.

(v) THE SOCIAL WORLD OF THE PLAY

In Brecht the behaviour of the individual is constantly determined by the social situation. A few characters have qualities which override this, and so they come into conflict with society: Kattrin in *Mother Courage*, Shen Teh in *The Good Person* and Grusha here. But around them are many others who are mere ciphers, altering their attitudes more or less as the wind blows them: the cook in *Mother Courage* is a good example, and *The Caucasian Chalk Circle* is full of them. The architects who dance attendance on the Governor are not lickspittles by nature: they need contracts (17, 1209). The doctors who abandon Michael are concerned to save their skins. The peasant who asks an impossible price for milk is not a profiteer and grasping, but poor: he gently helps Grusha to pick Michael up after their argument (17, 1209). The soldiers work for whoever pays them and change their attitude according to the news from above. In act 6 they string Azdak up on a denunciation, but on receipt of a despatch from the Grand Duke, their newly-restored master, they are on the spot. One of them immediately raises the fainting Azdak. The others are slower to grasp the situation: only after an embarrassing pause does one of them remove the focus of embarrassment, the noose, smiling at Azdak 'like a hairdresser who wants his tip' (Brecht).[17] The peasant woman who panics and gives away Grusha and Michael to the corporal, too, acts in a way determined by her social situation. None of them are all bad, but they do not break out of the vicious circle. Grusha's sister-in-law treats her coldly because she fears for her own respectability; Grusha's brother is annoyed but can do nothing about it, and his defence of his wife (2049; 47) expresses a bad conscience. And so it goes on. The world in which Grusha and Azdak move is made up of people with no impetus to change it, though very few of them benefit from it. The possible changes in the world would have to start with the activation of people like this, whose true interest it would be to put an end to their exploitation by those above them. Indeed, Brecht is more interested in showing this end of society and where the shoe rubs it than in attacking the exploiters directly. Socialist realist critics objected to the lack of positive revolutionary content in Brecht.

The time of the main action is basically similar to that in *Galileo*: the feudal hierarchy is in decline. The princes fish in troubled waters, using the war in which the Grand Duke is engaged to extend their power; the Governor by his effeteness and ineffectuality, shown by his lack of interest in despatches from the front, plays into their hands. The feudal powers are served by the judiciary and the armed forces, and logically reinforced by the Church. Lawyers, doctors, and architects are theoretically independent, but in practice only able to make money out of the feudalists, who alone have money. No beginnings of mercantilism are to be seen among this embryonic middle class.

The concomitant of feudalism, serfdom, is underplayed. Though in act 1 one of the older participants has been a serf, in the body of the play people behave like free peasants and townspeople, whose suffering at the hands of the nobility takes the form of taxation and the capricious exercise of violence by the powerful. The Governor and his wife think only of property;[18] she in particular has no attitudes that are specifically feudal rather than capitalistic. The most sensitive point of property is possession of a child (here Michael), determined by begetting and bearing: 'the ultimate *locus* of private property is in the private parts',[19] an aspect of capitalism that had attracted Brecht's satirical attention in the sonnet *On Kant's Definition of Marriage* . . . (9, 609; B. Poems, 312). The peasants vary from rich to poor, and they marry into property in the time-honoured way; Grusha's brother does it here in Grusinia just like his forerunner in Swabia. An urban artisanate, the carpet-weavers, is kept off stage; it apparently attempts from time to time to assert itself in revolts, but has never grown strong enough to hold its own for long against the feudalists. The servants, as seen mainly in act 2, have a rudimentary solidarity in that they help each other when the quarrels of the mighty involve the powerless too. They are also seen, in Brecht's production, stealing in the time of chaos.[20] This is typical of them. In the caravanserai episode of act 3, Grusha tries to pass herself off as a fine lady. When she is found out, only one construction can – as in the didactic piece *The Exception and the Rule* – be put on it: that she is out to kill or rob.[21] No one is expected to believe that she had honest, let alone positively good, intentions. But in fact she is rising above class bonding and showing fellow-feeling with a member of another class because he is himself, like the servants, powerless and helpless.

Azdak, the village clerk, makes a decision like Brecht's: he espouses the revolutionary cause out of an intellectual insight. When the revolution fails him, he finds himself, in his attempt to realise what social justice he can, allied with the robber – who in a time of oppression has a positive social function, helping the poor by robbing the rich. That Irakli is also St Banditus, an old hermit, is part of the play's criticism of Christianity. For his use of force is, as the Singer adumbrates (2084; 77; 5), the correct, primevally Christian way of loving one's neighbour. Christ came to bring not peace, but the sword. Otherwise the flaunted Christianity of various figures in the play, especially those Grusha meets, is just a mask for exploitation and indifference. The peasant woman with whom Grusha leaves Michael calls this abandonment a sin (2038; 37); the real sin has been committed, just after Sunday church, by the Governor's wife. The same peasant woman, thinking only of her harvest money, denounces Grusha as soon as the Ironshirts arrive, thus forcing her to use violence to save Michael. When she comes with him to the rotten bridge, the merchant woman can only pray and say that crossing the bridge constitutes the sin of tempting God (2043f.; 42); Grusha has to act alone. In the following scene Grusha's sister-in-law with the crucifix is more concerned about gossip than about helping the child; whilst one could not expect Brecht to miss the chance of portraying a drunken, obscene and money-grubbing monk. None of these Christians eases Grusha's lot; they censure her and let her down.

Yet Christianity is not only attacked. Grusha as virgin 'mother' of a child of high birth, whose father is not her fiancé, fleeing with it from the Prince's persecution into a far country, and married to Yussup (Joseph), has similarities to the Virgin Mary; so has the old woman, 'Mother Grusinia', who receives the gifts of St Banditus and the adoration of·Azdak. Azdak breaks the laws like bread to feed the masses, bringing a temporal rather than spiritual salvation to the needy (2086; 80; 5), is mocked by the soldiers with a robe and a burlesque crown (2078; 72), greets his apparently certain end with 'The fear of death is upon me' (2089; 82; 5). But he is no Messiah. Brecht uses parts of the story of Jesus for Michael too – hailed by Grusha in the song at the end of scene 3 with an echo of Isaiah, thrice denied by her on Simon's return. Brecht finds biblical references and echoes suitable for scenes set in the feudal past, where they serve to underline the real, egalitarian message of Christ against its perversion by the hypocritical oppressors. Thus Christianity is incorporated into the humane tradition Brecht would like to formulate. But biblical echoes are lacking in act 1: Brecht does not want to risk any hint that such a debased form of organised religion might be allowed to influence modern life.

(VI) GRUSHA'S PRODUCTIVITY

'Terrible is the temptation to do good!', the Singer tells us (2025; 25; 2). As Grusha takes the child, music expresses the threat of retribution for this theft. The Singer's paradox draws our attention to the state of an age in which the ageless quality of goodness (the abstract quality is invoked in the German text) is something to be resisted. But the theme of goodness – as general charity, and as doing one's best for a single child – has been treated in *The Good Person*, and Brecht does not just repeat himself. The particular twist in this play is that Grusha takes on a strange child out of joy at her betrothal to Simon. The temptation to do good is an almost sexual one: *Verführung*, seduction.[22] 'I took him because on that Easter Sunday I got engaged to you. And so it is a child of love', she tells Simon at the end (2105; 96; 6). And the child leads her into marriage to another, thus very nearly preventing the engagement to Simon from turning into marriage. Simon is invented by Brecht independently of the concept of Grusha's child not being her own, and his function is to complicate the plot.

But at the same time Simon represents the promise of a fulfilment. In *Mother Courage*, Kattrin was not only prevented from taking on orphan children by the colder attitude of her mother, but also unable to get herself a man. Grusha gets at one stroke the promise of a man, and the reality of a child. The promise is redeemed: despite her marriage to another, Simon declares himself willing to perjure himself for her (like Shen Teh for Wang), and in the comedy ending she is freed to marry him.

When Grusha actually takes on the child, under the influence of her personal joy, it is for quite direct and universal reasons. Her sensitivity is expressed in the magnificent narration (2024; 24; 2) of what she thinks she hears the child saying, and it is a threat: by closing one's ear to a cry for help one cuts oneself off from the simple contentment of existence for ever. She tries to resist the message, but in vain. In the eyes of the world she may be concerning herself with dangerous things that are none of her business, she may be infringing the sacred rule that charity begins at home; but humanitarian impulses overcome her. (The hesitation before she takes the child has been said to be borrowed from the Chaplin film *The Kid*[23]). In her own view she is merely keeping the peace with herself. She sighs when she lifts up the child, for she knows she is taking responsibility for a hunted boy with a price on his head, something which must bring her anxiety and perhaps danger.

She wants at first only to get Michael out of danger. She is quite ready to leave him with the peasant couple once she has realised it is impracticable for her to take him further without nappies or supplies. At this point she is so keen to get the child safely billeted and to take up the threads of her own life that she has changed her mind about going to her brother's and wants to return to Nukha to await Simon. So she has not thought about how to bring Michael up. Then comes the realisation that the Ironshirts are searching for the child in exactly the direction where she has left him, and the turning-point of the plot when in order to save him she has to hit the Corporal over the head. After this, she as well as Michael is hunted, both are in the same boat (2043 'Mitgegangen, mitgehangen'; cf. 42 'Live together, die together'). Grusha and the peasant woman have each done exactly what they wanted not to when they see Ironshirts. The woman betrays the child though she wanted to keep it; Grusha gives herself away and has to act desperately to keep the child, though she wanted to lose it. The apparently better situation for the child was really almost fatally catastrophic.

Now, having done much for Michael already, she makes him hers. She dresses him in her blanket instead of his fine linen and re-baptises him (2041; 40). Almost the first thing she said about him was: 'He hasn't got the plague. He looks at you like a human being' (2023; 23; 2). Now, from a sort of taboo object dangerous for the lower orders to touch, he is to be transformed into a true human being. The baptism is to signify conversion to positive (rather than hypocritical) Christianity. The song at the end of act 3 is about Michael (2044, 'auf dich'; missed in the translation). It has a social awareness which critics have paid too little attention to. She sets out consciously to divert Michael from the ways laid for him by heredity. His thief-father wanted to lay out a new wing to the palace, pulling down the houses of the poor to do so – all for Michael (2009, 2013; 11, 14; 1). His whore-mother is never seen without the Adjutant. Both have been a scourge to the poor, tiger and snake. But Michael is to feed children and foals. In act 4 his education is proceeding. Bent at the loom, Grusha sings a song with useful lessons about not making oneself too obvious, which she applies to their present situation as well as to war (2048; 46). After her marriage he is seen trying his hand at mending a straw mat (2058; 55): work-orientated play. Her defence before Azdak is based on her having brought him up 'to be friendly with everyone' and 'to work as well as he could' (2096; 88; 6), and she wants to teach him more words (2103; 95). Her unspoken reaction to Azdak's tempting offer that if she lets the child go to its real mother it will be rich completes the picture: 'He who wears the shoes of gold / Tramples on the weak and old . . .' (2102; 93) – and what is more, being so evil is too great a strain for a man, and it would be better for him to fear hunger than to fear the revenge of the hungry. So Grusha develops ideas on education which are typical of Brecht in their double basis: class-consciousness and humanitarianism. As in *The Good Person* the exploiting class is as alienated as the exploited, and suffers from the need to be harsh, so here. As it was not Shui Ta's fault that he was so hard, so here Grusha actually takes it on herself to save a potential exploiter from the consequences of birth into the ruling class – by making him a worker, a useful member of society.[24] In scene 6, finally, her attack on Azdak shows awareness of his apparent role as the judicial defender of private property and exploitation (2100; 92).

The other, more obvious, side of Grusha is her naïvety. At the beginning, the cook tells her she is none of the brightest (2023; 23; 2). Her kindness lacks anything to moderate it. She calls herself a sucker (2051, 'die Dumme', Brecht's translation of 'sucker' as explained 17, 1206 and *Mat. K.*, 19; cf. 48 'the fool'; 4). But really she is closer to Kattrin, who becomes self-sacrificingly good only after a series of catastrophic alienations, than to the unstoppable existential goodness of Shen Teh. Like Mother Courage's daughter she is a tireless worker, the one sent for the extra goose, a strong and willing girl – Brecht cast Angelika Hurwicz in both parts, solid and down-to-earth, her physique and face counteracting any desire to see her as a little-girl-lost. Grusha is the timeless, practical, four-square peasant, but with some of the monomania afflicting Bruegel's *Dulle Griet*, the madwoman rushing open-mouthed through a nightmare world on a mission she alone understands.[25] At the beginning, at least, she may be helpless and silly, but she has the stamina and obstinacy she will need for her task. Grusha was pure and goody-goody only in the first version written for Luise Rainer; immediately after sending the script off to her Brecht was discontented and rewrote the part completely (*Aj.*, 2, 671: 8.8.44; *Mat. K.*, 32f.). In rehearsal, he contemplated hinting that she stole on her journey with Michael in order to feed the two of them (*Mat. K.*, 72f.). In fulfilling her function *vis-à-vis* Michael, Grusha develops herself, 'changes herself, with sacrifices and through sacrifices, into a mother for the child' (*Mat. K.*, 23), from a naïve girl into a thinking woman.

She also undergoes the strangest twists and turns of the plot, as when the end of the war transforms her from a virgin widow with an adopted son and a lover far away, into an unwilling wife who must fear the return of her lover and cannot account to him or to her husband for the child. A final irony in the last scene is that, having looked after Michael when the Governor's wife could not be bothered with him, she wants nothing more badly than to be allowed to go on wearing herself out and involving herself in expense for it! Here she and her poor friends are contrasted in the stage grouping with the Governor's wife and lawyers: the productive against the parasites of society.[26] In the meantime she has survived a series of dangers so crassly presented as to verge on the comic. The way she hits the bending corporal is certainly funny; her crossing of a bridge which collapses immediately afterwards takes one into the world of Victorian melodrama. With each of these perils she adds to the self-sacrifice which is implicit in taking the child on in the first place. The more pressures are put on her, the more her refusal to let society alienate her stands out. What began as a quick rescue undertaken to salve her conscience turns gradually into a total commitment.

Finally Azdak's freak judgment gives her peculiar productive talent as a mother free rein; it is blessed by society, institutionalised. At last she can be herself without fighting everyone else. The ending emphasises that men are made what they are by social life, not by biology. For all practical purposes Michael is Grusha's child now. This application of the Marxian statement that social being determines consciousness has alienated some believers in *la voix du sang*, but is surely understandable even to them as an answer to the racial madness which is what National Socialism made of theories of heredity.

(VII) AZDAK'S PRODUCTIVITY

Perhaps Brecht's most energetic character, full of zest and quirkiness, Galileo and Schweyk rolled into one, Azdak from the outset gives lessons to Shauva, demonstrations to the Grand Duke. He runs of his own accord to the centre of what he hears is a revolution, just as Mother Courage sets off to the war, though with different intentions. He has an alert political consciousness and the mental agility and self-confidence to use it; he is ready to be appointed judge. His first political song (2071f.; 66f.) is a striking example of Brecht's technique of the missing third strophe. Because the king is carrying on a war and taxing everyone, because the government is ruinous and the workers impoverished – for these reasons, it says, we no longer bleed and weep, leaving bleeding to the calves and weeping to the willows. The missing link is, in this case, in the middle: because of war and injustice the workers have revolted and abolished the cause of their sorrow. The omission has a poetic and an ideological purpose. The poetic one is to force the reader to supply the missing link – and the structure of the song, consisting of a question, two strophes of description and the paradoxical assertion that they answer the question, scarcely makes it easier. The ideological purpose is to conform to the general ambivalence of Marxian theory according to which the dictatorship of the proletariat has indeed to be worked for, but is at the same time a historical necessity. The alienation described classically in the song in the image of the ragged weaver has in in itself the germ of its downfall.

The song nearly results in a catastrophe. Azdak's celebration of the 'new age' (1069; 65) was premature. The new age arrives in the unexpected form of the Fat Prince (1073; 68), just as Galileo's new age turned out to be a new age of exploitation. Azdak does not give up. Soon, to the Ironshirts, in the presence of the Fat Prince, he expresses utter contempt for the forms of law (2074f.; 69f.). He has recognised in the soldiers fellow-proletarians; even if at this moment they are not to be diverted from the service of their oppressors, they will not take a little satire amiss. Here he shows the cunning in finding and spreading the truth demanded in *Five Difficulties in Writing the Truth* (18, 222–39). His performance in the role of the Grand Duke unmasks the new rulers as no better than the old, their claims to change things for the sake of the people as hollow. This need to show up the apparently new as really old, mentioned in the essay, is basic in such anti-Hitler plays as *Roundheads and Peakheads* and *The Resistible Rise of Arturo Ui*. Here, the nephew claims to represent the People – 'Volk' (2076; 71), with no more justification than Hitler. Azdak works against this, which brands him in the Fat Prince's eyes as a revolutionary. His second song (2087; 81) ironically pretends to deprecate the state of chaos in which the common people come into their own.[27] It resembles the carnival ballad in *Galileo* in its Utopian expectations. As often with Brecht, order is the principle of exploitation, disorder the chance for the individual's self-realisation. This song is already used as an instance of cunning used to broadcast truth under a tyranny in *Five Difficulties* (18, 234f.); it is an adaptation of an Egyptian lament of *c.* 2500 B.C.[28]

Ernst Busch in the Berliner Ensemble played Azdak as a representative of the lower classes: lolling back incongruously in his red robe, watching the emotional Governor's wife's attempts to convince him of her right to the child with the air of an old trade-unionist listening to the employer justifying a pay cut.[29] To him everything is reducible to a class aspect. The Princes win their battle for profits in millions of piastres when Grusinia loses the war. Conversely, Mother Grusinia's surprise at a poor person being given a ham goes straight to his heart.[30] His justice is that of a disappointed revolutionary reduced to playing the fool (17, 1206). Brecht's intention of making him a purely selfish judge (*Aj.*, 2, 650: 8.5.44) is not realised: an ambiguity remains, Azdak is now selfish and now altruistic (in rehearsal Brecht stressed these aspects alternately). He uses his power in the interest of the poor, thus establishing an enclave of fairness in a general atmosphere of class justice. He works pragmatically: there being no hope of revolution, he is willing to try and alleviate the effects of tyranny. He is the good bad judge: morally good, professionally bad.[31] He takes bribes openly, a practice obviously to be expected of the regular judge, which he satirises by taking it to absurd lengths. He complains that the poor expect justice without payment (2099; 91; 6). The cynical openness is intended to show up the usual practice. 'It's good for Justice to do it in the open. The wind blows her skirts up and you can see what's underneath' (2081; 75; 5) is not only a reference to Ludovica. He turns the language of jurisprudence upside down, declaring Ludovica's waggling of her hips to be rape (2083; 77; 5). Sometimes he is content to modify somewhat the workings of the caricatured market economy: the doctor in his first case gets away with loss of his fee, the poor patient has to drown his sorrows in a bottle of brandy. In the case of Mother Grusinia the presence of Irakli allows a more direct judgment in favour of the poor, and rich farmers are sentenced to fines. Bribes and fines flow into Azdak's pocket; he is punctilious about collecting fines for contempt of court (even from Simon at the end). Social justice and self-interest concern him about equally. If he loves troubled waters, he does not forget his fishing-rod. He wants to gratify his senses, and like Galileo's scientific urge, his love of justice is bound up with sensuality. The set for his hut, with hung hare, onions and garlic as well as the demonstratively displayed handiwork of the scribe, says as much. Beauty for him is often connected with food; he cannot do without wine. 'With me, everything goes on food and drink' (2100; 91; 6). The theme centres on Azdak but is not confined to him: intelligent appreciation of food is a motif of act 1, whose goat-and-fruit-tree motif is repeated in act 3 where the Old Man mentions his goats (2027; 27) and the innkeeper his cherry and peach trees (2028f.; 28). Similarly Azdak's revaluation of the concept of justice is summed up by the girl tractor driver: 'The laws will have to be re-examined in any case to see whether they are still valid' (2003; 5), but only Azdak actually undertakes the examination.

If Grusha was subject to the seduction of goodness, he can be seduced by a question. He sees himself as an intellectual, a logician, not as good-hearted (2067; 63; 5). His anomalous activities culminate in act 6 – the climax of Brecht's whole *oeuvre*, with its riches of argument and paradox, and a comic perversion of the court scene. In Hauptmann's *Der Biberpelz*, a comedy which was among the early productions of the Berliner Ensemble, the magistrate von Wehrhahn is so blinkered by political prejudice that the rascally protagonist, Mother Wolffen, gets away with her blatant theft. Azdak distorts the law in a nicer way. Even the restoration of the Grand Duke cannot remove him from his place, and threats of what will happen if he gives judgment against the Governor's wife do not make him forget his pragmatic and philanthropic jurisprudence. He says beforehand (2089; 82; 5) that he will not show 'human greatness'; but unlike Galileo in a similar situation he remains true to himself and his work. What most attracts him about the Grusha case seems to be the chance to shake Grusha out of her bovine slowness into a more active assertion of her right to Michael; when she becomes excited and denounces his apparent class justice he is delighted (2100; 92). Not only does he allow this unmasking of feudal justice; he also distorts the point at issue, refusing to take seriously the evidence on the legally decisive matter of maternity (2096; 88), never touching on the mother's abandonment of the child, and finally wrongly claiming that the case is obscure and the duty of finding a mother for the child thus devolves on him (2103; 94). Thus he puts the utility of the judgment before its legality, as he does too in pronouncing the 'wrong' divorce and in declaring the Abashvili estates forfeit to be used as a playground because the city children need one (2104; 95).[32] His liking for Grusha and the poor performance put up by the lawyers on the other side make him determine to disregard the duress he is under. (He does not forget it: he prepares, and makes, a quick getaway after his judgment.)

In *The Augsburg Chalk Circle* Dollinger similarly put utility first, but with no intention of permanently damaging, still less of mocking, established law. Azdak has more in common with Till Eulenspiegel in another Brecht story, *Eulenspiegel als Richter* ('Eulenspiegel as Judge', 11, 371f.). He creates around himself a Saturnalia, a period of misrule, like that which in Greek comedies figures as a reminiscence of the Golden Age of Kronos[33] – the Golden Age is invoked by the Singer (2105; 96; 6). He is a rogue and jester, a parodist who excels himself when for once he sets up a positive principle. And after doing so he must disappear (with an echo of Goethe's poem *Der Fischer*: 'und ward nicht mehr gesehen', 2105): he is no longer safe. He has clarified and modified a few things about the feudal order, given impulses to action – and he leaves the seeds without seeing whether they will grow.

(VIII) THE PRODUCTIVITY OF THE COMMUNES

The Soviet citizens of act 1 have not only just fought Hitler, an expression of the political will of the Socialist system; they also live in a state which by its very nature is a constant challenge to all forms of capitalism. In contrast to the state of destructive competition in capitalism, of which Hitler's war was in Brecht's view only the most striking development, here the good of society and the good of the individual converge. The pleasures of living in Communism are the pleasures of production. The people we see are connoisseurs of cheese, whether themselves goat-keepers or not. They are fascinated by the tools of progress, such as plans for new technical advances: they vindicate Galileo's confidence that mankind is open to the workings of reason. They take pleasure in discussion, they can quote Mayakovsky, and they have enough leisure to rehearse the play of the *Chalk Circle*, which has been revised (2007; 8; 1) – this clearly refers to the fact that the biological mother does not get the child – to bring it into line with new ideas of productivity. They feel pleasure that their existence allows decisions for the benefit of all to be made so easily, whereas in the feudal world many chances were necessary to provide a happy ending. T. M. Holmes, however, points out that even in 1945 the wise communal decisions are only made possible by a bureaucrat, the visiting commissar, waiving his right to impose his will on the communes, so that there is in act 1 at least some of the same tension as in the rest of the play.[34]

The only thing to suffer in the communal life shown here is the individual's attachment to a particular piece of ground. The old man on the right appeals to law, history and sentiment – 'what kind of tree stands beside the house where one was born' (2003; 5) – in his attempt to keep the valley, and finds the cheese produced elsewhere 'barely decent' (2003; 4) on the unprovable ground that the goats like the strange grass less. But his opposite number disagrees about the cheese: it is excellent. This fits with the reversal of the Chalk Circle story. Another mother is not necessarily bad for the child; other ground is not necessarily bad for the goat. The two concepts attacked here are foundations of National Socialist ideology, the components of the slogan 'Blut und Boden', blood and soil: the ties of blood leading to the concept of race and Aryan purity, the attachment to the soil considered to justify the building of a Greater Germany. It is the modern Georgians who not only overcome Hitler, but also change the old play to give it lessons opposed to his ideology.

Brecht's answer to Hitler is not now, as in the first version of *Galileo* or in *Schweyk*, the answer of the little man who has to duck under until it is safe to show his head again. It is a triumphant assertion which need not stop to argue or question. Hitler and his ideology vanquished, the world is again safe for those who are truly modern, who in their working life are busy improving things, putting to work a productive critical attitude, and able to entertain themselves with plays which, as adapted, mixing old and new wisdom (2007; 8; 1), show the same attitudes in an embryonic stage. The topicality and relevance of the Grusha and Azdak plots thus depends on their being embedded in a post-Hitler reality.

A frequent excuse for cutting this scene – which is not a 'prologue'; Brecht dropped this designation of it in 1956 – is that it is impossibly starry-eyed in its view of Soviet Russia. Critics who believe that Brecht the Communist and Brecht the Writer kept tripping each other up explain it as the product either of wilful blindness to facts or of a cynical acquiescence in East German demands for ideology and socialist realism (though it was written before East Germany was invented). The truth is more complicated. Brecht had written 'the USSR is still very far from reaching the state of productive forces in which leadership, e.g., no longer means domination' (*Aj.*, 1, 77: 1.1.40). He did not believe Stalin's state would wither away: Walter Benjamin charmingly describes Brecht impersonating the Soviet Union: he 'assumes a cunning, furtive expression . . . and says, with a sly, sidelong glance . . .: "I know I *ought* to wither away".'[35] And Rosa Luxemburg, after whom one of the colchoses is named, was a Communist leader by no means happy with Russian developments between October 1917 and her death. Incidentally, Brecht almost named the goat-owning commune after her, but Eisler pointed out that 'goat' in German is a term for a silly female, not to be associated with a great revolutionary![36] Russian critics, notably Ilya Fradkin, are rightly sceptical about the scene as a portrayal of Russian actuality, and at least one Russian director has declared it unstageable in Russia.[37] Nor it is a tongue-in-cheek tractor-Utopia; if Brecht wrote such pieces at all, it was only after settling in East Germany. Nor is it a forecast about Soviet reality of 1985 or 2025, for in the course of historical development dialectical changes would by then have come about which a writer in Brecht's time could not anticipate.[38]

Perhaps we can best call it a provisional Utopia: people in the present represented as acting in ways which can only be expected, if at all, in a very distant future. Scene 10 of *Galileo* foreshortens history similarly, making an ideal state spring out of the seventeenth century. Brecht chooses to disregard all the evidence about the Russian reality of 1945 and to hold fast to one overriding aspect: as the most progressive country, Russia is the one to associate with an ideal of humane behaviour. That the visiting arbitrator-commissar finds no work to do adumbrates the Marxian withering-away of the state in a quite fantastic manner. Brecht presumably holds on to the apparent presentation of a real place in the present time only as a counterbalance to the vague chronology of the other two plots and their fairy-tale improbability. Discussion will continue as to whether the treatment is adequate; but we should do Brecht the justice of assuming that he sincerely wanted to portray, just for once, a positively better society such as he is striving towards, and that this was the best way he could find.

(IX) PRESENTATION AND LANGUAGE

The bridge episode of act 3 is a vehicle for empathy with Grusha, and – like the death of Swiss Cheese in *Mother Courage* – does a great deal to undo the effects of all the social comment, the coolness and the distancing techniques used elsewhere. The most notable of these are dealt with under the headings of narration and setting, but it should be pointed out here that whilst the Grusha plot has an epic narrator the Azdak plot is less in need of one. Thus by a bold stroke Brecht was able to make Ernst Busch double as Singer and Azdak in the 1954 production. This underlines that against Grusha's silence and hesitancy, Azdak is voluble and in control, the driving force of his plot,[39] just as in *Galileo*, which has a similar lack of epic effects, Galileo was. It also stresses that the Azdak we see is an actor, whom for the first part of the play we have seen as an actor-singer; and it allows Ernst Busch to show the range of his talents.

When Grusha does talk, she is down-to-earth. The pithy 'Mittagszeit, essen d'Leut' (2027; cf. 27 'Noon time, eating time') shows a South German stamp in its elision and impure rhyme, and the following sentences vary from the colloquial ('wie bei Fürstens', bringing the nobility down to the level of neighbours) to the vulgar ('earned our money sitting on our bottom'). False deference to superiors is not in her make-up; she calls Azdak a 'drunken onion' (2100; 92). Her songs are popular: that promising to wait for Simon (2018f.; 19; 2) echoes distantly a popular song of the Second World War by the Soviet writer Konstantin Simonov;[40] the song of Sosso Robakidse (2026; 26; 3), intended to give her courage, has also a topical reference at the time of a Persian war.

Azdak on the other hand has a rich plebeian language and a stock of proverbs which get great social statements into a small compass.[41] In a few lines of dialogue with Simon, 'When the horse was shod . . .' (2099; 91; 6), the truism that the weaker is subject to the stronger (from *Galileo*) is followed through a series of absurd consequences culminating in the weak person asserting the freedom he claims only by hurting himself (a theme from *Mother Courage*). Finally Azdak objects to Simon's crudity, but he himself is none too careful. Also part of his linguistic virtuosity is the parody of the Grand Duke's clipped speech, leading into the proof that all the princes have a way of speaking that should be suspect to the lower orders (2078; 72). The comic element is obvious in this overflowing energy, set against the muted lyricism of the Grusha scenes. The Singer too in his ballad of Azdak gleefully presents such pairs of concepts as 'Gibher und Abgezwack' (2083; cf. 77, '*Come Here's* and *Listen-You's*') among its colourful rhymes to the name Azdak.

The Singer's language is marked by rhetorical procedures, such as parallelism with variation: 'Then the Governor . . . / Then the fortress . . . / Then the goose . . .' (2013; 14; 2). Adjectives appositionally placed after their nouns lend emphasis: 'Die Panzerreiter nehmen das Kind fort, das teure' (2064; cf. 61, 'The Ironshirts took the child away, the precious child'). Apostrophe and invocation give a solemn tone: 'Oh, blindness of the great! . . . Oh, Wheel of Fortune! Hope of the people!' (2015; 15; 2) – but this is also parodied: 'Oh, confusion! The wife discovers that she has a husband!' (2058; 55; 4). His lyrical descriptions of the effect of passing time on Grusha are reminiscent, with their emphasis on transcience, of Brecht's early poems: 'As she sat by the stream to wash the linen . . .' (2059f.; 56; 4). 'Mit gehenden Monden' makes two poetic effects in the German which are lost in translation ('As the months passed by'). But a more sophisticated way of producing sympathetic awareness of Grusha's problems is to interpolate officialese and contorted syntax to contrast with the emotive terms: 'Sehnsucht hat es gegeben, gewartet worden ist nicht. / Der Eid ist gebrochen. Warum, wird nicht mitgeteilt' (2063; cf. 60, 'There was great yearning . . .'). Sentiment is prevented from relapsing into sentimentality by avoiding such obvious terms as 'empfinden', to feel emotions. Another way of encouraging sentiment without false pathos is by introducing everyday actions among the potentially emotive content: 'I had to care for what otherwise would have come to harm / I had to bend down on the floor for breadcrumbs / I had to tear myself to pieces for what was not mine . . .' (2064; 60; 4). The leisureliness of the singer's reports of Grusha's inner life, the cunning metrical variations, even the idyllic comment in some places, as in the evocation of the evening Angelus (2024; 24; 2) cannot blind one to the social context. Mention of the Angelus is part of Michael's threat to Grusha: if she does not heed him, she will not partake of life's satisfactions. But more in evidence in the play, and in the singer's comments, is the obverse: the punishment for heeding Michael's cries, the punishment inflicted by a hostile society on goodness.

There are frightening elements in the play. The Ironshirts in their stiff, shapeless clothing and grotesque attitudes repeat an effect which had been a success in the pre-Hitler *Man is Man*. Against a background of a severed head (the Governor's head is displayed in Nukha after his execution right to the end of the play) and a hanged judge they listen threateningly to Azdak's self-denunciation and then suddenly, with de‧moniac laughter, turn to his persecution, which ends just as abruptly. But the two who pursue Grusha are also comic, and a microcosm of the social order: one to give orders, the other to execute them. Brecht rubs in the unfairness of things by using N.C.O. clichés. The private is always a 'blockhead', his every movement shows he is 'insubordinate', he is subjected to orders in the infinitive (a nuance lost in the English) and little sermons: 'A good soldier has his heart and soul in it . . .' (2034; 33; 3). The corporal's rough sadism comes out in his coarse innuendoes in dealing with Grusha. Otherwise verbal humour is rare in the play: a restrained pun on *Trauung*, wedding, and *Trauer*, mourning (2053; cf. 50) comes in the wedding scene, an episode of wild movement. The apparently imminent death of the bridegroom makes everyone hurry over the mar‧riage: his mother rushes around making arrangements, the villagers rush in so as not to miss anything – and crowd the room intolerably. Finally the two women, unable to get round the guests, have to throw the bits of cake among the crowd, a buffeted and swaying knot of eating, chatter‧ing, singing, praying people among whom eventually the talk about the end of the war becomes audible. The dying husband, a pale and skeletal figure, suddenly appears at the door – a *memento mori* turned into a husband, the spectre at the feast who turns the mock wedding into a reality and stops Grusha's intention of using it as a social convenience. This night-shirted apparition causes a swift exodus of screaming guests.[42] Movement is important at the end of the play too. Brecht intended, in order to avoid intrinsically false folkloristic dancing, to arrange the final dance as a set of mimes by which all those present would demonstrate their work – emphasising the theme of productivity better than general pointless merrymaking could; but as this turned out hard to understand, it was cut to a few dance steps before the final curtain.[43]

As usual, Brecht added plenty of business in rehearsal. The peasant woman to whom Grusha wants to entrust the child, for instance, ex‧presses when she comes out her suspicion of anything left lying around in these uncertain times, her fear that someone may be lying in wait with a cosh to catch her off guard, her apprehension that the child has some infectious disease, her awareness that children picked up off the street usually turn out ne'er-do-wells whatever one does for them; then she finds the child has fine linen, is of good family; and suddenly she decides to give the child a home despite all doubts (*Mat. K.*, 65–7). And after she has put forward her arguments for keeping the child, her hus‧band does not follow her in immediately, which could mean he is going to continue arguing inside; he stays to shake his head at the folly of

women and, still more, at the folly of men who let the weaker sex get
the better of them (*Mat. K.*, 69). In the final scene, the first lawyer
advances to make his plea with self-satisfied bounds and an exaggerated
bow to the judge. A similar incongruity is that between the nephew's
diminutive figure and his family mask, clipped speech, marionette-like
movements, and pretensions to the office of judge.[44]

Dessau's music is difficult and controversial.[45] Some of the melodies
are taken from Azerbaijan folk music, with characteristic ornamentation;
but the melodic ornamentation of the Jewish synagogue tradition, and
a whole catalogue of other exotic effects, are also drawn on. Special
percussion, including three tomtoms, gives more atmosphere than Gru-
sinian authenticity, and the Berliner Ensemble used a special *Gongspiel* –
a set of eight gongs played by hammers like a piano and having pedals
for damping or for a special steely effect. Dessau desires nine in-
strumentalists; at least five are necessary. For Azdak's investiture as judge
Dessau provides a little march quoting the waltz from Act II of Tchai-
kovsky's *Eugene Onegin* – with melody in the accordion and accompaniment in the percussion! Controversy centres, however, around the long
part of the Singer, which is laid out for v-effects. Coldness in telling
Grusha's story suggests the horror of an era in which kindness is self-
destructive. Such phrases as 'Feuer schlugen sie aus meinem Nacken'
(2063; 59 'My neck was burnt by fire' is not so graphic and direct; 4)
are set in the cadence of a question and with musical accent on gram-
matically unstressed syllables, to aid the singer in expressing surprise
at the emotion or its formulation; but critics merely found this, like the
arbitrary melismatic treatment of some words intended to give oriental
atmosphere, made the words incomprehensible, and few hearers or
musicians have defended the difficulty of comprehension as a spur to
greater attentiveness.

(x) SETTING AND COSTUME

Among the techniques which relativise the reality of stage events and
work against uncontrolled empathy are Karl von Appen's sets. The backdrops are of silky white, painted in Chinese style and having the primary
function of being beautiful and giving pleasure in their own right.[46] They
are frequently changed during the individual acts, particularly act 3.
Not weighted by battens, they swirl over the stage like flags as they
are dropped.[47] For acts 2, 5 and 6 the town is painted – a mass of box-
like houses jumbled on top of one another, of central Asian inspiration.
In act 3 the delicate calligraphic style comes into its own for distant
mountains, gnarled trees and threatening percipices. In act 4 a broad
landscape suggests Simon's wanderings, in act 5 Azdak's perambula-

tions. At the end, when Azdak has invited those present to an open-air dance, the procession out takes place in front of a drawing of a group of musicians and a dancer with a tambourine.

What is placed before the backdrop should, according to Brecht, remind one of the Christmas crib: overloaded, precious and naïve. The palace has a richly worked silver gate – in which the red fires of rebellion can be reflected.[48] Another, less pretentious, gate represents the church; the two stand side-by-side on stage, not spatially tied to the idea of a building behind. A curving red carpet connects them. Props in act 2 include large, heavy, practical pieces of luggage: a wicker basket, studded trunks and so on. In act 3 the turntable stage is much used. Grusha runs against its turning, and sets for the various episodes come to her on it, having been quickly built up during the previous episode behind a drop screening the back third of the turntable. There is no real break between episodes. Walking from one episode to the next, Grusha sees the next building or landmark in front of her. The music supports the idea of a continuum in which the tension is not allowed to drop – a film-style chase sequence.[49] The peasant's hut is solid, heavy wood; at the climax of the scene, the bridge is realistically rickety, with missing floor laths and only one rope to hold on to. Act 4 is largely interiors: solid furniture, a loom as high as Grusha, and after the marriage an out-sized cask for Yussup's bath. When Simon returns, the river is shown by two ground-rows of rushes running from backdrop to proscenium, a true naïve effect. In act 5, the court has a heavy practical gate and gallows, in contrast to a light-framed, pointed construction which is the roomy judgment-seat in which Azdak can recline as he is carried round the assizes.

Karl von Appen took responsibility for costumes as well as for sets. The women of the communes, even the agricultural expert, are in voluminous shawls covering the head like a wimple and reaching over the upper arms and back; the same folksy headdress is worn by married women in the main plots. Among the men of 1944, if not in uniform, fur hats are in favour; in the historical scenes there are steeple hats for those in authority, spiked helmets for the soldiers, a high pudding-basin shape for peasants and servants. The architects wear cloche hats crowned with the emblem of a snail, architects being in von Appen's opinion slow-moving creatures.[50] The Governor's wife has a cross between coronet and tiara, crowned with peacock feathers. Grusha generally wears her own hair, parted in the middle and formed into long plaits; the female singers show a similar arrangement under their wimples.

The lords and ladies have masks, partly to complement their exaggerated costumes, partly because the actors are to be thought of as amateurs who will take pleasure in dressing up. Their servants and soldiers not involved in the action have partial masks, attaching them to the ruling class, but incompletely (and facilitating doubling). The poorer people could not have masks, as their costume was drab and inexpressive. The double function of Simon, who as a soldier should inspire fear, but as Grusha's lover must not, meant his having not the mask other Ironshirts had, but a very masculine beard instead. Masks do not separate the good from the bad: Grusha's sister-in-law did not have one. Rather, once limited to the upper classes, they show the rulers' immutability. Whereas the evil sister-in-law has changes of mood and rich expression, the Governor is always bored, the Fat Prince always grinning, the nephew always stupid. The Governor's wife has a half-mask, so that she can be seen to smile at the Adjutant.[51]

The Governor and his wife are in long, rich, light-coloured robes; the architects, doctors, lawyers, have darker dress. The Ironshirts, of apparently Samurai inspiration, have long, stiff, heavy tabards over long-skirted coachman's cloaks. The Fat Prince – that Goering-figure – also has quasi-Japanese armour, incongruously completed by a dainty fan. Servants, peasants and townspeople have more or less ragged clothes of rough material: leggings, short overcoats and tied belts are typical of the men, shapeless heavy jackets with skirts down to the ground and aprons almost as long of the women, the whole in brown and beige, occasionally a touch of red. The same clothes, in better material, better preserved and with the addition of a cross at the neck, show the prosperity of Grusha's sister-in-law. The girl whom Azdak finds guilty of rape has a skirt slit right up the front to show close-fitting ankle-length drawers. Michael was represented at first by a doll, but after the winter in the Northern Mountains a real boy appears.

8 Assessment

Practically all Brecht did is based on opposition: the split of Shen Teh and Shui Ta is the most obvious example. It is useless to object to the crassness of this duality, dismiss Brecht as simplistic, and go on to conclude that despite his errors he did quite well considering the era he had to live through.[1] The shock-effect of the extreme is only part of his uniqueness, and so is the tenacity with which he applies Marxian views to the business of men's communal life. Each one of the plays we have examined is influenced in its very structure by Marx's concepts of historical movement and of society. Another part of his impact is based on his willingness to differentiate within the contradictions. Shui Ta is not all bad. Grusha is not all good. Theoretical Marxism does not sit like an incubus on the characters either, but is thoroughly modified by the application of Chinese concepts of politeness, needed to complete the image of people living in harmony as an ideal. The battle against oppression makes those who participate in it tense and even evil, but its aim, never to be lost sight of, is goodness and relaxation. Art must (for, if one does not believe in a religion, no other area of life can) represent the aim too, however hard the struggle, and must exemplify the serenity which in real life there is little chance for.

When we consider the interplay of exaggeration and nuance, of mass constraints and individual dignity, of action and relaxation, of commitment and distance, in Brecht, and when we ask what other playwrights offer similar fruitful complexities, then we may come close to grasping his greatness. Next we might look at the unmatched lyrical form in which he can put his thoughts, for instance the words which the Singer in *The Caucasian Chalk Circle* attributes to Michael and which make Grusha pick him up. What use, Hanns Eisler asks, are distancing and Marx and Lenin to a non-politician, until they fall into the hands of 'one of the greatest poets of German literature'?[2] And Ronald Bryden some years ago expressed discontent that, until the English are converted to learning foreign languages, 'discussion of Brecht here seems doomed to centre on what he said rather than how he said it; on Brecht the translatable political didact rather than the greatest modern German poet.'[3] One can be more sanguine: few of Brecht's effects rely on pure sound, and many of the effects that rely on the riches of the German language and tradition can be approximated to by transposition into English; certainly the translations of the four plays we have dealt with show very much more than just politics in dialogue form.

If we then examine his plays as the writings of a man steeped in theatre practice, embodying a new vision of a possible theatre experience, we have the third element of Brecht's greatness before us. The epic components of the plays serve to open up the stage for the presentation of the dramatic action in the context of a wide historical development, and most of all they aim at a unique interplay of appeal to the head and appeal to the heart. In keeping with the general demand for serenity and relaxation, the play on the stage is to allow the audience to keep cool and laughing, not to put it into emotional tension which impairs possession of the faculties. Brecht-theatre should make us use our senses and our sense to the full, not sweep us off our feet and make us passive. In producing such effects, the collective of people who bring about the theatrical experience exemplify the kind of human co-operation which is Brecht's ethical ideal, and we are to be aware of this realised ideal at work for our pleasure.

Theatre, freed by the rise of film and television from the constraint to imitate reality, can develop as a means of commenting on reality in many different ways. In this development Brecht's conception of theatre must have a major role to play, since it uses to best advantage precisely the things about theatre which film cannot do or cannot do so well,[4] mainly because in the theatre living actors supported by a range of techniques of various kinds confront a living audience. The specifically theatrical experience is Brecht's first aim, never propaganda; and his theatrical imagination, his eye for stage movement, also adds an extra note to his style as a playwright. He is not so much of a political activist, certainly not in the plays we have considered, as were Piscator's writers before him or as is Peter Weiss after him. But the construction of situations and dialogue with the stage in mind allows him to incorporate, without apparent effort, at least as much basic political content as they can, without interfering with the gracefulness and humour he demands of theatre.

As a Marxist, an intellectual, a proponent of reason in the theatre, Brecht sometimes seems an outsider in an age whose drama seems to have moved towards sensual and a-logical adventures, from Sartre's *Huis clos* through Beckett, Ionesco and Pinter to the recent writers who each seem to have developed some sensational neurosis to call their own. As Martin Esslin has pointed out, the common core Brecht and his great contemporaries have is the disorientation of personality, and for this the contradictoriness of modern society is responsible. All these dramatists show an alienated vision of the existent, or a vision of the existent as alienated. Brecht was fascinated enough by Beckett to work on an adaptation of one of his plays. He is aware of the nightmare aspects of our communal schizophrenia. But he does not trap himself in an irrationality that would cut him off from giving any answers. For him man is good, if not perfectible, and he is able to see his work, in classical style, within a tradition of humane elements: Jesus, Luther, Bacon, Goethe, Marx, Mo Tzu – none of them accepted uncritically, but all pointing to the idea that it is worth while for men to attempt to alter their fate.

Notes

References to Brecht's works in German text are generally to the collected edition in 20 volumes:

Bertolt Brecht: *Gesammelte Werke* (werkausgabe edition suhrkamp), Frankfurt 1967.

Except in the case of the plays dealt with in detail in this book, the volume number is quoted first, the page following after a comma, thus: 15, 174. It is difficult to date many of Brecht's texts, so I have dispensed with dates, but it may be useful to the reader to know that a single, *very approximately* chronological sequence runs through volumes 8–10 (poems), another through volumes 15–16 (essays on theatre), another through volumes 18–19 (essays on literature and art) and another through volume 20 (essays on politics); and that these groups of volumes are (like volumes 1–7, plays) through-paginated. Thus:

vol. 8 pp. 1–424, poems 1913–33.
vol. 9 pp. 425–822, poems 1933–41.
vol. 10 pp. 823–1082, poems 1941–56.
vol. 15 pp. 1–498, theatre essays 1918–1942.
vol. 16 pp. 499–942. theatre essays 1937–1956.
vol. 18 pp. 1–284, literary essays 1920–1939.
vol. 19 pp. 285–556, literary essays 1934–1956.
vol. 20 pp. 1–350, political essays 1919–56.

His journals are quoted in the editions

Bertolt Brecht: *Arbeitsjournal*, 2 vols., Frankfurt 1973 (abbreviated *Aj.*; my translations from it retain Brecht's private convention of not capitalising) and Bertolt Brecht: *Tagebücher 1920–1922. Autobiographische Aufzeichnungen 1920–1954*, ed. Herta Ramthun, Frankfurt 1975 (abbreviated *Tb.*).

Theoretical works and poems contained in the following editions are quoted from them:

Brecht on Theatre – The Development of an Aesthetic, ed. and trs. John Willett, London (Methuen) 1964 (abbreviated *B. on Theatre*).
Bertolt Brecht: *The Messingkauf Dialogues*, trs. John Willett, London (Methuen) 1965 (abbreviated *M. Dial.*).
Bertolt Brecht: *Poems*, ed. John Willett and Ralph Manheim, London (Eyre Methuen) 1976 (abbreviated *B. Poems*).

References to plays in English text are to the *Methuen Modern Plays* series, London (Eyre Methuen):

The Life of Galileo, trs. Desmond I. Vesey, 1963, repr. 1974 (abbreviated *G.*).
Mother Courage and her Children, trs. Eric Bentley, 1962, repr, 1976.
The Good Person of Szechwan, trs. John Willett, 1965, repr. 1974.
The Caucasian Chalk Circle, trs. James and Tania Stern, with W. H. Auden, 1963, repr. 1975.

Quotations from these plays are supplied first with the page number in volumes 3, 4 or 5 of *Gesammelte Werke* (*Galilei* in vol. 3, *Kreidekreis* in vol. 5, the others in vol. 4); then comes the page number in the Methuen edition; finally (unless clear from the context) the number of the scene, for those not using either of these editions. Alternative editions, some using other translations, are published by Eyre Methuen, Blackie and Penguin in Great Britain; and Grove Press, Random House and Pantheon Books in the U.S. Grove Press publish individual editions of all four plays – *Galileo* in the second version with two scenes cut.
The following important or useful books on Brecht, or by his friends, are referred to in text and footnotes by author's name only.

Hanns Eisler: *Gesammelte Werke III/7 = Gespräche mit Hans Bunge*, Leipzig 1975.
Erich Engel: *Schriften. Über Theater und Film*, Berlin 1971.
Martin Esslin: *Brecht. The Man and his Work*, New York 1974 (previous editions under the title *Brecht, a Choice of Evils*).
John Fuegi: *The Essential Brecht*, Los Angeles 1972.
Therese Giehse: *'Ich hab nichts zum Sagen', Gespräche mit Monika Sperr*, 2nd. ed., Munich 1975.
Ronald Gray: *Brecht the Dramatist*, Cambridge 1976.
Fritz Hennenberg: *Dessau-Brecht. Musikalische Arbeiten*, Berlin 1963.
Claude Hill: *Bertolt Brecht*, Boston 1975.
Walter Hinck: *Die Dramaturgie des späten Brecht*, Göttingen 1959.
Helmut Jendreiek: *Bertolt Brecht. Drama der Veränderung*, Düsseldorf 1969.
Volker Klotz: *Bertolt Brecht. Versuch über das Werk*, 4th. ed., Bad Homburg 1971.
Karl Korsch: *Karl Marx*, New York 1963, (also earlier editions).
Karl-Heinz Ludwig: *Bertolt Brecht. Philosophische Grundlagen und Implikationen seiner Dramaturgie*, Bonn 1975.
Hans Mayer: *Brecht in der Geschichte*, Frankfurt 1971.

Rainer Pohl: *Strukturelemente und Entwicklung von Pathosformen in der Dramensprache Bertold* [sic] *Brechts,* Bonn 1969.

James M. Ritchie: *Brecht: Der kaukasische Kreidekreis,* London, 1976.

Käthe Rülicke-Weiler: *Die Dramaturgie Brechts. Theater als Mittel der Veränderung,* 2nd. ed., Berlin 1968.

Ernst Schumacher: *Drama und Geschichte. Bertolt Brechts 'Leben des Galilei' und andere Stücke,* 2nd. ed., Berlin 1968.

Theaterarbeit. 6 Aufführungen des Berliner Ensembles, ed. Ruth Berlau, Bertolt Brecht, *et al.,* 3rd. ed., Berlin n.d.

Klaus Völker: *Bertolt Brecht. Eine Biographie,* Munich 1976.

Manfred Wekwerth: *Schriften. Arbeit mit Brecht,* Berlin 1973.

John Willett: *The Theatre of Bertolt Brecht. A Study from eight Aspects,* London 1959 (also later editions).

Four useful volumes of commentaries, notes and factual data are published in the *edition suhrkamp* and edited by Werner Hecht:

Materialien zu Brechts 'Leben des Galilei', 1963 (abbreviated *Mat. G.*).

Materialien zu Brechts 'Mutter Courage und ihre Kinder', 1964 (abbreviated (*Mat. C.*).

Materialien zu Brechts 'Der gute Mensch von Sezuan', 1968 (abbreviated *Mat. S.*).

Materialien zu Brechts 'Der kaukasische Kreidekreis', 1969 (abbreviated *Mat. K.*).

The abbreviation *BJb.* refers to the *Brecht–Jahrbuch* of the International Brecht Society: the first three issues under the title *Brecht heute/Brecht today,* and dated 1971, 1972, 1973–74; the fourth as *Brecht-Jahrbuch 1974,* all edited by John Fuegi and collaborators.

Marx and Engels are generally quoted from their *Selected Works* in one volume, 2nd printing, London 1970.

The notes following supply further bibliography on particular points.

CHAPTER 1 (pp. 1–14)
This chapter is partly based on Völker's book, which is the most up-to-date, reliable and full account of Brecht's life, especially his relationships with women. Another fairly full biography is contained in Esslin's book, though some details must be treated with care; valuable details on Brecht's childhood in Werner Frisch and K. W. Obermeier: *Brecht in Augsburg, Erinnerungen, Dokumente, Texte, Fotos,* Berlin and Weimar 1975. Brecht is best put in the full historical and cultural context by Frederic Ewen: *Bertolt Brecht, His Life, His Art and His Times,* New York 1967 and London 1970.

1 Henning Rischbieter: *Brecht,* vol. 1, Velber 1966, p. 22.
2 Walter Benjamin: *Understanding Brecht,* London 1973, pp. 113f., 116.
3 Giehse, p. 195.
4 See Willy Haas: *Bert Brecht,* Berlin 1958, p. 5.
5 See Zuckmayer's contribution in Engel, pp. 251f.

6 See Fritz Kortner's memoir in Engel, pp. 237–9.

7 See Mayer, p. 78.

8 See Erwin Leiser: 'Der Neinsager. Notizen über Brecht und die Politik', in the collection *Bertolt Brecht*, Bad Godesberg 1966, 15–26.

9 Willett, pp. 116f.

10 It was first performed in Prague; see Kurt R. Grossmann: 'Die Exilsituation in der Tschechoslowakei', in Manfred Durzak (ed): *Die deutsche Exilliteratur 1933–1945*, Stuttgart 1973, p. 69.

11 Wekwerth, pp. 26–8.

12 Eisler, p. 50.

13 See especially letter from Brecht to Helene Weigel, 21.4.49, in Werner Hecht and Siegfried Unseld (eds): *Helene Weigel zu ehren*, Frankfurt 1970, pp. 62f.

14 André Müller and Gerd Semmer: *Geschichten vom Herrn B., 100 neue Brecht-Anekdoten*, Munich 1968, p. 93.

15 Up to the end of 1956, *Señora Carrar's Rifles* had achieved 24 professional productions in East Germany and *Puntila* 18; *Mother Courage* ten (nine of of them by 1951), *The Caucasian Chalk Circle* one; *Galileo* and *The Three-penny Opera*, among others, remained unperformed. Data exclude the Berliner Ensemble, and are from Werner Hecht (ed): *Brecht-Dialog 1968*, Berlin 1968, pp. 324–33. In 1954, after rationalisation, there were about 68 professional drama companies in East Germany.

16 See Christoph Funke *et al.* (eds): *Theater-Bilanz 1945–1969*, Berlin 1971, p. 226.

17 For attitudes to Brecht in the GDR see Manfred Jäger: 'Zur Rezeption des Stückeschreibers Brecht in der DDR', *Text + Kritik*, Sonderband Bertolt Brecht I, 1973, 107–18.

18 Giehse, p. 95.

19 Eisler, p. 72.

CHAPTER 2 (pp. 15–23)

1 See Keith A. Dickson: 'Brecht's Doctrine of Nature', *BJb*. 3, 106–21.

2 Wekwerth, p. 69; and the same author's *Brecht?*, Munich 1976, p. 16.

3 The approach particularly associated with Martin Esslin (see Chapters 9 and 10 of his book), though he puts his viewpoint with great sensibility. His approach is applied to particular plays by Charles R. Lyons: *Bertolt Brecht. The Despair and the Polemic*, Carbondale, Ill., 1968.

4 Engel, p. 38.

5 See Ludwig, pp. 126f., and Korsch, esp. p. 86.

6 Korsch, p. 49.

7 See Robert Brustein: *The Theatre of Revolt*, London 1965, pp. 252f.

8 See Korsch, p. 85.

9 See Klaus-Detlef Müller: *Die Funktion der Geschichte im Werk Bertolt Brechts*, Tübingen 1972, p. 68.

10 See Ludwig, pp. 163–5.

11 Käthe Rülicke-Weiler: 'Bemerkungen Brechts zur Kunst, Notate 1951–1955', *Weimarer Beiträge*, Brecht-Sonderheft 1968, 5–11, p. 8.

12 Brecht, letter to Korsch, November 1941, quoted by Wolfdietrich Rasch: 'Bertolt Brechts marxistischer Lehrer', in Rasch: *Zur deutschen Literatur seit der Jahrundertwende*, Stuttgart 1967, 243–73, p. 265.

13 See Ludwig, p. 111.

14 See Heinz Brüggemann: *Literarische Technik und soziale Revolution*, Reinbek 1973, pp. 76ff.

15 See Rasch, op. cit. (n. 12 above), esp. p. 252.

16 On Lukács and the (rather woolly) realism debate, see Völker, pp. 264–85; and Lothar Baier: 'Streit um den schwarzen Kasten', *Text + Kritik*, Sonderband Bertolt Brecht I, 1973, 37–44.

17 Müller and Semmer, op. cit. (n. 14 to Chapter 1), p. 47.

18 André Müller and Gerd Semmer: *Geschichten vom Herrn B., 99 Brecht-Anekdoten*, Frankfurt 1967, p. 37.

19 See *Me-ti: Buch der Wendungen* (12, 417–585) and Ludwig, p. 56 *Anmerkungen*.

20 On Brecht and the Soviet Union see Ludwig, pp. 117–21.

21 On productivity see Rülicke-Weiler, pp. 29ff.

22 Erich Engel: 'Zeittheater', in Engel, 17–26, p. 22.

CHAPTER 3 (pp. 24–52)
This chapter would have taken a different form but for Käthe Rülicke-Weiler's book, from which I take a number of points without further acknowledgement.

1 Esslin, p. 127.

2 See Klaus-Detlef Müller: 'Der Philosoph auf dem Theater', *Text + Kritik*, Sonderband Bertolt Brecht I, 1973, 45–71, esp. pp. 45–7.

3 In discussion with students of the Karl Marx University, Leipzig, 29.1.55, quoted by Rülicke-Weiler, p. 44.

4 See Klaus-Detlef Müller: *Die Funktion der Geschichte im Werk Bertolt Brechts*, Tübingen 1972, p. 151; and Ernst Schürer: *Georg Kaiser und Bertolt Brecht*, Frankfurt 1971, esp. pp. 47–54.

5 See Rolf Tarot: 'Ideologie und Drama', in Stefan Sonderegger *et al.* (eds): *Typologia Litterarum*, Festschrift Max Wehrli, Zurich 1969, 351–66.

6 Eisler, p. 127.

7 As implicitly assumed by Esslin, pp. 150f.

8 On criticism and function, see Ludwig, pp. 44–9.

9 This argument is based on Ernst Nef: 'Das Aus-der-Rolle-Fallen als Mittel der Illusionszerstörung bei Tieck und Brecht', *Zeitschrift für deutsche Philologie*, LXXXIII (1964), 191–215.

10 Willett, pp. 112f.

11 See Willett, pp. 179f., and his contribution in *Communications of the International Brecht Society*, IV, 2 (Feb 1975), pp. 3f.; also Marjorie L. Hoover: 'Brecht's Soviet Connection Tretiakov', *BJb.* 3, 39–56, esp. pp. 44–6.

12 On distancing see Ludwig, pp. 38–41.

13 See Ralph J. Ley: 'Francis Bacon, Galileo and the Brechtian Theater', in Siegfried Mews and Herbert Knust (eds): *Essays on Brecht. Theater and Politics*, Chapel Hill 1974, 174–89.

14 Erich Engel: 'Brecht, Kafka und die Absurden', in Engel, 57–60.

15 Letter to Ilya Fradkin, 10.1.56, quoted by Rülicke-Weiler, p. 64.

16 As Esslin, p. 240. thinks. But he qualifies the statement with regard to the late plays, p. 264.
17 On emotion in epic theatre see Rülicke-Weiler, pp. 51–3; the quotation p. 53.
18 See Rülicke-Weiler, op. cit. (note 11 to Chapter 2), p. 7.
19 On Brecht and comedy see above all Fritz Martini: *Lustspiele – und das Lustspiel*, Stuttgart 1973, section 'Überlegungen zur Poetik des Lustspiels'; also Peter Christian Giese: *Das 'Gesellschaftlich-Komische'*, Stuttgart 1974; and Kenneth S. Whitton: 'Friedrich Dürrenmatt and the Legacy of Bertolt Brecht', *Forum for Modern Language Studies*, xii (1976), 65–81.
20 Marx, *Zur Kritik der Hegelschen Rechtsphilosophie*, quoted by Giese, op. cit., p. 16.
21 See Mordecai Gorelik: 'On Brechtian Acting', *Quarterly Journal of Speech*, lx (1974), 265–78, p. 271.
22 Wekwerth, p. 72.
23 Eric Bentley: 'Portrait of the Critic as a Young Brechtian', *Theatre Quarterly*, no. 21 (1976), 5–11, p. 6.
24 See Karl-Heinz Schoeps: 'Bertolt Brecht und George Bernard Shaw', *BJb*. 3, 156–72. For further affinities of the two, see the same author's 'Epic Structures in the Plays of Bernard Shaw and Bertolt Brecht', in Mews and Knust, op. cit. (n. 13 above), 28–43.
25 On Brecht's language see Esslin, Chapter 5.
26 Some means of literary distancing are listed with examples by Gertrud Fankhauser: *Verfremdung als Stilmittel vor und bei Brecht*, Tübingen 1971, pp. 41–8.
27 Often quoted, e.g. by Pohl, p. 29.
28 See the defence of Brecht's characterisation by Werner Mittenzwei: *Bertolt Brecht. Von der 'Massnahme' bis zu 'Leben des Galilei'*, Berlin and Weimar 1965, pp. 323f.
29 See Esslin, pp. 38f.
30 See Fuegi, pp. 128f.
31 For a good summary of Brecht's early theory starting from this point, see Willett, pp. 169–74.
32 For Brecht's place in the history of theory and dramatic form see Hinck, pp. 24–9.
33 On gestus see Ludwig, pp. 17–22.
34 Werner Hecht: *Aufsätze zu Brecht*, Berlin 1970, pp. 80f.
35 Manfred Wekwerth: *Notate*, Frankfurt 1967, pp. 14f.
36 For sympathy and empathy see Gorelik, op. cit. (n. 21 above), p. 269.
37 As they seem to be taken by Esslin, p. 139.
38 Mayer, p. 147.
39 Thomas K. Brown: '*Verfremdung* in Action at the Berliner Ensemble', *German Quarterly*, xlvi (1973), 525–39.
40 Angelika Hurwicz: *Brecht inszeniert – Der kaukasische Kreidekreis*, Velber 1964, p. [3]. This text is also available in *Mat. K.*, 57–63.
41 Müller and Semmer, op. cit. (n. 18 to Chapter 2), p. 75.
42 Rülicke-Weiler, p. 113; Werner Hecht (ed): *Brecht-Dialog 1968*, Berlin 1968, p. 161.

43 Specimen in *Theaterarbeit*, 258–60.

44 On models see *Theaterarbeit*, 285–346; also *Mat. C.*, 95–104.

45 Werner Hecht: *Sieben Studien über Brecht*, Frankfurt 1972, p. 170.

46 Fuegi, p. 82.

47 Hecht, op. cit. (n. 34 above), p. 93.

48 Hurwicz, op. cit. (n. 40 above), p. [2].

49 See Kenneth Tynan's articles in *New York Times*, 11.1.76; *Communications from the International Brecht Society*, v, 2 (Mar 1976); *Plays and players*, xxiii, 6 (Mar 1976), 12–6.

50 See Funke, op. cit. (n. 16 to Chapter 1), pp. 292f.

51 See Henry Glade: 'Brecht and the Soviet Theater: a 1971 overview', *BJb.* 2, 164–73.

52 See *Communications from the International Brecht Society*, ii, 3 (May 1973), p. 12. For a Marxist analysis of Brecht's popularity in West Germany, see Ernst Schumacher: 'Brecht und seine Bedeutung für die Gesellschaft der siebziger Jahre', *BJb*, 2, 27–87, esp. pp. 42f.

53 See Jack Zipes: 'Ein Interview mit Peter Stein', *BJb.* 3, 210–20.

54 See *Communications from the International Brecht Society*, iv, 3 (May 1975), p. 4 (Betty Nance Weber).

55 See Ernst Wendt: 'Möglichkeiten, Brecht zu spielen. Ein Überblick', in the collection *Bertolt Brecht*, Bad Godesberg 1966, 5–14.

56 In *Bertolt Brecht in Britain*, catalogue (by Nicholas Jacobs and Prudence Ohlsen) of an exhibition at the National Theatre, London, 1977, p. 6. This catalogue is the best source of information on its subject. For the quality of 'British Brecht', see David Zane Mairowitz's reviews under this title in *Plays and players*.

CHAPTER 4 (pp. 53–84)

1 Marianne Kesting: *Bertolt Brecht in Selbstzeugnissen und Bilddokumenten*, Reinbek 1959, p. 91.

2 The stage direction for her return is at the end of Galileo's long speech (1341; 118), but Brecht had her in long before this. See *Mat. G.*, 112 (Rülicke).

3 See Mittenzwei, op. cit. (n. 28 to Chapter 3), pp. 309, 326ff.

4 See Schumacher, pp. 62f.

5 Schumacher, p. 41.

6 Schumacher, pp. 72–81.

7 Gerhard Szczesny: *Das Leben des Galilei und der Fall Bertolt Brecht*, Frankfurt 1966, p. 107; 12, 375f.

8 See Mittenzwei, op. cit. (n. 28 to Chapter 3), pp. 283f.

9 Quoted by Schumacher, p. 118.

10 See *Mat. G.*, 140 (Rülicke).

11 Günter Rohrmoser: 'Brecht. Das [sic] Leben des Galilei', in Benno von Wiese (ed): *Das deutsche Drama*, vol. 2, Düsseldorf 1958, p. 405.

12 See *Mat. G.*, 148 (Rülicke).

13 For science in the drama see Rémy Charbon: *Die Naturwissenschaften im modernen deutschen Drama*, Zurich and Munich 1974, pp. 134–6, 251f.

14 See Müller, op. cit. (n. 2 to Chapter 3), p. 48. For the full arguments on Bacon's influence, see Ley, op. cit. (n. 13 to Chapter 3).

15 In *The Times*, 19.6.60; see Schumacher, p. 488.

16 Dated 1939 in *Gesammelte Werke* but more relevant to the second version.

17 See Schumacher, pp. 207–18, 349–63.

18 Esslin, pp. 168ff.

19 See Charbon, op. cit. (n. 13 above), pp. 113–16.

20 Mittenzwei, op. cit. (n. 3 above), p. 271.

21 See Henning Rischbieter: *Brecht*, vol. 2, Velber 1966, p. 11.

22 Brecht in rehearsal, 20.3.56, after *Mat. G.*, 121 (Rülicke).

23 See Schumacher, p. 229.

24 Eisler, p. 152.

25 See Karl S. Weimar: 'The Scientist and Society', *Modern Language Quarterly*, xxvii (1966), 431–48, esp. p. 440.

26 Schumacher, pp. 175–89.

27 See Erich Engel: ' "Leben des Galilei" von Bertolt Brecht' in Engel, 99–103, esp. p. 99.

28 See Edward M. Berckman: 'Brecht's *Galileo* and the Openness of History', *Modernist Studies*, i (2) (1974), 41–50, p. 46.

29 Schumacher, pp. 40f.

30 Schumacher, pp. 158–74.

31 Schumacher, p. 46.

32 Schumacher, pp. 55ff.

33 See Fuegi, pp. 136f.

34 Korsch, p. 57.

35 Schumacher, p. 76.

36 See Richard Beckley: 'Adaptation as a Feature of Brecht's dramatic Technique', *German Life & Letters*, xv (1961–2), 274–84, p. 284.

37 Rainer Nägele: 'Zur Struktur von Brechts *Leben des Galilei*', *Der Deutschunterricht*, xxiii (1971), 86–99.

38 Rülicke-Weiler, p. 87.

39 Rülicke-Weiler, p. 149.

40 See Alfred D. White: 'Brecht's *Leben des Galilei*: Armchair Theatre?', *German Life & Letters*, xxvii (1973–4), 124–32.

41 John Sidney Groseclose: 'Scene Twelve of Bertolt Brecht's *Galilei* . . .', *Monatshefte für deutschen Unterricht*, lxii (1970), 367–82, p. 372.

42 See Herbert Knust: 'Brechts Dialektik vom Fressen und von der Moral', *BJb.* 3, 221–50, esp. p. 231, note 18.

43 See White, op. cit. (n. 40 above).

44 Werner Hecht: *Aufsätze zu Brecht*, Berlin 1970, p. 136.

45 Full details in Pohl, pp. 58f.

46 See Pohl, p. 131.

47 See Pohl, pp. 120f.

48 *Aufbau einer Rolle, Laughtons Galilei*, Berlin 1956, pp. 9–12, quoted by Rülicke-Weiler, pp. 270f.

49 On scene 12 see Groseclose, op. cit. (n. 41 above); on the eyes particularly p. 380, referring to a stage direction in the second version.

50 Rülicke-Weiler, p. 112.

51 Rülicke-Weiler, p. 140.
52 Völker, pp. 354f.

CHAPTER 5 (pp. 85–112)

1 Klaus Völker: *Brecht-Chronik*, 2nd ed., Munich 1971, p. 78.
2 The scene titles, diverging from those in the text, and the gestic divisions, are taken from the commentary in *Mat. C.*, 19–80, and in *Theaterarbeit*, 228f.
3 See Fuegi, pp. 90–2.
4 Rülicke-Weiler, p. 87.
5 See Keith A. Dickson: 'History, Drama and Brecht's Chronicle of the Thirty Years War', *Forum for Modern Language Studies*, VI (1970), 255–72.
6 See Peter Leiser: *Bertolt Brecht – Mutter Courage und ihre Kinder – Der kaukasische Kreidekreis*, Hollfeld 1973, p. 54. In this speech incidentally, as pointed out by Hill (p. 111), 'withdrawing' is a mistranslation; 'moving through' would be closer.
7 Rülicke-Weiler, p. 214.
8 Giehse, p. 71.
9 Giehse, p. 72.
10 See Jendreiek, p. 175.
11 Brecht would have known from Korsch that the phrase was coined by Hobbes in the seventeenth century. See Korsch, p. 57.
12 See Hecht, op. cit. (n. 45 to Chapter 3), p. 153.
13 See Jendreiek, p. 179.
14 See Wekwerth, p. 54.
15 See Jendreiek, pp. 160f.
16 George Steiner: *The Death of Tragedy*, pp. 353ff., quoted by Fuegi, p. 93, with photo.
17 Rülicke-Weiler, p. 204, with photo.
18 *Theaterarbeit*, p. 300.
19 See Richard Beckley: 'Adaptation as a Feature of Brecht's Dramatic Technique', *German Life & Letters*, XV (1961–2), 274–84, esp. pp. 282f.
20 See Franz Norbert Mennemeier: 'Mother Courage and her Children', in Peter Demetz (ed): *Brecht. A Collection of Critical Essays*, Englewood Cliffs 1962, 138–50, p. 144.
21 Dickson, op. cit. (n. 5 above), p. 270.
22 A point well made by Mennemeier, op. cit. (n. 20 above), p. 140.
23 See Jendreiek, p. 162.
24 See John J. White: 'A Note on Brecht and Behaviourism', *Forum for Modern Language Studies*, VII (1971), 249–58, esp. p. 255.
25 'Es kommt ein Tag, da wird sich wenden / Das Blatt für uns, er ist nicht fern. / Da werden wir, das Volk, beenden / Den grossen Krieg der grossen Herrn . . .'. *Norddeutsche Zeitung*, Schwerin, 10.11.51, quoted by Hennenberg, p. 511.
26 Rülicke-Weiler, op. cit. (n. 11 to Chapter 2), pp. 6f.
27 Völker, p. 293.
28 See Henning Rischbieter: *Brecht*, vol. 2, Velber 1966, pp. 27–9.

29 Ralph Brustein: *The Theatre of Revolt*, London, 1965, p. 273.

30 See E. Speidel: 'The Mute Person's Voice: Mutter Courage and her Daughter', *German Life & Letters*, XXIII (1969–70), 332–9.

31 Pohl, pp. 22–4.

32 Examples from Pohl, p. 28.

33 Pohl, p. 25.

34 See Pohl, pp. 37f., with extract.

35 John Willett: 'The Poet Beneath the Skin', *BJb*. 2, 88–104, p. 102.

36 See Hinck, p. 42.

37 Eisler, p. 377 (footnote by Hans Bunge); Pohl, p. 63.

38 For details on the music in this section I am much indebted to Hennenberg's book. See also Dessau's essay *Zur Courage-Musik*, in *Mat. C.*, 118–22, and with further musical examples in *Theaterarbeit*, 274–80.

39 See Hinck, pp. 37f.

40 Wekwerth, pp. 384f.; *Mat. C.*, 77.

41 Well described by Gray, pp. 123f.

42 Rülicke-Weiler, p. 175, with photo.

43 Rülicke-Weiler, p. 199, with photo.

44 See Wekwerth, pp. 86f.

45 *Theaterarbeit*, p. 297, with photo.

46 Giehse, pp. 115–18, with photos.

47 *Theaterarbeit*, p. 317.

48 See Nick Wilkinson: '*Mutter Courage* in Westafrika', *BJb*. 4, 117–24.

49 See the description by Paul Ryder Ryan in *The Drama Review*, XIX, 2 (June 1975), 78–93. On Jerome Robbins' New York production, see Lee Baxandall: 'The Americanization of Bert Brecht', *BJb*. 1, 150–67, esp. pp. 154–7.

CHAPTER 6 (pp. 113–39)

1 Hennenberg, p. 452.

2 My scene titles are taken from a list of scenic elements in Brecht's working notes, printed in *Mat. S.*, 86f.

3 See Reinhold Grimm: 'Bertolt Brecht: Der gute Mensch von Sezuan', in Manfred Brauneck (ed): *Das deutsche Drama vom Expressionismus bis zur Gegenwart*, Bamberg 1972, 168–73, esp. p. 169; and Henning Rischbieter: *Brecht*, vol. 2, Velber 1966, p. 39.

4 See Hill, pp. 125f.

5 Hill, p. 125, following other American scholars.

6 See Hinck, pp. 85–7.

7 Renata Berg-Pan: 'Mixing Old and New Wisdom: The "Chinese" Sources of Brecht's *Kaukasischer Kreidekreis* and Other Works', *German Quarterly*, 1975, 204–28, pp. 209f.

8 Willett, pp. 96f., 237.

9 Berg-Pan, op. cit. (n. 7 above), p. 210.

10 Much of this section is based on Antony Tatlow: 'China oder Chima?', *BJb*. 1, 27–47, esp. pp. 44–6.

11 Klotz, p. 19.

12 Klotz, p. 18.

13 After Friedrich Engels: *Socialism: Utopian and Scientific*, Special Introduction to the English edition of 1892.
14 Klotz, pp. 19f.
15 See Jendreiek, p. 216.
16 See Jendreiek, p. 240.
17 See Müller, op. cit. (n. 4 to Chapter 3), p. 62.
18 See Jendreiek, p. 238.
19 See Henning Rischbieter: *Brecht*, vol. 2, Velber 1966, p. 37.
20 See Karl-Heinz Schmidt: 'Zur Gestaltung antagonistischer Konflikte bei Brecht und Kaiser', in *Mat. S.*, 109–33, esp. p. 117.
21 On the sex-bound elements see John Fuegi: 'The Alienated Woman: Brecht's *The Good Person of Setzuan*', in Mews and Knust, op. cit. (n. 13 to Chapter 3), 190–6.
22 See Walter H. Sokel: 'Brecht's Split Characters and His Sense of the Tragic', in Demetz, op. cit. (n. 20 to Chapter 5), 127–37, esp. p. 128.
23 See Mayer, p. 179.
24 See Klotz, pp. 15f.
25 Klotz, p. 16.
26 Sokel, op. cit. (n. 22 above), p. 129.
27 Sokel, p. 130.
28 See Mayer, pp. 165–70.
29 Willett, p. 91.
30 See on this song Hinck, p. 43; Jendreiek, p. 224; Willett, op. cit. (n. 39 to Chapter 5), p. 90.
31 See Hinck, pp. 49–51.
32 See H. G. Huettich: 'Zwischen Klassik und Kommerz. Brecht in Los Angeles', *BJb.* 4, 125–37.
33 See Wendt, op. cit. (n. 55 to Chapter 3), p. 11.
34 See Mayer, p. 173.
35 Fuegi, pp. 135f.
36 Fuegi, pp. 136f.
37 See Pohl, p. 32.
38 This section is very dependent on Hennenberg's book; see also *Mat. S.*, 145–53.

CHAPTER 7 (pp. 140–70)
1 *Bertolt Brecht in Britain* (n. 56 to Chapter 3), p. 92.
2 Based on Angelika Hurwicz's narration in her photographic record of the Berlin production (n. 40 to Chapter 3; the narration is not included in *Mat. K.*).
3 See Leiser, op. cit. (n. 6 to Chapter 5), pp. 56–8.
4 Berg-Pan, op. cit. (n. 7 to Chapter 6), pp. 215f.
5 Ritchie, pp. 12f.
6 Ritchie, p. 17.
7 See Leiser, op. cit. (n. 6 to Chapter 5), p. 59.
8 As an anecdote in Müller and Semmer (n. 14 to Chapter 1), p. 56, has him claiming.

9 Ritchie, p. 17.

10 See Leiser, op. cit. (n. 6 to Chapter 5), p. 85.

11 Ritchie, pp. 52f.

12 Qayum Qureshi: *Pessimismus und Fortschrittsglaube bei Bert Brecht*, Cologne and Vienna 1971, p. 133.

13 Fuegi, p. 147.

14 See Hinck, p. 49.

15 See Jendreiek, p. 295.

16 See Fuegi, pp. 147f.; and the same author's 'The Caucasian Chalk Circle in Performance', *BJb*. 1, 137–49, p. 140.

17 Rülicke-Weiler, p. 176 – note from rehearsal of 6.2.54.

18 See Qureshi, op. cit. (n. 12 above), pp. 145–7.

19 Eric Bentley: 'An Un-American Chalk Circle?', *Tulane Drama Review*, no. 32 (summer 1966), 64–77, p. 67.

20 Kesting, op. cit. (n. 1 to Chapter 4), p. 123.

21 Ritchie, p. 28.

22 Ritchie, p. 26.

23 Kesting, op. cit. (n. 1 to Chapter 4), p. 109.

24 See Hill, pp. 136f.

25 See Robert Spaethling: 'Zum Verständnis der Grusche in Brechts Der kaukasische Kreidekreis', *Die Unterrichtspraxis*, 1971 (4), 74–81, on the analogy with this 'Mad Meg' drawn by Brecht (*Mat. K.*, 32).

26 Rülicke-Weiler, p. 190, with photo.

27 Hennenberg, p. 89.

28 Quoted by Bentley, op. cit. (n. 19 above), p. 71.

29 Wekwerth, p. 19.

30 See Qureshi, op. cit. (n. 12), p. 152.

31 See W. A. J. Steer: 'The Thematic Unity of Brecht's Der kaukasische Kreidekreis', *German Life & Letters*, xxi (1967–8), 1–10, esp. p. 3.

32 On this, and Azdak in general, see Jürgen Jacobs: 'Die Rechtspflege des Azdak', *Euphorion*, lxii (1968), 421–4.

33 Bentley, op. cit. (n. 19), pp. 69f.

34 See the collective work *Bertolt Brecht – Leben und Werk*, Berlin 1963, p. 143; and T. M. Holmes: 'Descrying the Dialectic . . .', *Journal of European Studies*, vii (1977), 95–106.

35 Benjamin, op. cit. (n. 2 to Chapter 1), p. 115.

36 Eisler, p. 78.

37 A. Kats, quoted by Glade, op. cit. (n. 51 to Chapter 3), p. 171.

38 On this rejection of Utopian anticipation see Ludwig, pp. 148–50.

39 See Fuegi, p. 149.

40 Ritchie, p. 25. Brecht incorporated an English version in his journal (*Aj.*, 1, 548: 24.11.42).

41 On the language of Azdak, and of the Singer and the corporal, see Pohl, esp. pp. 12f., 26, 39, 138f., 144.

42 See Hinck, pp. 106f.

43 See Hennenberg, p. 380.

44 See Hinck, p. 105.

45 On the music to the play see Hennenberg, pp. 216–23, 248f., 329–35, chap. 6 *passim*, pp. 378–80; and Paul Dessau: 'Zur *Kreidekreis*-Musik', in *Mat. K.*, 87–94.
46 Rülicke-Weiler, p. 210.
47 Karl von Appen: 'Über das Bühnenbild', *Mat. K.*, 95–100, p. 96.
48 Rülicke-Weiler, p. 214.
49 See Fuegi, pp. 151f.
50 Wekwerth, p. 16.
51 On masks see Hurwicz, op. cit. (n. 40 to Chapter 3), p. 4; Rülicke-Weiler, p. 216, with photos; and Joachim Tenschert: 'Über die Verwendung von Masken', *Mat. K.*, 101–12.

CHAPTER 8 (pp. 171–3)
 1 Gray, pp. 176–81.
 2 Eisler, p. 139.
 3 Ronald Bryden: 'Pop goes Imperialism', *Observer Review*, 7.3.71.
 4 See A. D. White: 'Brecht's Quest for a Democratic Theatre', *Theatre Quarterly*, no. 5 (Jan 1972), 65–70, esp. p. 70.

Index

BRECHT'S WORKS

GENERAL INDEX